VOLUME II CHAPTERS 14-26

STUDY GUIDE

for use with

INTERMEDIATE ACCOUNTING

♦

Revised Edition

Thomas R. Dyckman Roland E. Dukes Charles J. Davis

Prepared by
Rosita S. Chen
Sheng-Der Pan
Both of California State University, Fresno

IRWIN
Homewood, IL 60430
Boston, MA 02116

Previously copyrighted in 1976, 1979, 1982, 1986, and 1989 under Welsch and Zlatkovich.

Printed in the United States of America.

ISBN 0-256-10785-8

1 2 3 4 5 6 7 8 9 0 ML 9 8 7 6 5 4 3 2

Contents

Introduction

The two volumes of this **Study Guide** are designed as an aid to your study of **Intermediate Accounting,** Revised Edition, published by Richard D. Irwin, Inc. However, they can also be helpful to you when used with any other intermediate textbooks.

This study guide provides an organized analysis and concise summary of each chapter presented in the text. **Chapter Objectives,** which are mainly adopted from the text, identify those topics you should know after studying the chapter. **Chapter Highlights** introduce accounting issues, discuss accounting principles, describe accounting methods, and present comprehensive worksheets, as appropriate, using extensive examples and illustrations. At the end of the Chapter Highlights, there are **key concepts** provided as a glossary for your reference. The last section of each chapter consists of **Review Questions and Exercises** intended to aid and reinforce your understanding of the topics presented in the chapter. **Solutions** to the Review Questions and Exercises are provided at the end of each chapter. The solutions provide you with immediate feedback on the accuracy of your answers. By referring to the correct solutions after you have answered the questions you can **reinforce** and **evaluate** your understanding of the chapter.

This study guide also will be helpful to you when **preparing for examinations,** including the **CPA examination.** By reviewing the highlights of the chapters, you can gauge your recall of the subject areas and determine the topics in need of further review.

Good luck!

R. S. C.

S. D. P.

CHAPTER 14

Investments -- Temporary and Long Term

CHAPTER OBJECTIVES

This chapter is designed to enable students to:

A. Appreciate why firms invest in debt and equity securities.

B. Understand classification criteria.

C. Understand the conceptual basis for the accounting for investments.

D. Understand and be able to use various methods in accounting for investment in securities.

F. Be familiar with the disclosure requirements in accounting for investment in securities.

G. Understand how to account for the cash surrender value of life insurance.

CHAPTER OVERVIEW

A. Introduction

In addition to their major courses of business, many companies make a variety of **investments**, such as acquiring land or other properties for speculation, setting up special purpose long-term funds, buying life insurance policies for their executives and building up cash surrender values. However, the most important of all is probably purchasing securities issued by other entities. The motivation for such security investments might be to (1) earn a return on temporarily idle cash, or (2) to acquire the voting stock of another firm (perhaps a major customer, supplier or competitor) in order to gain influence, control, business expansion or some other business advantages.

B. Nature of Securities and Classification of Security Investments

The appropriate accounting for a security investment depends upon the nature of the securities and the classification of security investments as follows:

1. **Equity or debt securities.** An equity security is defined as any instrument representing ownership shares (e.g., a common stock or a preferred stock) or the right to acquire ownership shares (e.g., stock options). This term, however, does not encompass callable or redeemable preferred stock, treasury stock and convertible bonds. A debt security, on the other hand, is an instrument representing creditors' claim with a fixed amount and usually some interest obligation (e.g., a note or a bond).

2. **Marketable or nonmarketable.** An equity or a debt security is considered marketable if the sales price of the security is currently available on a national securities exchange or in the over-the-counter market.

3. **Current or noncurrent:** A security investment is classified as **current** (or **short-term**) if the security is (1) readily marketable, and (2) intended to be converted to cash within an accounting period or operating cycle, whichever is longer. Otherwise, it should be classified as **noncurrent** (or **long-term**).

4. **Significant influence.** Investor's ability to exercise significant influence over operating and financial policies of an investee may be indicated in several ways (such as representation in the board of directors, material intercompany transactions, etc.). In general, however, in the absence of evidence to the contrary, significant influence should be presumed if an investor holds 20% or more of the investee's voting stock.

Accounting methods applicable to specific circumstances are summarized in the following diagram and will be individually discussed thereafter:

Given:
- C = Cost method
- E = Equity method
- LCM = Lower-of-cost-or-market method
- MV = Market value method

	Equity Securities	**Debt Securities**
Current (or Short-term)	**LCM**	**C or LCM *** (optional)
Noncurrent (or Long-term)	**C,LCM,E or MV **** (mutually exclusive)	**C**

Notes: * For debt securities held as a **short-term** investment, both the **cost** and the **lower-of-cost-or-market** methods are acceptable.

** **Long-term** investments in equity securities should be accounted for using:

(1) the **cost** method,
(2) the **lower-of-cost-or-market** method,
(3) the **equity** method, or
(4) the **market value** method.

C. Accounting Methods for Investment in Equity Securities

1. **Cost method.** This method is applicable if the investor does not have significant influence, and the securities are not marketable. Under this method:

   a. The investment is initially recorded at cost.

   b. Investment income (revenue) is recognized whenever dividends are received, unless the dividends are liquidating (i.e., the total dividends received exceed the investor's cumulative share in the investee's earnings since the investment). Liquidating dividends are considered a return of the original investment and should be credited to the investment account.

   c. Gain or loss on the investment is recognized only when realized (i.e., the acquired securities are sold).

   d. At any time, if a decline in market value of any individual security is **other than temporary**, investment in the specific security should be written down to market directly, and a loss is recognized. The market value then becomes the new cost of the investment.

2. **Lower-of-cost-or-market (LCM) method.** Following **FAS 12**, the LCM method is applied to (a) investments classified as current, and (b) those noncurrent investments in marketable securities with which the investor does not have significant influence. Under this method:

   a. The investment is initially recorded at cost.

   b. The securities shall be grouped separately into a current portfolio and a noncurrent portfolio. The carrying amount of a portfolio shall be the lower of its **aggregate** cost or market value. The requirement for an aggregate comparison allows unrealized gains of some securities to offset unrealized losses of some other securities in the portfolio.

When the market value of a portfolio is less than its cost at the balance sheet date and the decrease in market value is considered temporary, an **unrealized loss** is recorded and a **valuation allowance account** is established to effect the reduction to market value. Then:

(1) If the investment is classified as **current**, the unrealized loss is a **nominal** account, and included as an other operating expense in the determination of income for the period.

(2) If the investment is classified as **noncurrent**, the unrealized loss is a **real** account, and presented on the balance sheet as a direct reduction in owners' equity.

c. In the **subsequent** years, the allowance account should be adjusted up and down to reflect changes in the excess of cost over current market value. If the market value goes further down, the above procedures still apply (i.e., the unrealized loss is debited, and the allowance account credited for the current change in market value). If the market value goes up, the allowance account should be debited, and:

(1) If the investment is classified as **current**, the **recovery of market value** account is credited, which is reported on the income statement as an other operating gain, or

(2) If the investment is classified as **noncurrent**, the **unrealized loss** account is credited in order to reduce the carrying balance of this contra equity account.

d. When an individual security is **reclassified** between the **current** and **noncurrent** portfolios, the security is transferred at the **lower of cost or market** at the date of transfer. If its market value is less than cost, the market value becomes the **new cost** basis, and the difference between the "old" and the "new" costs is recorded as a loss as if the security were sold and a loss realized.

e. When a decline in market value of a security is considered permanent, the unrealized loss is recognized, the investment account is written down to market, and the market value becomes the new cost for subsequent cost or market application.

f. When a security is sold, investment is credited at the original cost of the security, and the realized gain or loss is recognized. The allowance account should be adjusted, usually at the year end, to reflect the excess of cost over market value of those **securities remaining in the investment**.

ILLUSTRATION 1 -- LCM METHOD, SHORT-TERM EQUITY INVESTMENT

On January 2, 1991, Helmsey Industries invested temporarily idle cash in two common stocks as follows: Cotton Corporation, $12,000, and Grape Corporation, $25,000. During 1991, a cash dividend of $1,000 was received from Cotton Corporation. On December 31, 1991 the market prices of those investments were: Cotton Corporation, $12,500, and Grape Corporation, $20,000.

1991.

The following journal entries and financial statement presentation for 1991 are appropriate:

(1) **To record the investment:**

Investment in equity securities	37,000	
Cash ($25,000 + $12,000)		37,000

(2) **To record cash dividend received:**

Cash	1,000	
Investment income (or dividend income)		1,000

(3) **To adjust the investment to LCM at the year end:**

Unrealized loss on investments	4,500*	
Allowance to reduce investments to market		4,500

*Aggregate difference is calculated as follows:

	Cost	Market	Difference
Cotton Corporation	$12,000	$12,500	$ (500)
Grape Corporation	25,000	20,000	5,000
Aggregate (Cost - Market)	$37,000	$32,500	$ 4,500

(4) To close unrealized loss account:

Income summary	4,500	
Unrealized loss on investment		4,500

(5) **To present investment on the balance sheet:**

Investment in equity securities	$37,000	
Less: Allowance to reduce investment to market	(4,500)	$32,500

1992.

Assume that at the end of 1992, the aggregate market value increased to $35,000.

(1) To adjust allowance to the new required balance [($37,000 - $35,000) - $4,500]:

Allowance to reduce investments to market	2,500	
Recovery of unrealized loss on investment		2,500

(2) To close the cost recovery account:

Recovery of unrealized loss on investment	2,500	
Income summary		2,500

(3) To present investment on the balance sheet:

Investment in equity securities	$37,000	
Less: Allowance to reduce investment to market	(2,000)	$35,000

ILLUSTRATION 2 -- LCM METHOD, LONG-TERM EQUITY INVESTMENT

Use the above data, except the investment is classified as **noncurrent**. Accounting treatments are:

1991.

Items (1), (2), and (3): Same as those under short-term investment.

Item (4) is irrelevant because, the unrealized loss of a **noncurrent** equity security investment is a real account and will not be closed at year end.

Item (5) is the same as that under the **short-term investment** insofar as the presentation of allowance account is concerned. In addition, the unrealized loss should be reported on the balance sheet as a contra equity account as follows:

Total Owners' Equity	$ xxxxx	
Less: Unrealized loss on investment	(4,500)	$ xxxxx

1992.

At the end of 1992, the recovery of market value is recorded as:

Allowance to reduce investments to market	2,500	
Unrealized loss on investment		2,500

The resulting ending balance of unrealized loss account ($4,500 - $2,500 = $2,000) is again presented on the balance sheet as a contra equity account. The presentation of the allowance account is still the same as that under the **short-term investment.**

3. **Equity method.** For the investor, the cost and the LCM methods discussed above are based on the two-entity concept. That is, the investor considers the investee as a separate business entity. In contrast, the equity method views the investor and the investee as a special type of **single entity.** Under this concept, the investee is a part of the investor's entity, and the income of the investee is part of the investor's earnings.

   The equity method is required when the investor's long-term investment in the investee's common stock enables the investor to exercise significant influence over the investee. Under this method:

   a. The investment is initially recorded at cost.

   b. The investment is increased by the recognized investment income, which is measured as:

      Investment income = **Proportionate share of investee's income + /- Adjustments**

      where the **adjustments** include an:

      (1) amortization of the differences between the fair and book values of individual assets acquired and liabilities assumed,
      (2) amortization of the purchased goodwill, and
      (3) elimination of profits or losses from intercompany transactions (known as intercompany profits or losses).

      In the event that the investor's investment losses **exceed** the carrying amount of the investment, it ordinarily should **discontinue** applying the equity method and the **excessive losses** should not be recognized. Application of the equity method should be resumed when the investment income of subsequent periods has equaled the unrecognized investment losses.

   c. The investment account is decreased whenever cash dividends are declared by the investee. Under the equity method, there is no concern with the issue whether a certain dividend is liquidating or not.

   d. When the investor's level of influence changes, a change in accounting method may be required. If the change is from the equity method to another method, **no adjustment** is made to the carrying amount of the investment. However, when a change to the equity method is appropriate, **retroactive adjustments** are required to the investment account, the income statement and retained earnings. The adjusted amounts should be those which would have occurred if the equity method always had been used.

e. A gain or loss on security investment is recognized when realized, and the **LCM** rule does not apply.

ILLUSTRATION -- THE EQUITY METHOD

Parent Company purchased **55%** of Subsidiary Company's outstanding common stock for $45,000 on January 2, 1991. On that date, the balance sheet of Subsidiary and estimated market values of its assets and liabilities were as follows:

	Book Value	Market Value	Difference
Cash and receivables	$ 10,000	$ 10,000	
Equipment (net)	20,000	25,000	$ 5,000
Land	30,000	41,000	11,000
Total Assets	$ 60,000	$ 76,000	
Liabilities	$ 20,000	$ 20,000	
Owners' equity	40,000	56,000	
Total liab. & owners' equity	$ 60,000	$ 76,000	

Further assume that, on the date of acquisition, Subsidiary's equipment had a useful life of 5 years. For the year Subsidiary reported $8,000 of net income, and declared and paid $5,000 dividends. Any purchased goodwill is amortized over 40 years.

Required: Prepare journal entries to record the investment.

SOLUTION:

(1) **To record the investment:**

	Debit	Credit
Investment in Subsidiary	45,000	
Cash		45,000

(2) **To record dividends received:**

	Debit	Credit
Cash ($5,000 x 55%)	2,750	
Investment in Subsidiary		2,750

(3) **To record share of Subsidiary's reported income:**

	Debit	Credit
Investment in Subsidiary ($8,000 x 55%)	4,400	
Investment income		4,400

(4)	**To amortize the difference between the fair and book values of equipment:**		
	Investment income ($5,000 x 55% / 5)	550	
	Investment in subsidiary		550
(5)	**To amortize goodwill:** (goodwill = $45,000 - $56,000 x 55% = $14,200)		
	Investment income ($14,200 / 40)	355	
	Investment in Subsidiary		355

Note that:

(1) Only a real account (investment in subsidiary) and a nominal account (investment income) are used to record the investment transactions.

(2) The difference between the fair and the book values of the equipment acquired by Parent was $2,750 [($25,000 - $20,000) x 55%], which was to be amortized (depreciated) over the remaining useful life of the equipment at $550 ($2,750 / 5) per year.

(3) The acquired goodwill must be amortized over a period of no longer than 40 years, and adjusted to investment income.

4. **Market value method.** Unlike any other methods, the market value method is based on the current value concept, instead of the cost principle. This method is not generally accepted except that, following specialized industry accounting practices (i.e., industry peculiarities), certain **specialized industries** (e.g., an investment company, mutual fund, pension fund or insurance company) may use it to account for their investments in **marketable** securities. Under this method:

a. The investment is initially recorded at cost.

b. Dividends received are recognized as investment income.

c. A change in the market value of each individual security is directly adjusted to the investment account, and an unrealized gain or loss is recorded. Then:

(1) under the **current approach**, the unrealized gain or loss is included in current income, or

(2) under the **deferral approach**, the unrealized gain or loss is deferred and reported as a contra owners' equity account.

d. When the investment is sold, the carrying value of the investment (including the deferred unrealized gain or loss, if applicable) is closed and a resulting realized gain or loss is recognized.

D. Special Problems in Accounting for Equity Investment

1. **Stock dividends and stock split.** A **stock dividend** is a capitalization of a part of retained earnings and does not increase or decrease the net assets of the issuing corporation. The investor neither receives assets from, nor owns more of the issuing corporation. Therefore it should make no entry for the dividends other than a memorandum record for the number of additional shares received. Nevertheless, the new cost per share should be recalculated to take the additional shares into consideration.

   To the issuer a **stock split** is different from a **stock dividend**. However, the two are virtually identical from the point of view of the investor.

2. **Stock rights.** Stock rights are rights to acquire a specified number of shares of certain stock at a specified price within a specified period of time. When a right is issued by an investee to its stockholders (investors), the investor usually does not record the right unless it is detachable from the shares it holds. If the right is separable (detachable) from the original shares and the market value of the right is available, an entry is prepared to debit a separate account such as **investment in stock right**, with a counter credit to **investment income**. When the right is disposed of:

   (1) If the right is sold, cash less the carrying value of investment in stock right, if any, is recorded as a gain (loss).

   (2) If the right is exercised and new shares are acquired, the acquisition cost of these new shares should include cash paid and the carrying value of investment in stock right, if any.

   (3) If the right is expired, the carrying value of the right, if any, is closed to a loss account.

F. Disclosure Requirements in Accounting for Equity Security Investment

An investor firm must disclose the following for its investments in equity securities:

1. Aggregate costs of the **current** and **noncurrent** portfolios, respectively.

2. Aggregate market values of the Portfolios.

3. Gross unrealized gains and losses.

4. Net realized gain or loss, the basis for determining this gain or loss, and the change in the valuation allowance that is included in the determination of income.

G. Accounting Methods for Investments in Debt Securities

Investment in debt securities is accounted for using the **cost method.** The investment is carried at cost, interest revenue is recognized as accrued, and a gain or loss is recognized only if realized. If the decline in market value is significant and not due to temporary conditions, the investment account is directly adjusted to the market, and the unrealized loss is recognized and included in the determination of income. Any subsequent recovery in market value is disregarded. Two possible exceptions:

1. If the debt securities are **marketable** and the investment is classified as **current,** the **lower-or-cost-or-market method** may also be applied.

2. For any other debt securities, the cost method must be applied. However, if a debt security was acquired at a premium or discount, the premium or discount is amortized over the remaining term of the security. This topic is covered in Chapter 16.

H. Cash Surrender Value of Life Insurance

When a firm insures the lives of its top executives, with itself as the beneficiary, the firm is in essence making an investment. Some insurance policies allow the firm to build up a cash surrender value while the policy is in force. A cash surrender value is the amount that would be refunded should the policy be terminated at the request of the insured.

Cash surrender value increases over time as the firm pays the insurance premium. Therefore, a periodic premium payment covers not only the firm's insurance expense for the period, but also current contribution to the cash surrender value. The cash surrender value is recorded as an asset and usually reported on the balance sheet under **investments and funds.**

KEY CONCEPTS

Debt securities Instruments representing creditors' claim on a fixed amount and usually some interest obligation (e.g., notes and bonds).

Equity securities Any instrument representing ownership shares (e.g., common stock, or preferred stock), or the right to acquire ownership shares. Callable or redeemable preferred stock, treasury stock or convertible bonds are not considered as equity securities.

Marketable equity securities An equity security for which sales price is currently available on a national securities exchange or in the over-the-counter market.

Realized gain or loss The difference between the net proceeds from the sale of a security and its cost.

Significant influence Investor's ability to influence the investee's operating and financial policies. An investment of 20% or more of the voting stock of an investee should lead to a presumption that the investor has the ability to exercise the influence, unless there is evidence to the contrary.

The cost method An accounting method applied to investments in most debt securities and certain nonmarketable equity securities, under which the investment is initially recorded at cost, interest accrued or dividends received are recognized as income, and the investment account continues to carry the original cost unless there is a liquidating dividend, a substantial and permanent decline in market value, or a disposal of the security investment.

The equity method The accounting method required to be applied to long-term investment in the equity securities of another firm (the investee) over which the investor has significant influence. This method is based on the single-entity concept. Investment is initially recorded at cost. The investment account increases by the investor's investment income, and decreases by its share in dividends declared by the investee.

The lower-of-cost-or-market method An accounting method primarily applied to investments in marketable equity securities in which the investor does not have significant influence. This method is basically the same as the cost method, except that a valuation allowance is established to account for the unrealized loss of a portfolio at the end of an accounting period.

The market value method The only valuation method based on the current value concept. It is not generally acceptable, except for some specialized industries such as investment and insurance companies. Under this method, investment in marketable securities is initially recorded at cost. The investment account is then adjusted directly to the market value, and both the unrealized gain and loss are recorded.

Unrealized gain or loss The difference between the market value of a security and its cost at any given date.

Valuation allowance The **net** unrealized loss in a portfolio of marketable equity security investment (i.e., the amount by which aggregate cost exceeds market value of a portfolio).

REVIEW QUESTIONS AND EXERCISES

TRUE-FALSE

Indicate whether each of the following statements is true or false by circling the correct response.

T F 1. Regardless of the accounting method used, stock investments should **initially** be recorded at the total cost of the investment, including brokerage fees and commissions.

T F 2. Using the **cost method** the investor does not adjust the investment account to reflect temporary market value changes.

T F 3. The use of **lower-of-cost-or-market (LCM) method** requires that marketable equity investments be classified into current and noncurrent portfolios.

T F 4. In applying the **LCM method**, the cost of securities is **individually** compared with the corresponding market value to determine the appropriate valuation allowance.

T F 5. Once the aggregate carrying value of a **specific portfolio** has been written down following the **LCM method**, the carrying value may not be written back up for subsequent recovery of market value.

T F 6. The market value method is not in accordance with GAAP, and should thus **never** be applied to accounting for security investment.

T F 7. Using the equity method, the investor's share of investee's dividends should not be recorded as investment income.

T F 8. The equity method is required for long-term equity investment, regardless of whether the investor is able to exercise significant influence or not.

T F 9. Using the equity method the investor company records the amortization of goodwill by debiting amortization of goodwill (expense) and crediting goodwill.

T F 10. The unrealized loss from writing down short-term security investment to LCM is reported as a component of income from continuing operations.

T F 11. An investment in common stock is accounted for using the equity method only if the stock is marketable.

T F 12. Equity securities include common stock, preferred stock and stock rights, but exclude callable and redeemable preferred stock, treasury stock and convertible bonds.

T F 13. When a change in the level of ownership requires that an investor change from the equity method to the LCM method, the investment account should be adjusted retroactively to reflect the new method.

T F 14. When the fair value of a depreciable asset exceeds its book value at acquisition, the equity method requires a periodic increase in both the investment account and investment income.

EXERCISE 1

On January 2, 1991, Jordan Corporation purchased 5,000 shares of Wickman Company's common stock from a national stock exchange for $290,000. The investment represents 40 percent of Wickman's equity interest. Jordan received dividends of $2.5 per share on December 10, 1991, and Wickman reported net income of $120,000 for the year. At December 31, 1991, the market value of Wickman's common stock was $53 per share.

Additional information:

1. Immediately before the acquisition, Wickman reported a book value of its net assets as $500,000, and the fair value of an equipment was $50,000 above its book value. The equipment had a remaining useful life of 5 years.

2. The remainder of the excess of the cost of the investment over the book value of net assets purchased was attributable to goodwill, amortized over 20 years.

Required: Prepare the required journal entries for Jordan Corporation to record the investment.

1. January 2, 1991:

2. December 10, 1991:

3. December 31, 1991:

   a. To record Jordan's share in Wickman's reported income:

   b. To amortize the difference between the fair value and the book value of depreciable assets:

   c. To amortized the purchased goodwill:

EXERCISE 2

Based on the same data as in **Exercise 1** except that the acquired common stock represents a 15% of Wickman's equity interest.

Required: Prepare the journal entries required by Jordan for the investment.

1. January 2, 1991:

2. December 10, 1991:

3. December 31, 1991:

EXERCISE 3

Fleiman Corporation purchased common shares of Liebe Company and Wilson Company for short-term investment purposes as follows:

a. On January 2, 1991, purchased 300 shares of Liebe Company's stock at $25 per share, plus a brokerage fee of 2%.

b. On March 5, 1991, purchased 500 shares of Wilson Company's stock at $65 per share, plus a brokerage fee of $500.

c. On June 20, 1991, purchased additional 200 shares of Liebe Company's stock at $28 per share, plus brokerage fee of 2%.

d. On October 15, 1991, received from Wilson Company cash dividends of $1 per share. The dividends were not liquidating.

e. On November 1, 1991, sold 100 shares of Liebe's common at $32 per share. Incurred brokerage fee of $100.

f. On December 31, 1991, market prices were: Liebe's common, $28 per share, and Wilson's common, $62 per share.

g. On December 31, 1992, market prices were: Liebe's common, $21 per share, and Wilson's common, $60 per share.

Required:

Give an entry to record each of the investment transactions and year-end adjustments, applying the **LCM** method:

a. January 2, 1991:

b. March 5, 1991:

c. June 20, 1991:

d. October 15, 1991:

e. November 1, 1991:

f. December 31, 1991: (year-end adjustment)

g. December 31, 1992: (year-end adjustment)

MULTIPLE CHOICE

Enter the letter corresponding to the response which **best** completes each of the following statements or questions.

____ 1. For market value to be used as the basis for valuation of a firm's marketable equity securities under the LCM method:

a. management's intention must be to dispose of the securities within one year.
b. the market value must be less than cost for each equity security in the portfolio.
c. the market value must approximate historical cost.
d. the aggregate market value must be less than the aggregate cost of a portfolio.

____ 2. Which of the following statements is **untrue** regarding investments in equity securities?

a. If the investor owns less than 20% of the investee's marketable voting stock, the **LCM method** generally is required.
b. If the investor owns more than 20% of the investee's nonmarketable voting stock for long-term investment, the **equity method** is generally required.
c. If the investor owns less than 20% of the investee's common stock for long-term investment, the **equity method must not** be used.
d. If the investor owns 50% of the investee's voting stock for temporary investment, the **LCM method** is appropriate.

____ 3. Corporations invest in the securities of other companies for each of the following reasons except:

a. to earn a return on otherwise idle cash.
b. to ensure a supply of a required raw material.
c. to expand their business operations.
d. to report intercompany profit.

____ 4. The unrealized loss on **noncurrent** investment in marketable equity securities due to a decline in market price is:

a. reported in the shareholders' equity section of the balance sheet.
b. included in the determination of income from operations.
c. reported as extraordinary items.
d. reported in the liability section of the balance sheet.

____ 5. In the application of the equity method, dividends from the investee should be accounted for:

a. as an increase in the investment account.
b. as a reduction in the investment account.
c. as dividend revenue.
d. as an extraordinary item.

____ 6. What is the most appropriate basis for recording the acquisition of 40% of the voting stock of another corporation in a noncash transaction?

a. at the book value of the stock acquired.
b. at the par value of the stock acquired.
c. at the book value of the consideration given.
d. at the market value of the consideration given.

____ 7. A marketable equity security is transferred from a current portfolio to a noncurrent portfolio, the security should be transferred at:

a. the carrying value of the security, if higher than cost.
b. the original cost of the security, regardless of the market.
c. the market value of the security, regardless of the cost.
d. the lower-of-cost-or-market.

____ 8. When the equity method is changed to the LCM method:

a. no adjustment to the carrying amount of the investment is required.
b. the investment account should be adjusted to the original cost of the investment.
c. the investment account should be adjusted to the lower-of-cost-or-market.
d. the investment account should be adjusted to the market, regardless of the cost.

____ 9. Primary Investment Company purchased marketable equity securities for temporary investment. The cost and market value on December 31, 1991 of its current portfolio were as follows:

	Cost	Market
Alpha common	$1,000	$1,200
Beta common	5,450	5,000
Theta common	3,000	2,800
Total	$9,450	$9,000

Assuming that, at the beginning of 1991, Primary's valuation allowance account had a balance of $500, Primary should report in its 1991 financial statements:

a. unrealized loss of $450.
b. unrealized loss of $650.
c. unrealized gain of $500, and unrealized loss of $450.
d. recovery of unrealized loss of $50.

____ 10. Based on the same data as in Question 9, except that Primary sold its holding of Theta's common on December 31, 1991 for $3,500, and paid commission of $50. Primary should report in its 1991 financial statements:

a. a realized gain of $450, and a recovery of unrealized loss of $250.
b. realized gain of $700.
c. unrealized loss of $50.
d. recovery of unrealized loss of $150.

____ 11. On January 2, 1991, Hawk Inc. bought 40% of the outstanding common stock of Dove Company for $400,000 cash. Hawk accounts for this investment by the equity method. At the date of acquisition of the stock, Dove's net assets had a book value as well as a fair value of $800,000. Any purchased goodwill should be amortized over 40 years. Dove's net income for the year ended December 31, 1991, was $20,000. During 1991, Dove paid cash dividends of $10,000.

Hawk should recognize investment income for 1991 of:

a. $4,000.
b. $6,000.
c. $8,000.
d. $7,800.

____ 12. Based on the same data as in Question 11, Hawk's investment account should have a balance on December 31, 1991 of:

a. $400,000.
b. $478,800.
c. $438,800.
d. $402,000.

____ 13. Based on the same data as in Question 11 except that, at the acquisition of the stock, Dove's book value of net assets was $700,000. The difference between the book value and the fair value was attributable to a building, which had a remaining useful life of 10 years.

Hawk should recognize investment income for 1991 of:

a. $2,000.
b. $3,400.
c. $7,400.
d. $7,800.

____ 14. During 1991, its first year of operation, Twin Investment Company purchased several marketable equity securities, and at December 31, 1991, had the following investments:

	Cost	Market
Short-term:		
Security A	$1,000	$1,500
Security B	5,000	3,000
Total	$6,000	$4,500
Long-term:		
Security X	$4,000	$3,600
Security Y	4,400	3,000
Total	$8,400	$6,600

Using the LCM method Twin should establish valuation allowances at December 31, 1991 with a corresponding charge against:

	Income	**Stockholder's equity**
a.	$0	$3,300
b.	$3,300	$0
c.	$1,500	$1,800
d.	$1,800	$1,500

SOLUTIONS TO REVIEW QUESTIONS AND EXERCISES

TRUE-FALSE

1.	T	5.	F	9.	F	13.	F
2.	T	6.	F	10.	T	14.	F
3.	T	7.	T	11.	F		
4.	F	8.	F	12.	T		

EXERCISE 1

1. January 2, 1991:

Investment in common stock, long-term	290,000	
Cash		290,000

2. December 10, 1991:

Cash (5,000 Shares x $2.5)	12,500	
Investment in common stock, long-term		12,500

3. December 31, 1991:

a. To record Jordan's share in Wickman's reported income:

Investment in common stock, long-term	48,000	
Investment income ($120,000 x 40%)		48,000

b. To amortize the difference between the fair value and the book value of depreciable assets):

Investment income ($50,000 x 40% / 5)	4,000	
Investment in common stock, long-term		4,000

c. To amortized the purchased goodwill:

Investment income {[$290,000-($550,000 x 40%)]/20}	3,500	
Investment in common stock, long-term		3,500

EXERCISE 2

1. January 2, 1991:

Investment in marketable equity securities	290,000	
Cash		290,000

2. December 10, 1991:

Cash (5,000 shares x $2.5)	12,500	
Dividends income		12,500

3. December 31, 1991: Unrealized loss = ($290,000 - 5,000 shares x $53):

Unrealized loss on investment	25,000	
Allowance to reduce investment to market		25,000

EXERCISE 3

a. January 2, 1991: To record investment in Liebe's common:

Investment in stock, short-term	7,650	
Cash (300 shares x $25 x 102%)		7,650

b. March 5, 1991: To record investment in Wilson's common:

Investment in stock, short-term	33,000	
Cash (500 shares x $65 + $500)		33,000

c. June 20, 1991: To record investment in Liebe's common:

Investment in stock, short-term	5,712	
Cash (200 shares x $28 x 102%)		5,712

d. October 15, 1991: To record receipt of Wilson's cash dividends:

Cash (500 shares x $1)	500	
Dividends income		500

e. November 1, 1991: to record disposal of Liebe's common:
(FIFO cost = 100 shares x $25 x 102%)

Cash (100 shares x $32 - $100)	3,100	
Investment in stock, short-term		2,550
Realized gain on investment		550

f. December 31, 1991: To record unrealized loss:

Unrealized loss on investment	1,612 *	
Allowance to reduce investment to market		1,612

* Unrealized loss is calculated as follows:

	Cost	Market	Difference
Liebe's stock	$10,812	$11,200	$ (388)
Wilson's stock	33,000	31,000	2,000
Total	$43,812	$42,200	$1,612

g. December 31, 1992: To record incremental unrealized loss:

Unrealized loss on investment	3,800 *	
Allowance to reduce investment to market		3,800

* Accumulated unrealized loss is calculated as follows:

	Cost	Market	Difference
Liebe's stock	$10,812	$ 8,400	$2,412
Wilson's stock	33,000	30,000	3,000
Total	$43,812	$38,400	$5,412

Adjustment to allowance = $5,412 - $1,612 = **$3,800.**

MULTIPLE CHOICE

1.	d	5.	b	9.	d	13.	a
2.	c	6.	d	10.	a	14.	c
3.	d	7.	d	11.	b		
4.	a	8.	a	12.	d		

Computations and explanations:

9. (d) To determine change in valuation allowance:

January 1, 1991	$500
December 31, 1991 ($9,450 - $9,000)	450
Adjustment for recovery of unrealized loss	$ 50

10. (a)

(1) To determine realized gain on investment:

Cash proceeds	$3,500
Less: Commission	50
Cost of investment	3,000
Realized gain	$ 450

(2) To determine change in valuation allowance:

January 1, 1991	$500
December 31, 1991 ($6,450 - $6,200)	250
Adjustment for recovery of unrealized loss	$250

11. (b) To calculate investment income:

Share in reported income ($20,000 x 40%)	$8,000
Amortization of goodwill: [($400,000 - $800,000 x 40%) / 40]	(2,000)
Investment income	$6,000

12. (d) To calculate the carrying value of investment account:

Initial cost of investment	$400,000
Recognized investment income	6,000
Dividends received ($10,000 x 40%)	(4,000)
Balance, December 31, 1991	$402,000

13. (a) To calculate investment income:

Share in reported income ($20,000 x 40%)	$8,000
Amortization for difference between fair and book value of building ($100,000 x 40%) / 10	(4,000)
Amortization of goodwill [($400,000 - $800,000 x 40%) / 40]	(2,000)
Investment income	$2,000

14. (c) To calculate unrealized losses:

	Short-term	Long-term
Aggregate cost	$6,000	$8,400
Aggregate market	4,500	6,600
Unrealized loss	$1,500	$1,800

Note that the unrealized loss of short-term investment is closed to income summary, and that of the long-term investment is reported as a contra equity account.

CHAPTER 15

Short-Term Liabilities

CHAPTER OBJECTIVES

This chapter is designed to enable students to:

A. Be able to define a liability and specify its characteristics.

B. Know how to distinguish short-term from long-term liabilities.

C. Know when it is appropriate to recognize a liability and how to measure the amount attached to the liability.

D. Understand the accounting for interest- and noninterest-bearing current liabilities as well as how to treat notes with unrealistic interest rates.

E. Be able to explain why cash collected in advance of delivery of a good or service creates a liability for the firm.

F. Be able to properly account for the incurrence and payment of short-term liabilities.

G. Know what contingent and estimated liabilities are and the accounting appropriate to such liabilities.

CHAPTER OVERVIEW

A. As defined in **FAC 6**, liabilities are probable, future sacrifices of economic benefits arising from the present obligations of a particular entity to transfer goods or provide services to other entities in the future resulting from past transactions or events. The **FASB** further specifies the characteristics of a liability as:

1. It is a present duty or responsibility.
2. The duty or responsibility obligates a particular entity.
3. The transaction or other event obligating the entity has already happened.

For financial reporting, liabilities are classified as current (short-term) or noncurrent (long-term). This chapter discuss the concept of and items typically classified as short-term liabilities.

B. Following **FAS 6**, short-term liabilities (obligations) are those that are scheduled to mature within one year after the date of balance sheet or within an operating cycle that is longer than one year. This definition is consistent with **ARB 43** in which **current liabilities** are specified as those whose liquidation is reasonably expected to require the use of existing resources properly classified as current assets, or the creation of other current liabilities.

The usual types of current liabilities are discussed as follows:

C. Accounts Payable (or Trade Accounts Payable)

Accounts payable are obligations to suppliers of goods or services that arise from ongoing business operations including the acquisition of merchandise, materials, supplies, and services which are used in the production and/or sale of goods and services.

In general, accounts payable are recognized when legal title to the goods passes or when the services are received. They are typically recorded at the amount due. If a cash discount is involved, the related accounts payable may be recorded using either the **gross** or the **net approach** similar to their counterparts in accounts receivable as discussed in Chapter 8. It is noted that the amount of cash discount is usually immaterial and the issue is relatively minor.

D. Short-Term Notes Payable

A short-term note payable might be a **trade note payable** that arises from the same source as an account payable, or a **nontrade note payable** that arises from other sources including the current maturity of a certain long-term debt. A trade note is customarily recorded at its **face amount**. A nontrade note, on the other hand, should be reported at its **present value**. The present value of a note issued solely for cash is the cash amount received, whereas the present values of other notes are calculated in terms of the respective types of notes and the applicable interest rates. Basically, accounting procedures which deal with notes payable are similar to their counterparts dealing with notes receivable as introduced in Chapter 8.

Depending on whether a rate of interest is explicitly stated, notes are generally classified as interest-bearing and noninterest-bearing. The stated interest rate of an interest-bearing note, furthermore, may or may not be realistic (i.e., the same as the market interest rate). In any case the calculation of the present value of a note is based on the following general equations:

Maturity value (MV) = Face value (1 + r x n)

Present value (PV) = MV / (1 + i x n)
= Face value (1 + r x n) / (1 + i x n)

where: **i** = Effective (market) interest rate
r = Stated interest rate
n = Term of the note

1. **Interest-bearing note with realistic stated interest rate:** Assume that Normandy Bakery acquired a machine by issuing a six-month note with a face value of $8,000 and a stated interest rate of 10% to be paid at maturity. Further assume that the stated interest rate is realistic (i.e., the stated and the market interest rates are identical), and that the note is issued and matures in the same accounting period:

   a. **To determine the present value of the note:**

   Since **i = r:**

   Present value = $8,000 (1 + 10% x 6/12) / (1 + 10% x 6/12)
   = **$8,000**

   b. **To record the issuance of the note:**

Machinery	8,000	
Notes payable		8,000

   c. **To record the payment of the note at maturity:**

Notes payable	8,000	
Interest expense ($8,000 x 10% x 6/12)	400	
Cash		8,400

2. **Interest-bearing note with unrealistic stated interest rate:** Assume that when Normandy Bakery issued the above note, the market interest rate is 16%:

   a. **To determine the present value of the note:**

   Present value = $8,000 (1 + 10% x 6/12) / (1 + 16% x 6/12)
   = **$7,778**

b. To record the issuance of the note:

Machinery	7,778	
Discount on notes payable	222	
Notes payable		8,000

c. To record the payment of the note at maturity:

Notes payable	8,000	
Interest expense ($8,000 x 10% x 6/12)	400	
Cash		8,400

d. To amortize note discount and to adjust interest expense:

Interest expense	222	
Discount on notes payable		222

3. **Noninterest-bearing note:** If the note does not bear interest, the face value would include both the cash price of the machine and the implied interest expense. Assuming the $8,000 note does not bear interest and the market interest rate is 16%:

a. To determine the present value of the note:

Since the note is noninterest-bearing, the maturity value of the note is simply its face value:

Present value = $8,000 / (1 + 16% x 6/12)
= $7,407

b. To record the issuance of the note:

Machinery	7,407	
Discount on notes payable	593	
Notes payable		8,000

c. To record the payment of the note at maturity:

Notes payable	8,000	
Cash		8,000

d. To amortize note discount and to recognize interest expense:

Interest expense	593	
Discount on notes payable		593

Note that the acquisition cost of the machine is measured by the present value of the note, and the present value of a note is less than its face value if the note does not bear interest or its stated interest rate is unrealistically lower than the market. In these cases the note is discounted. To record a discounted note the following approaches are both acceptable:

1. **The gross approach (as illustrated above):** The note is recorded at its face value and the excess of the face value over the present value of the note is debited to a contra liability account, i.e., discount on notes payable. The discount is then amortized over the term of the note by making adjustment to interest expense.

2. **The net approach:** The note is recorded at its present value, note discount is not separately recorded, and the amount paid over the present value of the note is recognized as interest expense.

Note also that if a note is issued in one accounting period and paid in another, a year end adjusting entry to accrue interest expense may be required.

E. Dividends Payable

The declaration of cash or property dividends by the board of directors creates a legal obligation for a corporation and should be recorded and reported as a current liability if they are to be paid within the coming year, or operating cycle, whichever is longer. Undeclared dividends of any kind are not recorded because the corporation has no obligation to its stockholders. Nevertheless, undeclared dividends on cumulative preferred stock, known as preferred dividends in arrears, should be disclosed in the notes. A declared stock dividend, on the other hand, is a transfer of retained earnings to contributed capital without sacrificing any future economic benefit, and should thus be reported in the owners' equity section of the balance sheet.

F. Advances and Returnable Deposits

When cash is collected from a customer as an advance payment for products or services or as a deposit which is refundable, the firm is obliged to transfer goods, to render services, or to return the deposits to the customer under certain conditions. Upon receipt of the cash, a liability account (i.e., unearned revenues, or customers deposits) is credited, which is then reported as a current liability if the obligation is expected to be discharged within one year, or an operating cycle if longer. The same rule is applicable to deposits collected from the employees of the firm. Any unclaimed deposits are reported as a miscellaneous revenue.

G. Accrued Liabilities

An expense incurred but for which cash has not been paid is referred to as an accrued expense (liability) and should be recorded by an adjusting entry usually at year end. Accrued liabilities generally due within one year, or an operating cycle, and are classified as short term. Examples of accrued expenses are unpaid salaries earned by employees, unpaid interest owed to creditors and property taxes due to the local government. If salaries of $2,000 incurred but have not been paid by the end of the period, the expense and related liability should be recorded as follows:

Salaries expense	2,000	
Salaries payable		2,000

This adjusting entry may be reversed at the beginning of the following period. With the original adjusting entry reversed, the later payment will be recorded simply by debiting expense, and crediting cash.

In addition to an accrual of employees' regular salaries expenses, an employer should also accrue a liability for employees' **compensated absences** (such as vacation or holiday pay) if the following conditions are all met:

1. The employer's obligation is attributable to employees' services **already rendered.**
2. The obligation relates to rights that **vest.**
3. Payment is **probable.**
4. The amount can be reasonably **estimated.**

Note that an employer is not required to accrue a liability for **nonvesting** accumulating rights (i.e., can be carried forward) to receive sick pay benefits because of the lower degree of reliability of the estimates and the cost of making those estimates. At the end of each year an adjusting entry should be made to recognize an expense and a liability for those **unused** vacations and holidays earned by employees during the period.

H. Collection for Third Parties

Business enterprises frequently make **collections for third parties** from customers or employees and periodically remit those amounts to the appropriate governmental or other units. Amounts so collected represent liabilities until remitted. Examples are sales taxes, payroll taxes, employee withholding taxes, insurance and union dues. A typical entry to record sales revenue and the collection of sales tax is illustrated below, assuming a sale of $200, and a sales tax rate of 8%:

1. To record the sale:

Cash [$200 (1 + 8%)]	216	
Sales revenue		200
Sales tax payable ($200 x 8%)		16

2. To record the remittance:

Sales tax payable	16	
Cash		16

The typical withholdings on payrolls include (1) federal income tax, (2) FICA (Federal Insurance Contribution Act) tax, generally known as social security tax, and (3) FUTA (Federal Unemployment Tax Act) tax. Note that the employer is also taxed under the FICA and the FUTA. The amounts withheld by the employer are recorded as liabilities, whereas the employer's own shares in the taxes are additions to payroll expenses.

I. Reclassification of Liabilities

1. **Reclassify long-term obligation as short-term liability.** A long-term obligation generally should be reclassified as a current liability when it becomes payable (or callable) within one year (or operating cycle), **unless** the payment is to be made with a **noncurrent** asset (e.g., if a long-term bond issue is to be paid at maturity with the amounts accumulated in a bond sinking fund). For instance, a 20-year bond is classified as a long-term liability for 19 years, then normally is reclassified as a current liability the 20th year. Furthermore, if the creditor has at the balance sheet date, or will have within one year (or operating cycle, if longer) from that date, the **unilateral right** to demand immediate repayment of the debt under any provision of the debt agreement, the obligation should be reported as a current liability even its stated maturity date is still years away (**FAS 78**).

2. **Reclassify short-term liability as long-term liability.** If a short-term liability is expected to be **refinanced** with a long-term obligation (e.g., if new bonds will be issued at the maturity of old bonds due within one year, and the proceeds from the second issue will be used to pay the maturity amount of the first issue), the liability should be reported as a **long-term liability** if the following criteria are both met:

   a. The debtor has the **intent** to refinance.

   b. The **ability** to refinance is **demonstrated** by either an existing refinancing agreement, or actual financing prior to the issuance of the financial statements.

J. Contingencies and Estimated Liabilities

As defined in **FAS 5,** a contingency is an existing condition, situation, or set of circumstances involving uncertainty as to possible gain (i.e., gain contingency) or loss (i.e., loss contingency) that ultimately will be resolved when one or more future events occur or fail to occur. A gain contingency is rarely recognized. Rather, it is disclosed in notes to the financial statements, provided the note does not give misleading implications. Accounting treatment of loss contingency, on the other hand, depends on:

1. Whether the contingency is:

    a. **Probable.** The future event or events are likely to occur.

    b. **Reasonably possible.** The chance of occurrence of the future event or events is more than remote but less than likely.

    c. **Remote.** The chance of occurrence of the future event or events is slight.

2. Whether the amount of the loss can be at least **reasonably estimated (measurable).**

A loss is recognized and a liability is accrued if the loss contingency is **both** probable and measurable. If the occurrence of the loss is remote, no disclosure is required. If the occurrence of the loss is probable, but the amount cannot be reasonably estimated, or if the occurrence of loss is only reasonably possible, a footnote may suffice to disclose the contingency. These accounting treatments are summarized as follows:

Reasonably Measurable	Occurrence of Future Event(s)		
	Probable	Reasonably Possible	Remote
Yes	Accrue liability	Footnote	Disclosure not required
No	Footnote	Footnote	Disclosure not required

Typical loss contingencies include estimated loss on receivables, litigations, claims and assessments, and anticipated losses on the disposal of a segment of the business. In addition, the following transactions are also related to the occurrence of future event(s):

1. **Warranties and guarantees.** Warranties and guarantees are often offered by a seller or a manufacturer to correct deficiencies of or to give refund for the product sold to its customers for a specified period of time. Some firms report warranty and guarantee expenses when the expenditures are made. Theoretically, however, these expenses, if reasonably measurable, should be accrued in the period of the sale. The estimated warranty and guarantee expenses are recorded by debiting an expense account and crediting a liability account (e.g., estimated warranties payable).

   In addition to the manufacturers' warranties and guarantees, many firms sell separately service contracts for the goods sold. In this case, the sales price of the service contract should be recorded as an unearned service revenue, which will then be transferred to a revenue account when earned.

2. **Premiums.** To promote sales, many firms acquire premium items (e.g., dinner ware) and offer to give them away to their customers at no charge, or to sell them at a reduced price below cost upon receiving coupons, box tops, labels, etc. as a proof of their purchase of a certain quantity of a certain product. The cost of such a premium offer over the reduced price, if any, represents an expense and should be recognized in the period of sale of the product. At year end the expense of the outstanding claims expected to be redeemed should be estimated, accrued and reported as a current liability. Typical entries pertinent to premium offers are as follows:

   1991 -- Year of sale

   To record the purchase of $3,000 premium items for cash:

Account	Debit	Credit
Inventory of premiums	3,000	
Cash		3,000

   To record premiums with a cost of $2,000 distributed to customers at a reduced price of $200:

Account	Debit	Credit
Cash	200	
Premium expense	1,800	
Inventory of premiums		2,000

   To accrue estimated premium expense of $900 at year end:

Account	Debit	Credit
Premium expense	900	
Estimated liability under premium plan		900

1992 -- Year after sale:

To record distribution of premiums with a cost of $1,000 and a reduced price of $100:

Cash	100	
Estimated liability under premium plan	900	
Inventory of premiums		1,000

3. **Purchase contracts.** Executory (unperformed) contracts or agreements usually are **not** recorded because a transfer of assets or liabilities has not yet occurred. If the anticipated consideration is material, a note disclosure may be sufficient. For a purchase contract, however, if the commitment is firm (i.e., the contract is noncancelable) and the price declines, a loss on the firm commitment is recognized by debiting loss on purchase commitment and crediting a liability account, e.g., estimated liability on purchase commitment. Later price recovery is disregarded and no gain is recognized for the purchase agreement. On the date of purchase, (a) inventory (or purchase) is debited at the market price on the date when the loss was recognized, or on the date of purchase if lower, (b) estimated liability is debited at the existing amount, (c) cash or accounts payable is credited at the contract price, and (d) to balance the entry if necessary, loss on purchase commitment is debited, indicating a further decline in the price.

K. Current Liabilities Conditional to Operating Results

Certain liabilities of a business entity such as follows are based on the results of operations and should be measured and accrued:

1. **Income tax payable.** All the incorporated business entities are legally required to file income tax return and to pay income taxes. At year end income tax payable is recorded and reported as a current liability. Due to the inevitable discrepancies between tax rules and GAAP, income tax payable as reported in the tax return differs from income tax expense as presented on the financial statements. The accounting procedures used to deal with such discrepancies are covered in Chapter 17 in detail.

2. **Bonus payable.** Many firms pay cash bonuses to selected employees based on revenues, outputs or income. Bonuses increase salaries expenses, which are tax deductible, and establish current liabilities. At year end, bonus expenses should be computed and accrued. Presented below are several commonly employed formulas for computing bonus amounts. Given that:

Income before deducting bonus and tax	= $10,000
Bonus rate	= 10%
Tax rate	= 30%

a. The bonus is based on income before deducting bonus and tax

Bonus = Bonus rate x Income before bonus and tax
= 10% x $10,000
= $1,000

b. The bonus is based on income before deducting bonus but after deducting tax:

Tax = Tax rate x Income before tax but after bonus
= 30% ($10,000 - Bonus)
= $3,000 - 30% x Bonus

Bonus = Bonus rate (Income before bonus and tax - Tax)
= 10% [$10,000 - ($3,000 - 30% x Bonus)]
= $1,000 - $300 + 3% x Bonus
= $700 + 3% x Bonus
= $700 / 97%
= $722

c. The bonus is based on income after deducting bonus and tax:

Tax = $3,000 - 30% x Bonus (see b above)

Bonus = Bonus rate (Income before bonus and tax - Bonus - Tax)
= 10% [$10,000 - Bonus - ($3,000 - 30% x Bonus)]
= $1,000 - 10% x Bonus - $300 + 3% x Bonus
= $700 - 7% x bonus
= $700 / 107%
= $654

For the accrual of bonus expenses, the following journal entries are pertinent:

a. To accrue the bonus:

Compensation expense	xxxx	
Bonus payable		xxxx

b. To record the payment:

Bonus payable	xxxx	
Cash		xxxx

KEY CONCEPTS

Contingencies A contingency is an existing condition, situation, or set of circumstances involving uncertainty as to possible gain or loss that ultimately will be resolved when one or more future events occur or fail to occur. A gain contingency is rarely recorded. A loss contingency should be recognized if it is probable and measurable.

Current liabilities Short-term obligations scheduled to mature within one year or operating cycle, if longer, whose liquidation is expected to require the use of existing current assets.

Liabilities Probable, future sacrifices of economic benefits arising from the present obligations of a particular entity to transfer goods or provide services to other entity in the future resulting from past transactions or events.

Purchase contracts Unperformed executory contracts which are usually unrecorded. However, if a purchase contract is noncancelable and the market price declines, a liability is recognized for the estimated loss.

Reclassifying long-term liabilities Long-term liabilities are reclassified as current liabilities if they become due within one year or operating cycle and whose liquidation is expected to require the use of existing current assets.

Refinancing short-term liabilities Short-term liabilities expected to be refinanced with a long-term obligation are reported as non-current liabilities if (1) the debtor has the intent to refinance, and (2) the debtor has the ability to refinance.

REVIEW QUESTIONS AND EXERCISES

TRUE-FALSE

Indicate whether each of the following statements is true or false by circling the correct response.

T F 1. Notes payable generally should be recorded at their present values, but trade notes due within a year may be recorded at their face values.

T F 2. Notes payable are distinguished from accounts payable by whether or not they arise in connection with the firm's normal operations.

T F 3. A liability may be recognized and reported even though the **exact** amount of the liability is unknown.

T F 4. The existence of a legally enforceable claim is not a prerequisite for an obligation to qualify as a liability.

T F 5. In order for a liability to be recognized, the event or transaction causing the liability must have occurred.

T F 6. Current maturities of long-term debt should always be reclassified as current liabilities.

T F 7. A liability payable within one year should always be classified as a current liability.

T F 8. A short-term liability should never be reclassified as a long-term liability.

T F 9. Dividends in arrears on cumulative preferred stock should be accrued as a current liability.

T F 10. It is not required to accrue a liability for employees' sick pay that accumulates but is **nonvesting.**

T F 11. A liability for a loss contingency should be accrued if (a) it is reasonably possible that assets have been impaired and (b) the amount of the loss can be reasonably estimated.

T F 12. Footnote disclosure is required for those loss contingencies for which an impairment of assets is reasonably possible.

T F 13. A gain contingency usually is recognized in the statement of income when an increase in assets is reasonably possible and the amount is reasonably measurable.

T F 14. A noninterest-bearing note does not give rise to the problem of interest expense.

EXERCISE 1

Indicate with the appropriate code the manner in which each of the following usually should be reported on a balance sheet.

ITEMS

___ 1. Accounts payable.

___ 2. Six-month note payable.

___ 3. Preferred dividends in arrears.

___ 4. Cash and property dividends payable.

___ 5. Two-year note payable.

___ 6. Revenues collected in advance.

___ 7. Accrued expenses.

___ 8. Customers' deposits returnable within a year.

___ 9. Remote possibility of losing a lawsuit.

___ 10. Reasonably possible loss of $35,000 from pending lawsuit.

___ 11. Probable loss contingency of $53,000 expected to incur in one year.

___ 12. Long-term debt which is subject to creditor's legal right to demand immediate repayment within one year.

___ 13. Short-term obligation expected to be financed on a long-term basis.

___ 14. Bonus payable.

REPORTING

CL = Current liability

LTL = Long-term liability

ND = Note disclosure

NR = Not reported

EXERCISE 2

Mohegans Company acquired a piece of equipment by issuing a 8%, one-year, $12,000 note on October 1, 1991.

Required: For each of the following situations determine the present value of the note and prepare journal entries as indicated:

1. The stated interest rate is realistic:

a. Determine the present value of the note.

b. Record the issuance of the note.

c. Record year end adjustment.

d. Record the payment of the note.

2. The market interest rate is 14%.

a. Determine the present value of the note.

b. Record the issuance of the note.

c. Record year end adjustment (Straight-line amortization):

d. Record the payment of the note and amortization of discount:

EXERCISE 3

Cherry Corporation entered into an agreement on July 10, 1991 to acquire 10,000 units of merchandise at $12 per unit. On December 31, 1991 the market price of the merchandise fell to $10 per unit. Assume the agreement was noncancelable, and the merchandise was delivered on May 15, 1992, when the market price was (a) recovered to $11, and (b) further declines to $9.

Required: Record the above transactions and year end adjustment as appropriate.

1. July 10, 1991 -- To record the agreement:

2. December 31, 1991 -- To record loss on purchase contract:

3. a. May 15, 1992 -- To record the purchase (Market price = $11):

   b. May 15, 1992 -- To record the purchase (Market price = $9):

EXERCISE 4

Green Turtle Cereal offers an Almighty Calculator in exchange for 10 return box tops. The cost of the calculator is $15 per piece. In 1991, Green Turtle sold 50,000 boxes of cereal at $5 per box, 60% of which will be redeemed. At the end of 1991, 10,000 box tops had been redeemed.

Required: Prepare entry for each of the following:

1. To record the sale for 1991.

2. To record the redemption of box tops in 1991.

3. To adjust premiums expense at the end of 1991:

MULTIPLE CHOICE

Enter the letter corresponding to the response which **best** completes each of the following statements or questions.

____ 1. The essential characteristics of a liability do **not** include:

a. It represents an ownership interest.
b. It is a present duty or responsibility to transfer assets or provide services.
c. It is an obligation of a particular entity.
d. The transaction or event obligating the entity has happened.

____ 2. Which of the following typically would **not** be classified as a current liability?

a. bonds payable maturing within one year.
b. a guarantee of the indebtedness of another party.
c. nontrade notes payable.
d. rent revenue received in advance.

____ 3. Which of the following statements concerning dividends is **untrue?**

a. Once declared, a cash dividend on common stock becomes a liability of the corporation.
b. Since a dividend is generally paid within a month or so, it usually is classified as current.
c. Preferred dividends in arrears should not be accrued as a liability.
d. Once declared, preferred dividends should be disclosed via footnote.

____ 4. An employer should accrue a liability for compensation of employees' future absences if certain conditions exist. Each of the following is a condition for accrual except:

a. the payment for those benefits is probable.
b. the employee has the right to carry forward the vesting benefits beyond the current period.
c. the amount of payment is known.
d. the benefits have been earned.

__d__ 5. Which of the following loss contingencies generally does not require accrual?

a. product warranties.
b. lawsuits with probable negative outcome.
c. premium offers to customers.
d. obligations related to unasserted claims.

__d__ 6. A loss on a purchase contract should be recognized if:

a. The contract is cancelable.
b. The contract is noncancelable and the market price remains stable.
c. The contract is noncancelable and the market price is higher than the contract price.
d. The contract is noncancelable and the market price is lower than the contract price.

__d__ 7. After a loss on a purchase contract is recognized, a later acquisition of the merchandise under the contract should be valued at:

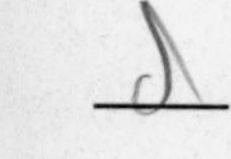

a. the contract price.
b. the market price at the date of purchase.
c. the market price at the date of recognizing the loss.
d. the market price at the date of purchase, or at the date of recognizing the loss, whichever is lower.

___ 8. The occurrence of a loss contingency is probable, but the amount cannot be reasonably estimated, the loss contingency should be:

a. recorded.
b. disclosed in notes.
c. ignored.
d. either of the above.

___ 9. On January 1, 1991 Prima Company agreed to grant its employees two weeks vacation each year, with the provision that vacations earned in a particular year could be taken the following year. For the year ended December 31, 1991, all six of Prima's employees earned $600 per week each. Five of these vacation weeks were not taken during 1991. In Prima's statement of income, how much expense should be reported for compensated absences for 1991?

a. $ 600
b. $1,200
c. $7,200
d. $3,000

___ 10. Marks Corporation has $1,000,000 of notes payable due on April 1, 1992. On January 2, 1992, Marks signed an agreement to borrow up to $800,000 to refinance the notes payable on a long-term basis. On the December 31, 1991 balance sheet, Marks should classify:

a. $200,000 of notes payable as short-term and $800,000 as long-term obligations.
b. $200,000 of notes payable as long-term and $800,000 as short-term obligations.
c. $1,000,000 as short-term obligations.
d. $1,000,000 as long-term obligations.

___ 11. Jena Fabrics borrowed cash from a local bank by issuing a $5,000, 6-month, noninterest-bearing note. Assuming an effective interest rate of 10%, the principal amount that Jena borrowed from the bank is:

a. $5,000
b. $4,500
c. $4,762
d. $5,500

____ 12. During 1991 Atlanta Company introduced a new line of appliances that carry a two-year warranty against manufacturer's defects. Based on industry experience, warranty costs are estimated at 3% of sales in the year of sale and 7% in the year after sale. Sales and actual warranty expenditures for the first two-year period were as follows:

	Sales	Actual warranty expenditures
1991	$30,000	$ 900
1992	$45,000	$3,450

What amount should Atlanta report as the warranty expense for 1992?

a. $3,000
b. $4,500
c. $7,500
d. $3,450

____ 13. Based on the same data as in Question 12, what amount should Atlanta report as estimated warranty liability at December 31, 1992?

a. $4,050
b. $3,450
c. $3,150
d. $3,300

____ 14. A company entered into an agreement with its employees to provide bonus at 10% of income before deducting bonus but after deducting tax. Income before tax and bonus for 1991 is $50,000, and the applicable tax rate is 34%. The bonus liability to be accrued for 1991 is:

a. $3,416
b. $1,700
c. $3,300
d. $4,211

SOLUTIONS TO REVIEW QUESTIONS AND EXERCISES

TRUE-FALSE

1.	T	5.	T	9.	F	13.	F
2.	F	6.	F	10.	T	14.	F
3.	T	7.	F	11.	F		
4.	T	8.	F	12.	T		

EXERCISE 1

1.	CL	5.	LTL	9.	NR	13.	LTL
2.	CL	6.	CL	10.	ND	14.	CL
3.	NR	7.	CL	11.	CL		
4.	CL	8.	CL	12.	CL		

EXERCISE 2

1. **The stated interest rate is realistic:**

   a. **October 1, 1991 -- Determine the present value of the note.**

   Since the stated interest is realistic:

   Present value = Face value = $12,000.

   b. **October 1, 1991 -- Record the issuance of the note.**

Equipment	12,000	
Notes payable		12,000

   c. **December 31, 1991 -- Record year end adjustment.**

Interest expense ($12,000 x 8% x 3/12)	240	
Interest payable		240

Assuming no reversing entry was made.

d. October 1, 1992 -- Record the payment of the note.

Account	Debit	Credit
Notes payable	12,000	
Interest payable	240	
Interest expense ($12,000 x 8% x 9/12)	720	
Cash		12,960

2. The market interest rate is 14%.

a. October 1, 1991 -- Determine the present value of the note.

Present value = $12,000 (1 + 8%)/(1 + 14%)
= $11,369

b. October 1, 1991 -- Record the issuance of the note.

Account	Debit	Credit
Equipment	11,369	
Discount on notes payable	631	
Notes payable		12,000

c. December 31, 1991 -- Record year end adjustment (Straight-line amortization):

Account	Debit	Credit
Interest expense	398	
Discount on notes payable ($631 x 3/12)		158
Interest payable ($12,000 x 8% x 3/12)		240

Assuming no reversing entry.

d. October 1, 1992 -- Record the payment of the note and amortization of discount:

Account	Debit	Credit
Notes payable	12,000	
Interest payable	240	
Interest expense	1,193	
Cash ($12,000 x 108%)		12,960
Discount on notes payable ($631 - $158)		473

EXERCISE 3

1. **July 10, 1991 -- To record the agreement:**

   None.

2. **December 31, 1991 -- To record loss on purchase contract:**

Unrealized loss on purchase contract [10,000 x ($12 - $10)]	20,000	
Estimated liability on purchase contract		20,000

3. a. **May 15, 1992 -- To record the purchase (Market price = $11):**

Purchases (10,000 x $10)	100,000	
Estimated liability on purchase contract	20,000	
Cash		120,000

   b. **May 15, 1992 -- To record the purchase (Market price = $9):**

Purchases (10,000 x $9)	90,000	
Estimated liability on purchase contract	20,000	
Loss on purchase contract	10,000	
Cash		120,000

EXERCISE 4

1. **To record the sale for 1991.**

Cash	250,000	
Sales (50,000 x $5)		250,000

2. **To record the redemption of box tops in 1991.**

Premium expense [(10,000 / 10) x $15]	15,000	
Inventory of premiums		15,000

3. **To adjust premium expense at the end of 1991:**

Premium expense [(50,000 x 60% - 10,000) / 10] x $15	30,000	
Estimated premium liability		30,000

MULTIPLE CHOICE:

1.	a	5.	d	9.	c	13.	c
2.	b	6.	d	10.	a	14.	a
3.	d	7.	d	11.	c		
4.	c	8.	b	12.	b		

Computations:

9. (c) Compensated absence expense
= 6 x 2 weeks x $600
= $7,200.

10. (a) Long-term liability
= $800,000, the amount to be refinanced on long-term basis.

Short-term liability
= $200,000, the amount not to be refinanced.

11. (c) Present value of noninterest-bearing note
= $5,000 / (1 + 10% x 6/12)
= $4,762.

12. (b) Premiums expense for 1992
= Sales in 1992 x total percentage of redemption
= $45,000 (3% + 7%)
= $4,500.

13. (c) Estimated premiums liability at December 31, 1992
= Estimated premiums expense to date - Premiums expenditures to date
= [($30,000 + $45,000) x (3% + 7%)] - ($900 + $3,450)
= $7,500 - $4,350
= $3,150 (or $45,000 x 7% = $3,150).

14. (a) The bonus is on income before deducting bonus but after deducting tax:

Tax = Tax rate x Income before tax but after bonus
= 34% ($50,000 - Bonus)
= $17,000 - 34% x Bonus

Bonus = Bonus rate (Income before bonus and tax - Tax)
= 10% [$50,000 - ($17,000 - 34% x Bonus)]
= $5,000 - $1,700 + 3.4% x Bonus
= $3,300 + 3.4% x Bonus
= $3,300 / 96.6%
= $3,416.

CHAPTER 16

Long-Term Liabilities

CHAPTER OBJECTIVES

This chapter is designed to enable students to:

A. Be familiar with long-term liabilities and how to value them.

B. Understand the nature of bonds and how to compute the price of a bond at issuance.

C. Know how to account for basic and more complex bond situations from the viewpoint of both the issuer and investor.

D. Appreciate the accounting issues surrounding long-term debt instruments issued with equity rights.

E. Be familiar with the different ways long-term debt is extinguished.

F. Be able to value long-term notes and measure periodic interest.

G. Know how to account for serial bonds.

H. Understand the issues underlying accounting for troubled debt restructuring.

CHAPTER OVERVIEW

A. As discussed in Chapter 15, liabilities are characterized by (1) there being a present obligation, (2) of a particular entity to transfer assets or provide services to another entity in the future, and (3) resulting from a transaction or event which has already happened. Any existing obligations whose liquidation will **not** require the use of current assets are reported as long-term liabilities. Typically they include obligations such as bonds, long-term notes, and mortgages which extend beyond one year from the balance sheet date, or an operating cycle if longer.

B. Bonds -- General

1. **Bond selling (market) price:** A bond payable obligates the issuing corporation to (1) repay a stated sum, referred to as **face value** (or principal, maturity, or par value) at a definite **maturity date**, and (2) make specified periodic cash interest payments, usually semiannually, based on the face value of the bond and the **stated interest rate** (or coupon, nominal, bearing rate) on the bond. The selling price of a bond is the present value of all these fixed future cash flows discounted at the actual interest rate, also referred to as the market rate, yield rate or the effective interest rate. That is, the bond issue is priced to yield the effective rate, and an investor paying that price will earn an rate of return equal to that rate. As shown below, given a stated rate, interest periods and face value, there exists an inverse relationship between the effective interest rate and the present value of a bond:

Given	**FV**	=	Face (or maturity) value of the bond
	n	=	Number of interest payment periods
	r	=	Stated interest rate
	i	=	Effective (market) interest rate
and:	**PV**	=	Present value of the bond
		=	Present value of the face value + Present value of the periodic interest payments
		=	$FV \times pv1_{n,i} + (FV \times r) \times pva_{n,i}$

If	Then
$i = r$	PV = FV, bonds issued at FV
$i > r$	$PV < FV$, bonds issued at a discount
$i < r$	$PV > FV$, bonds issued at a premium

Bonds issued at face value present no accounting complications. If they are issued at a discount or premium, however, the discount or premium should be amortized over the term of the bonds to adjust (a) the carrying value of the bonds, and (b) the interest expense reported by the issuer and interest revenue reported by the investor. On the balance sheet, any unamortized discount (premium) is deducted from (added to) the face value of the bonds to show the carrying (book) value of the bonds.

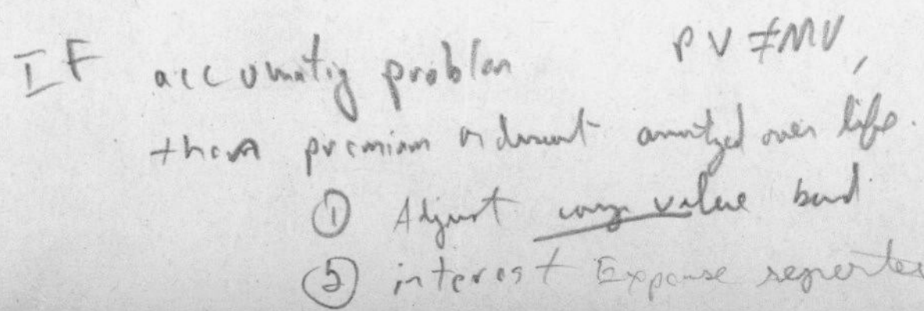

2. **Amortization of bond discount or premium:** Two methods are in use:

   a. **Straight-line method.** An equal dollar amount of discount or premium is amortized throughout the bond term. This method is conceptually defective because a constant rate of interest is not maintained. Under GAAP it can be used only when the interest amounts obtained are not materially different from those produced under the interest method.

   b. **Interest method.** **A constant effective rate** of interest is maintained. The dollar amount of interest is calculated by multiplying the effective rate to the beginning book (carrying) value of the bond, i.e., face value - (+) unamortized discount (premium). Since the book value of the bond changes as the discount or premium is amortized, the dollar amounts of amortization vary from period to period.

   Under the interest method, an amortization schedule is often prepared showing interest expense (revenue) to be recorded, discount (premium) to be amortized and the carrying value of the bonds over the term of the bonds.

ILLUSTRATION 1 -- Bonds issued at a discount:

On January 1, 1991, Jackson & Kreger, Inc. issued $20,000, 10% bonds, which mature in five years. Damen Corporation purchased the entire bond issue. The market rate for bonds of similar risk and maturity is 12%. Interest of $1,000 ($20,000 x 10% x 6/12) is payable **semiannually** on June 30, and December 31.

(1) To determine the present value (i.e., issuing price) of the bonds:

$$\begin{aligned}
\textbf{PV} &= \textbf{FV x pv1}_{n,i} + \textbf{(FV x r) x pva}_{n,i} \\
&= \$20{,}000 \times pv1_{n=10,i=6\%} + \$1{,}000 \times pva_{n=10,i=6\%} \\
&= \$20{,}000 \times .55839 + \$1{,}000 \times 7.36009 \\
&= \$11{,}168 + 7{,}360 \\
&= \$18{,}528
\end{aligned}$$

Note that, since interest is paid semiannually:

n = 5 x 2 = 10
r = 10% / 2 = 5%
i = 12% / 2 = 6%

(2) To prepare an amortization schedule:

Date	Cash Interest (10% x 6/12)	Effective Interest (12% x 6/12)	Discount Amortiza-tion	Unamortized Bond Discount	Carrying Amount of Bond
	(1)	(2)	(3)	(4)	(5)
1/1/1991				$1,472.00	$18,528.00
6/30/1991	$1,000	$1,111.68	$111.68	1,360.32	18,639.68
12/31/1991	1,000	1,118.38	118.38	1,241.94	18,758.06
6/30/1992	1,000	1,125.48	125.48	1,116.46	18,883.54
12/31/1992	1,000	1,133.01	133.01	983.45	19,016.55
6/30/1993	1,000	1,140.99	140.99	842.46	19,157.54
12/31/1993	1,000	1,149.45	149.45	693.01	19,306.99
6/30/1994	1,000	1,158.42	158.42	534.59	19,465.41
12/31/1994	1,000	1,167.92	167.92	366.67	19,633.33
6/30/1995	1,000	1,178.00	178.00	188.67	19,811.33
12/31/1995	1,000	1,188.67	188.67	0	20,000.00
Total	$10,000	$11,472.00	$1,472.00		

Notes: (1) Cash interest = Face value x Stated interest rate.

(2) Effective interest expense (revenue) = Beginning carrying amount x Effective interest rate.

(3) Discount amortization = Effective Interest - Cash Interest.

(4) Unamortized discount = Beginning unamortized discount - discount amortization for the interest period.

(5) Carrying amount (book value) of bonds = Face value - unamortized discount.

The above amortization table shows that the amortization of discount (or premium) adjusts the carrying value of the bonds towards their face value. This table can be used by both the issuer and the investor of the bonds.

(3) To record bond transactions and report bond liability for the issuer and bond investment for the investor:

Jackson & Kreger (Issuer)			Damen Corporation (Investor)		
To record issuance of bonds:			To record bond investment:		
Jan. 1, 1991:			Jan. 1, 1991		
Cash	18,528.00		Investment in bonds	18,528.00	
Discount on bonds	1,472.00		Cash		18,528.00
Bonds payable		20,000.00			
To record interest payments:			To record interest receipts:		
June 30, 1991:			June 30, 1991:		
Interest expense	1,111.68		Cash	1,000.00	
Discount on bonds		111.68	Investment in bonds	111.68	
Cash		1,000.00	Interest revenue		1,111.68
Dec. 31, 1991:			Dec. 31, 1991:		
Interest expense	1,118.38		Cash	1,000.00	
Discount on bonds		118.38	Investment in bonds	118.38	
Cash		1,000.00	Interest revenue		1,118.38
To report bond liability:			To report bond investment:		
Dec. 31, 1991:			Dec. 31, 1991:		
Long-Term Liabilities:			Investment and Funds:		
Bonds payable	$20,000.00		Investment in bonds	$18,758.06	
Less: Discount on bonds	1,241.94				
Net book value	$18,758.06				
Repeat the above interest entries using the appropriate figures obtained from the amortization table for the remaining term of the bonds.					
To record retirement of bonds:			To record disposal of bonds:		
Dec. 31, 1995:			Dec. 31, 1995:		
Bonds payable	20,000.00		Cash	20,000.00	
Cash		20,000.00	Investment in bonds		20,000.00

Note that while the issuer records bonds payable at fact value and uses a separate discount or premium account, the investor usually records bond investment at the net amount [i.e., book (carrying) value]. Note also that if the straight-line method is applied, interest expense (revenue) would be $1,147.20 ($1,000 + $1,472 / 10) every six months.

D. Bonds -- Additional Issues

1. **Bond issue cost:** Following **APB Opinion No. 21**, costs incurred in connection with the issuance of bonds, such as legal costs, printing costs, and underwriting fees, are recorded separately as **deferred charges** and are amortized over the term of the related bonds. The straight-line method of amortization generally is used for materiality reasons.

2. **Bonds sold between interest dates:** When bonds are sold between interest dates, the bonds will be sold at the appropriate market price **plus** accrued interest. That is, the proceeds from the sale of a bond include the selling price of the bond and interest accrued since the last interest date to the date of issuance.

ILLUSTRATION 2 -- Bonds issued between interest dates:

On March 1, 1991, Anderson Company issued $10,000 of 8%, 5-year bonds at face value. Cash interest is payable at year end.

Since the bonds were issued two months after the last interest date, the accrued interest for the two-month period is:

Accrued interest = $10,000 x 8% x 2/12
= $133

Anderson (Issuer)			Investor		
To record issuance of bonds:			To record bond investment:		
Mar. 1, 1991:			Mar. 1, 1991		
Cash	10,133		Investment in bonds	10,000	
Bonds payable		10,000	Interest revenue	133	
Interest expense		133	Cash		10,133
To record the next interest payment:			To record interest receipt:		
Dec. 31, 1991:			Dec. 31, 1991:		
Interest expense	800		Cash	800	
Cash		800	Interest revenue		800
Interest expense (1991) = $800 - $133 = $667.			Interest revenue (1991) = $800 - $133 = $667.		

3. **Accounting period does not coincide with interest period:** When the accounting period ends between interest dates, it is necessary to accrue interest since the last interest date to the end of accounting period. Assume Brilliant Company issued $100,000 of 8%, 5-year bonds for $92,278 on October 1, 1991. Interest is payable each September 30 and March 31. At the end of 1991, three months' interest must be recorded in a year-end adjusting entry, assuming an effective rate of 10%:

    Dec. 31, 1991:

Interest expense ($92,278 x 10% x 3/12)	2,307	
Interest payable ($100,000 x 8% x 3/12)		2,000
Discount on bonds payable		307

4. **Bonds with detachable warrants:** Occasionally bonds are sold with **detachable** stock warrants as part of the security issue. A stock warrant allows the investor to purchase a specified number of shares of common stock at a specified price. Since stock warrants have value and are usually traded in the market separately from bonds, in essence, two different securities, i.e., the bonds (debt) and the warrants (equity), are being sold as a "package."

    Accordingly, at issuance, the package price should be allocated between the two different securities on the basis of their relative market values. If the separate market value of only one of the two securities is determinable, the market value determines the allocation.

ILLUSTRATION 3 -- Bonds with detachable warrants:

On January 1, 1991, Portland Company issued $100,000 of bonds for $109,000. Attached to the bonds were 5,000 detachable stock warrants, exercisable for 5,000 shares of Portland's $10 par common stock at $12 per share. At issuance, the market value of the bonds sold separately was $101,000. Assume that 80% of the warrants were exercised on December 31, 1991, and the remainder forfeited.

Pertinent journal entries are presented as follows:

Portland (Issuer)			Investor		
To record issuance of bonds:			To record bond investment:		
Jan. 1, 1991:			Jan. 1, 1991:		
Cash	109,000		Investment in bonds	101,000	
Bonds payable		100,000	Investment in stock warrants	8,000	
Premium on bonds payable		1,000	Cash		109,000
Stock warrants outstanding		8,000			
To record the issuance of stock:			To record the exercise of stock warrants:		
Dec. 31, 1991:			Dec. 31, 1991:		
Cash (4,000 x $12)	48,000		Investment in stock	54,400	
Stock warrant outstanding	6,400		Investment in stock warrants ($8,000 x 80%)		6,400
Common stock (4,000 x $10)		40,000	Cash		48,000
Paid-in capital in excess of par		14,400			
To record forfeited warrants:			To record forfeited warrants:		
Stock warrants outstanding	1,600		Loss on investment in warrants	1,600	
Paid-in capital - from forfeited warrants		1,600	Investment in stock warrants		1,600

5. **Bonds convertible to common stock:** A convertible bond is one which can be exchanged for a specified number of shares of capital stock of the issuing company. Although the conversion privilege has market value, no **separate** measure of the market value exists for the conversion feature. Thus, the entire sale price of a convertible bond issue is recorded as debt in exactly the same manner as if the bonds were nonconvertible.

If **converted**, the bonds are removed from the accounting records at their current carrying (book) values. The new stock issued in exchange for the bonds is recorded in terms of either (a) the book value of the retired bonds (i.e., **the book value method**), or (b) the market value of the stock issued (i.e., **the market value method**). The book value method, however, appears more popular.

ILLUSTRATION 4 -- Issuance of convertible bonds:

On January 1, 1991, Federated Corporation issued $200,000 of 10-year, 10% convertible bonds at 110 (i.e., 110% of face value). Interest was payable on December 31. The conversion privilege specified that at the option of the investor, each $1,000 bond was convertible into 100 shares of Federated's $5 par common stock. On December 31, 1991 when the common stock was selling for $11 per share, the bonds were entirely converted. Assume that premium on bonds was amortized using the straight-line method:

Federated (Issuer)			Investor		
To record issuance of bonds:			To record bond investment:		
Jan. 1, 1991:			Jan. 1, 1991		
Cash ($200,000 x 110%)	220,000		Investment in bonds	220,000	
Bonds payable		200,000	Cash		220,000
Premium on bonds payable		20,000			
Dec. 31, 1991:			Dec. 31, 1991:		
To record interest:			To record interest:		
Interest expense	18,000		Cash	20,000	
Premium on bonds payable	2,000		Investment in bonds		2,000
Cash		20,000	Interest revenue		18,000
To record conversion:			To record conversion of bonds to stock:		
Book value method:			Book value method:		
Bonds payable	200,000		Investment in common stock	218,000	
Premium on bonds payable	18,000		Investment in bonds		218,000
Common stock (20,000 x $5)		100,000			
Paid-in capital in excess of par		118,000			
Market value method:			Market value method:		
Bonds payable	200,000		Investment in common stock	220,000	
Premium on bonds payable	18,000		Investment in bonds		218,000
Loss on conversion	2,000		Gain on conversion of bond investment		2,000
Common stock (20,000 x $5)		100,000			
Paid-in capital in excess of par [20,000 x ($11 - $5)]		120,000			

6. **Induced conversion.** To **induce** prompt conversion of the bond, the issuing company may offer cash or other privilege for the conversion. **FAS 84** requires that, upon conversion, the fair value of such an inducement (i.e., the fair value of consideration transferred in excess of the fair value of the stock issuable under the original conversion terms) be recognized as an expense if the inducement has only a limited exercisable time.

7. **Serial Bonds.** **Serial bonds** are bonds that mature in periodic installments. A serial bond issue may be accounted for as if the bonds represent different issues with separate maturity dates.

E. Long-Term Notes and Mortgages

1. **A long-term note** is a formal document that specifies the terms of a debt. Notes generally are not traded in organized exchanges or markets, and have shorter maturities than bonds. The accounting procedures for long-term and short-term

notes payable are almost identical, except that most long-term notes are interest-bearing, and that the interest method is usually applied to record interest expenses.

When a long-term note is exchanged for property, goods or services, the transaction is recorded at the market value of the property, goods or services received or the market value of the note, whichever is more clearly evident. If neither market value is known, the transaction is recorded at the present value of the note, discounted at the effective interest rate as illustrated below:

ILLUSTRATION 5 -- Long-term notes payable:

On January 1, 1991, Fundamental Corporation purchased a machine and signed a three-year, $15,000, 6% note. Interest of $900 is payable annually. Assume neither market value is known and the market interest rate is 10%.

(1) Determine the acquisition cost of the machine:

$$\begin{aligned} PV &= FV \times pv1_{n,i} + (FV \times r) \times pva_{n,i} \\ &= \$15{,}000 \times pv1_{n=3,i=10\%} + (\$15{,}000 \times 6\%) \times pva_{n=3,i=10\%} \\ &= \$15{,}000 \times .75131 + \$900 \times 2.48685 \\ &= \$11{,}270 + \$2{,}238 \\ &= \$13{,}508 \end{aligned}$$

(2) Record the purchase of the machine and issuance of the note:

January 1, 1991:

Machinery	13,508	
Discount on notes payable	1,492	
Notes payable		15,000

(3) Prepare the amortization schedule:

Date	Cash Interest (6%)	Effective Interest (10%)	Discount Amortiza-tion	Unamortized Note Discount	Carrying Amount of Note
1/1/1991				$1,492.00	$13,508.00
12/31/1991	$900	$1,350.80	$450.80	1,041.20	13,958.80
12/31/1992	900	1,395.88	495.88	545.32	14,454.68
12/31/1993	900	1,445.32*	545.32*	0	15.000.00
Total	$2,700	$4,192.00	$1,492.00		

* rounded

(4) Record the interest expenses and interest payments:

Dec. 31, 1991:

Interest expense	1,350.80	
Discount on notes payable		450.80
Cash		900.00

Repeat this interest entry for 1992 and 1993, using the appropriate figures presented in the amortization schedule.

(5) Record the payment of the note:

Dec. 31, 1993:

Notes payable	15,000	
Cash		15,000

2. Special kinds of **mortgage notes** are increasingly used to supplement traditional debt arrangements:

   a. In a **point-system mortgage**, the lender charges a specified number of "points" at the loan origination, instead of an otherwise higher interest rate. a **point** reduces the amount of cash the borrower receives by 1% of the loan's face value. Thus, for a $200,000 note specifying four points, the borrower would actually receive $192,000 [$200,000 - ($200,000 x 4%)], but would repay $200,000 at maturity, as well as pay periodic interest based on the stated rate and the $200,000 face value.

      Periodic interest expense is recorded at the **effective rate** -- the discount rate which provides a present value of future cash flows on the note equal to the net proceeds (i.e., face value minus points).

   b. In a **shared appreciation mortgage**, the interest rate typically is lower than normal. In return for the lower rate, the lender receives a specified share of the appreciation in the value of the mortgaged assets. Similar to a point-system mortgage, periodic interest expense is recorded at the effective rate, which is the discount rate which provides a present value of future cash payments equal to the face value minus an estimate of the current value of the shared appreciation.

   c. In an **adjustable rate (or variable-rate, or floating-rate) mortgage**, the stated rate changes at specified intervals to reflect changes in the market rate. When the interest rate is adjusted, a new payment is computed to equate the note's principal balance to the present value of all remaining payments using the new interest rate. No other complications arise.

F. Extinguishment of Debt

Bonds and long-term notes outstanding are normally retired when due and the debtor is thus relieved of all the obligations related to the debt. The debtor's obligations may also be relieved by means of debt extinguishment. **Extinguishment** of debt is defined as a transaction or event in which any of the following occurs:

1. The debtor pays the creditor and is relieved of all obligations with respect to the debt.

2. The debtor is legally released from being the primary obligor under the debt by having the debt (e.g., mortgage) assumed by a third party or having a third party (e.g., an affiliated company) agreed to become the primary obligator for the debt; or

3. The debtor places cash or other monetary assets in an irrevocable trust to pay the debt. It is referred to as **in-substance defeasance** because the debtor remains legally liable for the debt. However, the possibility that the debtor will be required to make future payments must be remote.

Debt extinguishment may occur before, at or after maturity. Accounting for debt extinguishment involves:

1. **Updating related accounts.** Interest expense, discount or premium and related issue costs are updated to the extinguishment date.

2. **Recording the extinguishment.** Record (a) the removal of the liability, unamortized discount (or premium) and related issue costs, (b) the transfer of cash and other resources or new issue of debt securities, and (c) the resulting gain or loss on the extinguishment.

3. **Reporting the extinguishment.** Gains and losses on extinguishment (e.g., the difference between the reacquisition price and the carrying value of the debt), net of tax, are aggregated and presented on the income statement as an **extraordinary item**, unless they are from cash purchases of debt made to satisfy sinking-fund requirement. In addition, the nature of the transaction including the means used for extinguishment is disclosed in notes.

G. Troubled Debt Restructuring

A restructure of troubled debt occurs when a debtor encounters difficulties in making payments on debt and its creditor (i.e., lender) **grants a concession** related to the debt obligation to the debtor. A troubled debt restructuring may involve either of the following:

1. **Settlement of debt.** A debt is settled outright by transferring assets or equity interest of the debtor to the creditor. The debtor will record a **extraordinary gain,** and the creditor will record an **ordinary loss** for the difference between the book value of the debt and the fair value of the assets or equity interest transferred. The debtor may also need to record first an ordinary gain or loss for the difference between the book value and the fair value of the assets prior to the transfer.

2. **Modification of terms.** Terms of a troubled debt are modified in favor of the debtor. The accounting treatment depends on whether the total **future cash payments** under the modified terms are **less** or **greater than** the carrying amount of the debt before restructuring:

   a. If the gross amount of future cash payments is less than the carrying value of the debt, the difference is recorded as an extraordinary gain to the debtor and an ordinary loss to the creditor at the date of restructure. No interest should be recorded thereafter. That is, all subsequent cash payments result in a reduction of principal.

   b. If the gross amount of future cash payments is greater than the carrying value of the debt, no gain or loss is recognized. Instead, a new effective rate of interest is determined (i.e., the rate that discounts the future cash payments to the carrying value of the debt), and that rate is then used to record interest expense by the debtor and interest revenue by the creditor over the modified term of the debt.

KEY CONCEPTS

Bond issue cost Bond issue costs such as legal fees and printing costs should be separately recorded as a deferred charge, and are amortized using the straight-line method over the term of the related bonds.

Discount (premium) on bonds (notes) The difference between the face value and the present value of bonds (notes) is either a discount or a premium, arising from the difference between the stated and the effective interest rates. Any discount (premium) should be amortized over the term of the debt, using the interest method. The straight -line method is allowed only if the resulting difference is immaterial.

Extinguishment of debt The debtor's obligations are relieved before, at or after the maturity date by (1) reacquiring the debt, (2) having a third party assume the debt, or (3) by placing cash or other monetary assets in an irrevocable trust, known as **in -substance defeasance.** Gains and losses on the extinguishment are aggregated and reported as **an extraordinary item**, except those gains or losses from cash purchase of the debt made to satisfy sinking-fund requirements.

Long-term debt Probable future sacrifice of economic benefits arising from present obligations whose liquidation will not require the use of current assets. Typically it consists of bonds and notes which extend beyond one year or an operating cycle, whichever is longer.

Troubled debt restructuring A troubled debt restructuring occurs when a debtor encounters difficulties in making payments on debt and the creditor grants a concession to the debtor. If the debt is settled outright, an extraordinary gain is recognized by the debtor, and an ordinary loss is recognized by the creditor. If the concession is made by a modification of debt terms and if the book value of existing debt exceeds the future cash payments under new terms, the difference is recorded as an extraordinary gain to the debtor, and an ordinary loss to the creditor. If the book value is less than the future cash payments under new terms, a new effective rate should be computed and applied to the calculation of interest.

Selling (issuing) price of bonds (notes) Bonds and notes are sold (issued) at the present value of all the future cash flows of the debt, i.e., the present value of the principal payable at maturity plus the present value of the periodic cash interest payments. The effective interest rate is used in the calculation of the present values.

Serial Bonds Bonds mature in periodic installment. A serial bond issue may be accounted for as if the bonds represent different issues with separate maturity dates.

Valuation of long-term debt Long-term debt is valued by the present value of future principal and cash interest payments, discounted at the effective interest rate.

REVIEW QUESTIONS AND EXERCISES

TRUE-FALSE

Indicate whether each of the following statements is true or false by circling the correct response.

T F 1. In general, liabilities should be valued at their present value. This requires that the future cash outflows needed to discharge the obligation be discounted at the **stated rate** of interest.

T F 2. The cash interest payment on bonds should be calculated using the effective interest rate.

T F 3. Although a long-term liability is recorded at present value, the carrying value of the liability should not be adjusted for subsequent changes in the market rate of interest.

T F 4. A discount related to a bond issue should be recorded as a deferred charge and reported as an intangible asset.

T F 5. A reverse relationship exists between the prevailing market rate of interest and the market price of bonds.

T F 6. In a typical **point-system mortgage**, the lender assesses a specified number of points, reducing the amount of cash the borrower receives to some amount less than the face value.

T F 7. The straight-line method is **required** in amortizing bond discounts or premiums, unless the use of the interest method would not produce materially different results.

T F 8. Current GAAP requires that bond issue costs be combined with any discount or premium upon the issuance of bonds.

T F 9. Upon the early extinguishment of debt, any gain or loss is classified as an extraordinary item only if the gain or loss is both unusual and infrequent.

T F 10. The carrying value of a bond increases over the term to maturity if the bond is sold at a discount.

T F 11. The amortization of a premium by the interest method creates successive increases in interest expense over the life of the bond.

T F 12. The entire issue price of a convertible bond issue is recorded as debt in exactly the same manner as if the bonds were nonconvertible.

T F 13. The issue price of bonds sold with detachable stock warrants is recorded entirely as debt if either the market price of the bonds, or the market price of the warrants is not available.

T F 14. A troubled debt restructuring may involve either an immediate settlement of the debt or a continuation of the debt under modified terms.

EXERCISE 1

On January 1, 1991, Fundamental Corporation issued $100,000 of 4-year, 10% bonds to yield a market rate of 14%. Cash interest is payable on each December 31.

Required:

1. **Compute the selling price of the bonds:**

2. **Prepare journal entry to record the issuance of bonds on January 1, 1991:**

3. **Record the first cash interest payment on December 31, 1991:**

4. **Record the second cash interest payment on December 31, 1992:**

5. **Record the retirement of the bonds on December 31, 1994:**

EXERCISE 2

On April 1, 1991, Gonzales Corporation issued $20,000 of 12%, 10-year bonds to yield interest of 8%. Interest was payable on each April 1. The amortization of bond premium was recorded using the effective interest method. The issue cost of the bonds was $500.

Required:

1. To determine the selling price of the bonds:

P.V. 20,000 × (8% . 10)

P.V.A 1600 × (.8) 10)

+ 500

2. To record the issuance of the bonds on April 1, 1991:

Selling price

Premium 25

Cash 25.

B/P 20,000

Premium 5

3. To record issue cost incurred on April 1, 1991:

Bond issue cost 500

Cash 500

4. To prepare an amortization schedule:

Date	Cash Interest (12%)	Effective Interest (8%)	Premium Amortiza-tion	Unamortized Bond Premium	Carrying Amount of Bonds
				5367.99	25367.99
/92	2400	2029.44	370.56	4997.43	24997.43
/93	2400.				
/94	2400.				
/95	2400.				
/96	2400.				
/97	2400.				
/98	2400.				
/99	2400.				
/00	2400.				
/01	2400.				

5. **To amortize bond issue cost on December 31, 1991:**

6. **To accrue interest on December 31, 1991:**

7. **To reverse the above accrual entry on January 1, 1992:**

8. **To record interest payment on April 1, 1992:**

9. **To record early extinguishment of bonds at 115 on April 1, 1993: (Assume interest payment on that date was appropriately recorded)**

EXERCISE 3

On April 1, 1991, the Clementine Groups issued $100,000 of 10% convertible bonds, dated January 1, 1991 for $95,320 plus accrued interest. the 10-year bonds mature 9 9/12 (i.e., 9.75) years from date of issuance and pay interest semiannually on June 30 and December 31. The fiscal period for Clementine Groups is the calendar year.

The bonds were entirely converted to 8,000 shares of $10 par common stock on December 31, 1991 when the market price per share of common stock was $11.25.

Required: Prepare all journal entries for Clementine during 1991, assuming that the straight-line method of amortization is used.

1. To record the issuance of the bonds on April 1, 1991:

2. To record interest payment on June 30, 1991:

3. To record interest payment on December 31, 1991:

4. To record the conversion of the bonds on December 31, 1991:

Book value method:

Market value method:

MULTIPLE CHOICE

Enter the letter corresponding to the response which **best** completes each of the following statements or questions.

____ 1. Competent Corporation exchanged land with a fair value of $56,000 for Reliance Company's $80,000, noninterest-bearing, 2-year note. For Competent the $24,000 difference represents:

a. an ordinary gain on the sale of land.
b. a premium on notes receivable.
c. a discount on notes to be amortized over two year period.
d. an extraordinary item.

____ 2. When bonds are issued between interest dates:

a. accrued interest since the last interest date is deducted from the market price of the bond issue.
b. the initial journal entry at issuance is unaffected by the time of sale.
c. the determination of the price of the bonds is simplified.
d. the entry to record the issuance of the bonds will include a credit to interest expense.

____ 3. In an amortization table that amortizes bond discount by the interest method:

a. the amount of discount amortized decreases with each interest payment.
b. the carrying value of the bonds decreases gradually to face value.
c. the total interest expense is equal to the discount on bonds plus the cash interest paid over the term to maturity.
d. Bond interest expense decreases over the term to maturity.

____ 4. With respect to the pricing of a bond issue, which of the following statements is true?

a. The bond issue will sell at a premium if the stated rate exceeds the market rate.
b. A bond issue will sell at a discount if the stated rate exceeds the market rate.
c. The price of a bond issue will be equal to the face value if the nominal rate is equal to the stated rate.
d. As the market interest rate increases, bond prices generally increases.

____ 5. A gain on the extinguishment of debt:

a. should be reported as an extraordinary item if it is unusual or occurs infrequently.
b. should be reported as an extraordinary item if it is unusual and occurs infrequently.
c. should always be reported as an extraordinary item.
d. should be reported as an extraordinary item unless it is from a cash purchase of debt made to satisfy sinking fund requirement.

____ 6. If a corporation issues bonds on January 1, 1991 and uses the straight-line method to amortize the discount on its bonds payable, Its interest expense for 1991 will be:

a. less than if the interest method were used.
b. greater than if the interest method were used.
c. the same as if the interest method were used.
d. none of the above.

____ 7. When bonds are issued at a premium, the carrying amount of long-term liability reported on the balance sheet:

a. decreases or increases each year depending upon the changes in market interest rate.
b. decreases each year during the life of the bond.
c. increases each year during the life of the bond.
d. decreases or increases each year depending upon the method of amortization used.

____ 8. When a troubled debt restructuring involves only modification of terms (not settled at the date of restructure), the creditor should recognize a loss when the carrying amount of the debt:

a. exceeds the present value of future cash payments specified by the new agreement.
b. is less than the total future cash payments specified by the new agreement.
c. exceeds the total future cash payments specified by the new agreement.
d. is less than the present value of future cash payments specified by the new agreement.

____ 9. Given the following:

Face value of bonds	$500,000
Term of bonds	5 years
Stated interest rate	9%
Date of issuance	Jan. 1, 1991
Interest payment dates	June 30 and December 31
Effective interest rate	10%
Present value of 1:	
for 5 periods at 10%	.62092
for 10 periods at 5%	.61391
Present value of an annuity of 1:	
for 5 periods at 10%	3.79079
for 10 periods at 5%	7.72173

The selling price of the bonds is:

a. $482,248
b. $481,046
c. $480,694
d. $500,000

____ 10. Floating Company issued $100,000 of bonds on January 1, 1991 for $101,000 with an effective rate of 11%. If interest is payable on each July 1 and January 1, the interest expense for the first six-month period is:

a. $10,000
b. $11,110
c. $5,555
d. $5,000

____ 11. On September 1, 1991 Niem Brothers issued $10,000 of five year bonds with a selling price of $10,675. The bonds were dated January 1, 1991 and had a stated rate of 12% payable on January 1. The cash amount received by Niem Brothers at issuance is:

a. $11,075
b. $10,675
c. $11,175
d. $11,475

____ 12. On January 1, 1991, Omega Company issued 100 of its 10-year, $1,000 bonds for $85,279. The bonds were issued to yield 12% interest. Stated interest rate is 8% payable each June 30 and December 31. Under the interest method, the amount of discount amortized for 1991 is:

a. $1,117
b. $1,184
c. $2,250
d. $2,301

____ 13. Ethical Company is indebted to Blank Bank through a $15,000 noninterest-bearing note dated December 31, 1991. On December 31, 1993, Blank agreed to settle the note for land having a fair market value of $12,000. Ethical acquired the land at a cost of $5,000. As a result of the troubled debt restructuring, Ethical should report an (pretax):

	Ordinary Gain	Extraordinary Gain
a.	0	$10,000
b.	$10,000	0
c.	3,000	7,000
d.	7,000	3,000

____ 14. Tyzan Company had $250,000 of outstanding convertible bonds. Each $1,000 bond is convertible to 100 shares of Tyzan's $10 par common stock. On March 31, 1991 when the bonds had an unamortized premium of $15,000, 80% of the bonds were converted. Under the book value method, paid-in capital in excess of par resulting from the conversion is:

a. $10,000
b. $12,000
c. $15,000
d. $20,000

SOLUTIONS TO REVIEW QUESTIONS AND EXERCISES

TRUE-FALSE

1.	F	5.	T	9.	F	13.	F
2.	F	6.	T	10.	T	14.	T
3.	T	7.	F	11.	F		
4.	F	8.	F	12.	T		

EXERCISE 1

1. Compute the selling price of the bonds:

$$\begin{aligned} Pv &= \$100{,}000 \times pv1_{n=4,i=14\%} \\ &\quad + (\$100{,}000 \times 10\%) \times pva_{n=4,i=14\%} \\ &= \$100{,}000 \times .59208 + \$10{,}000 \times 2.91371 \\ &= \$59{,}208 + \$29{,}137 \\ &= \$88{,}345 \end{aligned}$$

2. Jan. 1, 1991 -- Record the issuance of bonds:

Cash	88,345	
Discount on bonds	11,655	
Bonds payable		100,000

3. Dec. 31, 1991 -- Record the first cash interest payment:

Interest expense ($88,345 x 14%)	12,368	
Discount on bonds		2,368
Cash		10,000

4. Dec. 31, 1992 -- Record the second cash interest payment:

Interest expense [($88,345 + $2,368) x 14%]	12,700	
Discount on bonds		2,700
Cash		10,000

5. Dec. 31, 1994 -- Record the retirement of the bonds:

Bonds payable	100,000	
Cash		100,000

EXERCISE 2

1. To determine the selling price of the bonds:

$$PV = \$20{,}000 \times pv1_{n=10,i=8\%} + (\$20{,}000 \times 12\%) \times pva_{n=10,i=8\%}$$
$$= \$20{,}000 \times .46319 + \$2{,}400 \times 6.71008$$
$$= \$9{,}263.80 + \$16{,}104.19$$
$$= \$25{,}367.99$$

2. April 1, 1991 -- To record the issuance of the bonds:

Cash	25,367.99	
Premium on bonds		5,367.99
Bonds payable		20,000.00

3. April 1, 1991 -- To record issue cost incurred:

Bond issue cost (deferred charge)	500.00	
Cash		500.00

4. April 1, 1991 -- To prepare the amortization schedule:

Date	Cash Interest (12%)	Effective Interest (8%)	Premium Amortiza-tion	Unamortized Bond Premium	Carrying Amount of Bonds
4/1/1991				$5,367.99	$25,367.99
4/1/1992	$2,400.00	$2,029.44	$370.56	4,997.43	24,997.43
4/1/1993	2,400.00	1,999.79	400.21	4,597.22	24,597.22
4/1/1994	2,400.00	1,967.78	432.22	4,165.00	24,165.00
4/1/1995	2,400.00	1,933.20	466.80	3,698.20	23,698.20
4/1/1996	2,400.00	1,895.86	504.14	3,194.06	23,194.06
4/1/1997	2,400.00	1,855.52	544.48	2,649.58	22,649.58
4/1/1998	2,400.00	1,811.97	588.03	2,061.55	22,061.55
4/1/1999	2,400.00	1,764.92	635.08	1,426.47	21,426.47
4/1/2000	2,400.00	1,714.12	685.88	740.59	20,740.59
4/1/2001	2,400.00	1,659.41	740.59	0	20,000.00
Total	$24,000.00	$18,632.01	$5,367.99		

5. December 31, 1991 -- To amortize bond issue cost:

Account	Debit	Credit
Bond issue expense ($500 x 9/120)	37.50	
Bond issue cost		37.50

6. December 31, 1991 -- To accrue interest:

Account	Debit	Credit
Interest expense ($25,367.99 x 8% x 9/12)	1,522.08	
Premium on bonds payable	277.92	
Interest payable ($2,400 x 9/12)		1,800.00

7. January 1, 1992 -- To reverse the above accrual entry:

Account	Debit	Credit
Interest payable	1,800.00	
Interest expense		1,522.08
Premium on bonds payable		277.92

8. April 1, 1992 -- To record interest payment:

Account	Debit	Credit
Interest expense ($25,367.99 x 8%)	2,029.44	
Premium on bonds payable	370.56	
Cash		2,400.00

9. April 1, 1993 -- To record early extinguishment of bonds (at 115):

(Assume interest payment on that date was appropriately recorded)

Account	Debit	Credit
Bonds payable	20,000.00	
Premium on bonds payable (see amort. schedule)	4,597.22	
Bonds issue cost ($500 x 96/120)		400.00
Cash ($20,000 x 115%)		23,000.00
Gain on extinguishment of debt (Extraordinary)		1,197.22

EXERCISE 3

1. **April 1, 1991 -- To record the issuance of the bonds:**

Account	Debit	Credit
Cash ($95,320 + $100,000 x 10% x 3/12)	97,820.00	
Discount on bonds payable	4,680.00	
Bonds payable		100,000.00
Interest expense ($100,000 x 10% x 3/12)		2,500.00

2. **June 30, 1991 -- To record interest payment:**

Account	Debit	Credit
Interest expense ($5,000 + $120)	5,120.00	
Discount on bonds payable [($4,680 / 9.75) x 3/12]		120.00
Cash ($100,000 x 10% x 6/12)		5,000.00

3. **December 31, 1991 -- To record interest payment:**

Account	Debit	Credit
Interest expense ($5,000 + $240)	5,240.00	
Discount on bonds payable [($4,680 / 9.75) x 6/12]		240.00
Cash ($100,000 x 10% x 6/12)		5,000.00

4. **December 31, 1991 -- To record conversion of the bonds:**

Book value method:

Account	Debit	Credit
Bonds payable	100,000.00	
Discount on bonds payable ($4,680 - $120 - $240)		4,320.00
Common stock (8,000 X $10)		80,000.00
Paid-in capital in excess of par		15,680.00

Market value method:

Account	Debit	Credit
Bonds payable	100,000.00	
Discount on bonds payable ($4,680 - $120 - $240)		4,320.00
Common stock (8,000 X $10)		80,000.00
Paid-in capital in excess of par (8,000 x $1.25)		10,000.00
Gain on conversion of bonds		5,680.00

MULTIPLE CHOICE:

1.	c	5.	d	9.	c	13.	d
2.	d	6.	b	10.	c	14.	b
3.	c	7.	b	11.	d		
4.	a	8.	c	12.	d		

Computations:

9. (c) Bonds selling price
= $500,000 x $pv1_{n=10,i=5\%}$ + ($500,000 x 9% x 6/12) x $pva_{n=10,i=5\%}$
= $500,000 x .61391 + $22,500 x 7.72173
= $306,955 + $173,739
= $480,694

10. (c) Interest expense for the first six months
= $101,000 x 11% x 6/12
= $5,555

11. (d) Cash amount received
= $10,675 + $10,000 x 12% x 8/12
= $11,475

12. (d)

	1/1 to 6/30	7/1 to 12/31	Total
Beginning carrying value of bonds	$85,279	$86,396	
Effective interest (6%)	$ 5,117	$ 5,184	$10,301
Cash interest (4%)	4,000	4,000	8,000
Discount amortization	$ 1,117	$ 1,184	$ 2,301

13. (d) Ordinary gain
= Fair value of land - Book value of land
= $12,000 - $5,000
= $7,000

Extraordinary gain
= Carrying value of debt - Fair value of land transferred
= $15,000 - $12,000
= $3,000

14. (b) Paid-in capital in excess of par
= Book value of bonds converted - Par value of common stock issued
= ($250,000 + $15,000) x 80%
- ($250,000 / $1,000) x 80% x 100 x $10
= $212,000 - $200,000
= $12,000

CHAPTER 17

Accounting for Income Taxes

CHAPTER OBJECTIVES

This chapter is designed to enable students to:

A. Understand the major problems in accounting for income taxes.

B. Be familiar with the conceptual differences underlying the basic alternative methods in accounting for income taxes.

C. Understand the theory and application of the asset/liability method of accounting for income taxes.

D. Be familiar with the disclosure requirements as they relate to accounting for income taxes.

E. Be able to account for and provide required disclosures of tax loss carrybacks and carryforwards.

F. Understand the basic alternatives in accounting for the investment tax credit.

CHAPTER OVERVIEW

A. Taxable income is determined in accordance with tax rules and regulations, whereas the pretax accounting income (also known as financial income) is measured using generally accepted accounting principles. Since tax rules differ from GAAP in many aspects, differences between taxable income and pretax accounting income are almost inevitable. To deal with these differences, the **APB** issued its **Opinion No. 11** in 1967. Twenty years later, the **Opinion** was replaced by **FAS 96.** However, due to strong objection from business community, the effective date of **FAS 96** has been delayed several times. In hopes of resolving controversies surrounding **FAS 96**, the **FASB** is expected to issue a new statement, effective for years beginning after December 15, 1992. It is also likely that many firms will adopt this new standard early. This chapter is mainly based on this forthcoming statement, referred to as **the Proposed FAS 109.**

B. Permanent and Temporary Differences

The **FASB** as well as the **APB** identifies two types of differences between taxable income and pretax accounting income:

1. **Permanent differences:** If a revenue or an expense is reported on the income statement in a particular year, but will **never** be required to be reported on the tax return (or vice versa), pretax accounting income and taxable income will differ that year. This type of difference is referred to as a **permanent difference** because it **never reverses**, or "turns around," in one or more subsequent periods. Permanent differences do not have tax consequences and are never involved in interperiod tax allocation. Examples are:

   a. Accounting revenues exempt from income taxes, e.g., non-taxable interest revenues on municipal bonds, corporate dividend exclusion, and non-taxable death benefits of insurance policies carried by the firm on key officers.

   b. Accounting expenses not deductible in calculating taxable income, e.g., amortization of goodwill, fines and payments resulting from a violation of law and payments for life insurance policies carried by the firm on key officers.

   c. Tax deductible Items which cannot be recognized as expenses under GAAP, e.g., percentage depletion in excess of cost.

2. **Temporary Differences:** If a revenue or an expense is reported on the income statement in one year, but on the tax return in an earlier or later year, pretax accounting income and taxable income will differ in two or more years. The resulting difference between pretax accounting income and taxable income is referred to as a temporary difference. A temporary difference has tax consequences because it originates in one period and **reverses**, or "turns around," in one or more subsequent periods.

   Most of the temporary differences are caused by the application of the accrual basis to accounting income measurement, whereas the cash basis is basically required for income tax purposes. The ever changing income tax incentives also contribute to these differences. Some examples are listed below:

Revenues/Expenses	Financial Accounting	Taxation
1. Gross profit from installment sales	Recognized at point of sale	Taxable when collected
2. Investment income	Recognized as earned	Taxable when collected
3. Construction contracts	Percentage of completion method	Completed contract method
4. Unearned revenues	Recognized as earned	Taxable when collected
5. Interest on self-constructed fixed assets	Capitalized and then depreciated	Deductible when paid
6. Warranty and other estimated expenses or losses	Recognized if measurable and probable	Deductible when paid
7. Prepaid expenses	Expensed as incurred	Deductible when paid
8. Depreciation expenses	Straight-line method	Accelerated cost recovery system

C. Accounting for Permanent Differences

1. **Determine income tax expense:** By definition, a permanent difference never reverses. Accordingly, Income tax expense is determined directly by multiplying the current tax rate by pretax accounting income adjusted for permanent differences originated in the accounting period. In the absence of temporary differences, the adjusted pretax accounting income equals taxable income, and income tax expense, as indicated in the following equation, is the same as income tax payable:

   Income Tax Expense
   = [Pretax accounting income + (-) Permanent differences] x Current tax rate

2. **Prepare journal entry:** Since a permanent difference does not involve interperiod tax allocation, the required journal entry is simply:

Income tax expense	xxxx	
Income tax payable		xxxx

ILLUSTRATION 1 -- Accounting for permanent differences

In 1993 Jordan Company paid $50,000 of premiums on officers' life insurance, earned $60,000 interest on municipal bonds investment, and amortized goodwill of $35,000. Pretax accounting income including these items is $625,000. The applicable tax rate is 30%.

Required:

(1) Determine income tax expense:

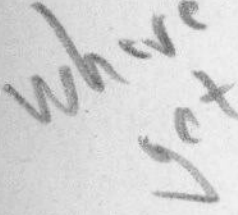

Pretax accounting income		$625,000
Add (Less) permanent differences:		
Insurance premiums	$ 50,000	
Bonds interest	(60,000)	
Goodwill amortization	35,000	25,000
Adjusted pretax accounting income		$650,000
Tax rate		30%
Income tax expense		$195,000

(2) Record income tax expense:

Income tax expense	195,000	
Income tax payable		195,000

D. Conceptual Controversies over Temporary Differences

The conceptual issues on accounting for temporary differences involve the following:

1. **Interperiod tax allocation:** Some accountants argue that, income tax expense results only from taxable income and should be measured in terms of income tax payable. As such there would be no difference between taxable and pretax accounting income, and interperiod tax allocation would not become an issue. In their view, income tax expense thus determined is a good indicator of future cash flows of a firm.

   However, many contend that income taxes are expenses of doing business, and, like other expenses, should be measured on the accrual basis. It is believed that interperiod tax allocation is consistent with the matching concept and could result in better prediction of future cash flows.

2. **Partial vs. comprehensive allocation:** In view of the fact that interperiod tax allocation is a costly process and that the reversal of certain recurring temporary differences, e.g., installment sales, is remote and unlikely, some accountants prefer partial allocation, i.e., to allocate only taxes owing to those temporary differences that will reverse in the near future.

   Nevertheless, many believe that interperiod tax allocation should include all temporary differences. It is argued that, for a firm as a going concern, any temporary difference is expected to have tax consequences and will reverse sooner or later. Furthermore, such a comprehensive allocation eliminates the need for arbitrary decision on which temporary differences should be subject to interperiod tax allocation.

3. **Methods of Allocation;** There are two methods of interperiod tax allocation:

   a. **Deferred method.** This method is income statement oriented with an attempt to match tax expense with revenues. Currently overpaid or underpaid tax expense is deferred at the **current** tax rate, and the same rate will be applied when the difference reverses. Arguments in favor of this method include that temporary differences result from historical transactions and events, and current tax rate is an objectively verifiable historical record that is not subject to manipulation.

   b. **Asset/Liability method.** This method is balance sheet oriented with the intention of reflecting economic reality of a firm. As presented on the balance sheet, a deferred tax is either an asset or a liability that is measured using the presently enacted **future** tax rates when temporary differences reverse. It is believed that this method, also referred to as liability method, would make future cash flows more predictable.

4. **Limitation of deferred tax assets.** Future taxable amounts give rise to deferred tax liabilities, whereas future deductible amounts generate deferred tax assets. Some accountants place emphasis on the conservatism principle and suggest that, while deferred tax liabilities should be recognized whenever there is any future taxable amount, the recorded deferred tax assets should be limited to those future tax benefits which are **assured of being realized** using carryback and carryforward procedure. It is contended, however, that this treatment is simply inconsistent and that the deferred tax assets should be recognized as long as it is more likely than not that the tax benefits will be realized some time in the future.

5. **Classification on the balance sheet.** There has been a general agreement that deferred taxes should be classified into current and noncurrent, but opinions differ regarding the basis of such a classification. Some accountants are in favor of using the accounting period in which the specific temporary difference is expected to reverse as the classification basis. Others prefer to classify deferred taxes based on the classification of the related assets and liabilities.

A comparison of **APB No. 11**, **FAS 96** and Proposed **FAS 109** on these conceptual issues is presented below:

	APB No. 11	FAS 96	Proposed FAS 109
1. No allocation vs. Allocation	Allocation	Allocation	Allocation
2. Partial vs. Comprehensive Allocation	Comprehensive	Comprehensive	Comprehensive
3. Deferred vs. Asset/liability Method	Deferred method	Asset/Liability Method	Asset/Liability Method
4. Limitation of Deferred Tax Assets	Essentially none	To the amount assured of being realized	To the amount more likely than not to be realized
5. Balance Sheet Classification	Primarily on related assets and liabilities	On expected accounting period of reversal	Primarily on related assets and liabilities

E. Accounting for Temporary Differences

Proposed **FAS 109** identifies the following basic principles to be applied in accounting for income taxes:

1. A current or deferred tax liability or asset is determined for the current or deferred tax consequences of all events that have been recognized in the financial statements.

2. The current or deferred tax consequences of an event are measured by applying the provisions of presently enacted tax laws.

3. The amount of deferred tax asset is limited only if it is more likely than not that some portion of the deferred tax asset will not be realized. A valuation allowance is provided to reduce deferred tax asset to such a limit.

4. Deferred tax assets or liabilities are classified as current or noncurrent based on the classification in the financial statements of the related asset or liability. Deferred taxes not related to asset or liability are classified in terms of the expected period of reversal.

These principles are procedurally implemented each period as follows:

Step 1. **Analyze tax data:** For convenience, a spreadsheet can be used to analyze tax data and to compute the amount of income tax payable and deferred taxes:

1. **Identify and schedule temporary differences:**

   Itemize existing temporary differences and, for each item, determine the scheduled reversal of the difference.

2. **Determine taxable income and income tax payable:**

   Add current pretax accounting income, separately determined, to the scheduled temporary difference in the **current year** to obtain taxable income. Current income tax payable is then determined by multiplying the taxable income by the enacted tax rate.

3. **Determine the required end-of-period deferred taxes:**

   Apply the enacted tax rate(s) to (1) the scheduled future taxable temporary differences to determine the end-of-period deferred tax liability, and (2) the scheduled future deductible temporary differences to determine the end-of-period deferred tax asset.

Step 2. **Determine income tax expense:**

Income tax expense
= Income tax payable - (+) Current increase (decrease) in deferred tax asset + (-) Current increase (decrease) in deferred tax liability

Note that the current change (increase or decrease) in deferred tax asset or liability is measured by the difference between the required end-of-period balance as calculated in (3) above and the beginning balance of the asset or liability account.

Step 3. **Record income tax expense:** The following journal entry is typical:

Income tax expense	xxxx	
Deferred tax asset	xxxx	
Deferred tax liability		xxxx
Income tax payable		xxxx

Step 4. Provide valuation allowance and adjust income tax expense:

A valuation allowance is to be provided to reduce deferred tax asset if it is more likely than not (i.e., a 50% or greater probability) that some portion of the deferred tax asset will not be realized. Determine the required end-of-period balance of the valuation allowance and adjust the account to that balance:

Income tax expense	xxxx	
Valuation allowance		xxxx

Step 5. Balance sheet presentation:

Income tax payable (or income tax refund receivable) is reported as current liability (or asset). Deferred taxes are separated into a current amount and a noncurrent amount based on the classification of the related assets or liabilities on the balance sheet. If a deferred tax is not related to any asset or liability, the classification as current or noncurrent depends on the expected period of reversal of the temporary difference.

ILLUSTRATION 2 -- Accounting for temporary differences (1)

Allard Company reported $5,000 pretax accounting income for the year ended December 31, 1992, the first year of operation. Allard made installment sales with a gross profit of $600 on January 1, 1992 to be collected evenly over 3 years. The entire gross profit was recognized for book purposes in 1992. The applicable tax rate was 40% for 1992-1993, but 30% for 1994.

Required: Complete the following:

Step 1. Analyze tax data:

	1992 (Current Year)	1993	1994
1. Schedule temporary differences.			
Gross profit from Installment sales:			
Per tax return	$200	$200	$200
Per book	600	0	0
Scheduled temporary differences	**$(400)**	**$200**	**$200**
2. Determine income tax payable.			
Pretax accounting income	5,000		
Taxable income	$4,600		
Tax rate	40%	40%	30%
Tax payable	**$1,840**		
3. Determine deferred taxes.			
Deferred tax liability		**$80**	**$60**

Step 2. Determine income tax expense:

Income tax payable	$1,840
Increase in deferred tax liability ($80 + $60)	140
Income tax expense	$1,980

Step 3. Record income taxes:

Income tax expense (plug)	1,980	
Income tax payable		1,840
Deferred tax liability		140

Step 4. Provide valuation allowance:

Not applicable because there is no deferred tax assets.

Step 5. Balance sheet presentation:

Current Liabilities:	
Income tax payable	$1,840
Deferred tax liability*	140

* Note that the related installment receivable is normally classified as a current asset.

ILLUSTRATION 3 -- Accounting for temporary differences (2)

To extend **ILLUSTRATION 2** and assume that in 1993, Allard Company reported a pretax accounting income of $6,000. In addition to the temporary difference originated in 1992, the following transactions with tax consequences occurred:

(1) Allard acquired a piece of equipment for $1,200 at the beginning of 1993. It was estimated that the equipment had a useful life of 4 years without salvage value. Depreciation was computed on the straight-line basis for book purposes, and the sum-of-the-years-digit basis for tax purposes.

(2) Allard reported a contingent litigation loss of $1,000 in 1993, which was expected to reverse in 1994.

The enacted tax rate was 40% for 1993, but 30% for years thereafter. Assume that there was a less than 50 percent probability that the excess of deferred tax asset over deferred tax liability would be realized.

Required: **Complete the following:**

Step 1. Analyze tax data:

	1993 (Current year)	Future Years	Effect on Future Taxable Income: Deductible	Effect on Future Taxable Income: Taxable
1. Schedule temporary differences.				
Gross profit from installment sales	$ 200	$ 200		$ 200
Depreciation expenses*	(180)	180	(60)	240
Contingent loss	1,000	(1,000)	$(1,000)	
Scheduled temporary differences	$1,020	$ (620)	$(1,060)	$ 440
2. Determine tax payable.				
Pretax accounting income	6,000			
Taxable income	$7,020			
Tax rate	40%		30%	30%
Income tax payable	$2,808			
3. Determine deferred taxes.				
Deferred tax asset			$ (318)	
Deferred tax liability				$ 132

* Depreciation schedule for book (SL) and tax (SYD) purposes:

	Depreciation Method: SL	Depreciation Method: SYD	Difference	
1993	$300	$480	$(180)	Deductible
1994	300	360	(60)	Deductible
1995	300	240	60	Taxable
1996	300	120	180	Taxable

Step 2. Determine income tax expense:

Income tax payable	$2,808
Increase in deferred tax asset	(318)
Decrease in deferred tax liability ($140 - $132)	(8)
Income tax expense (before valuation allowance)	$2,482

Step 3. Record income taxes:

Income tax expense	2,482	
Deferred tax asset	318	
Deferred tax liability	8	
Income tax payable		2,808

Step 4. Provide valuation allowance:

Deferred tax asset, ending	$318
Less deferred tax liability, ending	132
Required valuation allowance, ending	$186
Less valuation allowance, beginning	0
Increase in valuation allowance	$186

General journal entry:

Income tax expense	186	
Valuation allowance		186

Step 5. Balance sheet presentation:

Classify current and noncurrent deferred taxes:

	Deferred tax asset		Deferred tax liability	
	Current	Noncurrent	Current	Noncurrent
Gross profit from installment sales	-	-	$200	-
Depreciation	-	$60	-	$240
Contingent litigation loss	$1,000	-	-	-
Total	$1,000	$60	$200	$240
Tax rates	30%	30%	30%	30%
Tax effect	$300	$18	$60	$72

Balance sheet presentation:

Current assets:

Deferred tax asset ($300 - $60)	$ 240
Less valuation allowance (see Step 4)	186
Deferred tax asset, net	$ 54

Current Liabilities:

Income tax payable (see Step 1)	$2,808

Noncurrent Liabilities:

Deferred tax liability ($72 - $18)	$ 54

F. Accounting for Net Operating Losses (NOL)

For tax purposes, net operating loss is defined as the excess of tax-deductible expenses over taxable revenues. Current tax laws permit taxpayers to use the loss of a taxable year to offset the taxable income of other years. They are allowed to have an option to elect between (1) carrying the loss backward for 3 years, started with the earliest year, and then forward for up to 15 years, and (2) carrying the loss forward only for up to 15 years. Most companies elect the first alternative to get immediate tax refund. The second alternative is attractive, however, if the company is expected to move into higher tax brackets.

The tax benefits of NOL carryback are recorded as **tax refund receivable**, whereas the tax effect of NOL carryforward is recorded as **deferred tax asset**. Both are recognized in the year of loss. However, if it is more likely than not that the loss carryforward will not be realized, a valuation allowance is provided to reduce the deferred tax asset.

To illustrate, assume the following:

	Taxable Income	Tax Rate
1989	$ 60,000	40%
1990	10,000	35%
1991	25,000	35%
1992	(225,000)	-
After 1882	...	35%

1. **NOL carried first back and then forward:** The 1992 **NOL** partially carried backward for 3 years is $95,000 ($60,000 + $10,000 + $25,000) with a total tax refund receivable of $36,250 ($60,000 x 40% + $10,000 x 35% + $25,000 x 35%). The remainder ($225,000 - $95,000 = $130,000) is carried forward to offset future taxable income. Assuming that it is more likely than not the future tax benefits will be realized, the pertinent journal entries are presented below:

   December 31, 1992:

   (1) To record 1992 NOL carryback:

Income tax refund receivable	36,250	
Gain, income tax refund from NOL carryback		36,250

(2) To record 1992 NOL carryforward:

Deferred tax asset	45,500	
Gain, income tax savings from NOL carryforward ($130,000 x 35%)		45,500

December 31, 1993 (assuming pretax income of $200,000):

Income tax expense	70,000	
Deferred tax asset ($130,000 x 35%)		45,500
Income tax payable ($70,000 x 35%)		24,500

2. NOL carried forward only:

December 31, 1992:

Deferred tax asset	78,750	
Gain, income tax savings from NOL carryforward ($225,000 x 35%)		78,750

December 31, 1993:

Income tax expense	70,000	
Deferred tax asset ($200,000 x 35%)		70,000

December 31, 1994 (assuming pretax income of $100,000):

Income tax expense	35,000	
Deferred tax asset ($25,000 x 35%)		8,750
Income tax payable ($75,000 x 35%)		26,250

Note that:

(1) If it is more likely than not the future tax benefits will not be realized, the following additional entry would be required to provide valuation allowance:

Gain, income tax savings from NOL carryforward	xxxx	
Allowance to reduce deferred tax asset		xxxx

(2) Gains from NOL carried back and forward are reported as loss reductions, instead of extraordinary gains. The allowance account, furthermore, is reported as a contra deferred tax asset item.

G. Investment Tax Credit

The investment tax credit (ITC) is a tax provision that allows tax payers to receive a direct reduction in income tax liability for the acquisition of certain qualified assets such as plant, machinery and equipment. Even though this provision has been suspended since 1986, the related financial accounting standards are still in effect. According to these standards, there are two alternative methods dealing with the ITC:

1. **Flow-through (or current reduction) method.** Under this method, the ITC is to be related to the **acquisition** of the qualified asset, and the entire credit is recorded and reported as a direct reduction of income tax expense in the period in which the asset is acquired.

2. **Deferral (or allocated reduction) method.** Under this method, the ITC is to be related to the **use** of the qualified asset. It is first recorded as deferred investment tax credit (a contra asset account) and then allocated to each period over the useful life of the asset as a reduction of income tax expense.

H. Financial Statement Disclosure:

Deferred tax assets and/or liabilities are classified into two categories, i.e., **current** and **noncurrent**. In addition, Proposed **FAS 109** also requires **intraperiod tax allocation**, to allocate current taxes to continuing operations, discontinued operations, extraordinary items, cumulative effects due to accounting changes and other items charged or credited directly to stockholders' equity.

On the income statement, furthermore, the following significant components of income tax expense attributable to continuing operations must be presented:

1. current tax expense (or benefits).

2. deferred tax expense (or benefits).

3. Investment tax credit.

4. government grant recognized as a reduction of income tax expense.

5. the benefits of operating loss carryforwards.

6. adjustments of a deferred tax liability or asset for enacted changes in tax laws or rates.

KEY CONCEPTS

Asset/liability method Tax deferred is reported as an asset or a liability that is measured using the presently enacted tax rates.

Deferred tax assets Potential tax benefit resulting from existing net operating loss carryforward, and the scheduled future deductible temporary differences.

Deferred tax liabilities Potential tax payable for future taxable temporary differences.

Interperiod income tax allocation Tax consequences of temporary differences are identified and allocated to those years affected by the differences. Interperiod tax allocation is justified mainly on the ground of matching income tax expenses against revenues.

Investment tax credit A tax provision which allows tax payers to receive a tax credit for the acquisition of certain qualified assets such as machinery and equipment. The credit may be either entirely deducted from current income tax expense (the flow-through method), or allocated over the useful life of the asset acquired (the deferral method).

Net operating loss The excess of tax-deductible expenses over taxable revenues. It is currently allowed to be carried back and/or forward to offset taxable income of those years.

Permanent differences Differences between taxable and pretax accounting income caused by transactions or events that do not have tax consequences. These differences once originate would never reverse. To determine income tax expense, the enacted tax rate is applied to the pretax accounting income adjusted for permanent differences.

Temporary differences Differences between the taxable income and the pretax accounting income caused by the difference between accounting standards and tax rules as to when and how a specific item is to be recognized. These differences originate in one year and reverse in one or more subsequent years. Interperiod tax allocation is required to deal with temporary differences.

Valuation allowance Allowance provided to reduce deferred tax asset for that portion of future tax benefit which is less likely to be realized.

REVIEW QUESTIONS AND EXERCISES

TRUE-FALSE

Indicate whether each of the following statements is true or false by circling the correct response.

T F 1. Both accounting income and taxable income are measured in compliance with Generally Accepted Accounting Principles.

T F 2. A difference between pretax accounting income and taxable income without tax consequences is a permanent difference.

T F 3. Interperiod tax allocation is mandatory for both permanent and temporary differences.

T F 4. Proposed **FAS 109** requires comprehensive income tax allocation of temporary differences using the asset/liability method.

T F 5. In compliance with Proposed **FAS 109**, the tax consequences of an existing temporary difference that will result in a net taxable amount in future years must be measured at the tax rate in effect when the difference originates.

T F 6. A temporary difference, once originated, will result in either taxable or deductible amounts in future years when the difference reverses.

T F 7. In the absence of temporary difference, there should be no difference between income tax expense and income tax payable.

T F 8. Following Proposed **FAS 109**, a valuation allowance should be provided to reduce deferred tax assets, regardless of whether the future tax benefits are likely to be realized.

T F 9. Following Proposed **FAS 109**, a deferred tax liability related to a current asset (or current liability) should be classified as current.

T F 10. For individual items creating temporary differences (e.g., depreciation of a specific asset), a balance will be created in a deferred tax liability (or asset) account and then reduced to zero as the temporary differences reverse.

T F 11. Intraperiod tax allocation refers to determining the appropriate income tax expense for each reporting period; whereas interperiod tax allocation refers to allocating a given year's tax expense among the financial statement items giving rise to the expense.

T F 12. An actual net operating loss must first be carried back for 3 years and then forward for up to 15 years.

T F 13. Under no circumstances should the tax benefits due to actual net operating loss carried forward be recognized in the year of loss.

T F 14. Tax benefits due to actual net operating loss carryback should be measured at the tax rate for the year of loss.

EXERCISE 1

Presented below is a reconciliation of pretax accounting income and taxable income of Kerman Company for 1992, the first year of operation, and the differences between pretax accounting and taxable income:

	1992	1993	1994
Pretax accounting income	$8,600		
Temporary differences:			
Rental revenue	2,400	$(1,200)	$(1,200)
Depreciation expense	(4,500)	3,000	1,500
Warranty expense	2,000	(1,000)	(1,000)
Permanent difference:			
Tax-exempt interest	(1,400)		
Taxable income	$ 7,100		

The current tax rate is 30% which is not expected to change in the foreseeable future.

Required:

Required: **Complete the following:**

Step 1. Analyze tax data:

	1992 (Current year)	Future Years	Effect on Future Taxable Income: Deductible	Effect on Future Taxable Income: Taxable
1. Schedule temporary differences.	9600			
Rental revenue	$ 2,400	(2400)	2400	
Depreciation expense	(4,500)	4500		4500
Warranty expense	2,000	(2000)	2000	
Scheduled temporary differences		100		
2. Determine tax payable.				
Adjusted pretax accounting income	8700			
Taxable income				
Tax rate	30%		30%	30%
Income tax payable	2880			
3. Determine deferred taxes.				
Deferred tax asset			1320	
Deferred tax liability				13500

Step 2. Determine income tax expense:

Income tax payable	8900
Increase in deferred tax asset	1320
Increase in deferred tax liability	1350
Income tax expense	

Step 3. Record income taxes:

Income tax expense	8930	
Deferred tax asset	1320	
Deferred tax liability		1350
Income tax payable		2880

EXERCISE 2

Metablitz uses the straight-line method for book depreciation, and the ACRS for tax purposes. The applicable tax rate is 40% for 1992-1995.

Required: Complete the following tax schedule and prepare journal entries to record income taxes in each of the four years for Metablitz, assuming taxable revenues minus deductible expenses (other than ACRS depreciation deductions) of $100,000 each year, and no deferred tax at the beginning of 1992.

Year	Straight-line	ACRS	Temporary Differences (Current)	(Accumulated)	Deferred Tax Liability (40%) Current Change	Ending Balance
1992	$ 5,000	$ 5,000	$ 0	$ 0	$ 0	$ 0
1993	5,000	7,600				
1994	5,000	7,400				
1995	5,000	0				
	$20,000	$20,000	$ 0			

Journal entries:

1992:

1993:

1994:

1995:

EXERCISE 3

Ulalt Corporation reported net income (loss) for the years 1991, 1992, 1993 and 1994 for both tax and accounting purposes as follows:

	Net income	Tax rate
1991	$ 100,000	40%
1992	80,000	30%
1993	90,000	30%
1994 (current)	(300,000)	30%

Required:

a. Assume that there is no difference between pretax accounting and taxable income, and that Ulalt elects the carryback-carryforward option for the 1994 NOL. Record the appropriate journal entry at the end of **1994** for any tax benefits of the NOL, assuming that future tax benefits due to 1994 NOL carryforward is more likely than not to be realized.

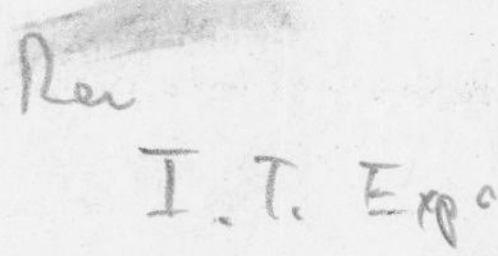

b. Use the same date as in (a) above except that it is more likely than not that the future tax benefits due to 1994 NOL loss carryforward will not be realized.

MULTIPLE CHOICE

Enter the letter corresponding to the response which **best** completes each of the following statements or questions.

____ 1. Interperiod income tax allocation should be used for:

	Permanent differences	Temporary differences
a.	Yes	Yes
b.	Yes	No
c.	No	Yes
d.	No	No

____ 2. Interperiod tax allocation is not appropriate when:

a. contingent loss is recognized for accounting purposes.
b. accelerated depreciation is used for tax purposes and the straight-line method is used for accounting purposes.
c. goodwill is amortized for the period.
d. different depreciable lives are used for machinery for tax and accounting purposes.

____ 3. Transactions and events originating temporary differences create the need for:

a. net operating loss carryforward.
b. net operating loss carryback.
c. an adjustment to pretax accounting income in order to make income tax expense equal to income tax payable.
d. interperiod tax allocation.

____ 4. Permanent differences are unlike temporary differences in that:

a. Permanent differences occur more infrequently than temporary differences.
b. A permanent difference cannot change its status once designated, but a temporary difference may be reclassified in a later period.
c. Permanent differences do not reverse themselves in subsequent periods.
d. Permanent differences are both unusual and infrequent.

___ 5. Under comprehensive allocation of income taxes:

a. only nonrecurring temporary differences require tax allocation.
b. only temporary differences expected to reverse in a reasonable period of time require tax allocation.
c. deferred tax asset is recorded only if the realization of future tax benefits is assured.
d. all temporary differences require tax allocation.

___ 6. Which of the following income items would generate permanent difference between pretax accounting and taxable income?

a. Proceeds from the death of an officer covered by the life insurance policy.
b. Proceeds from the sale of unused equipment.
c. proceeds from the sale of corporate voting stock held as a long-term investment.
d. Proceeds from the sale of a fully depreciated building.

___ 7. Harbin Corporation reports pretax accounting income of $500,000. Its taxable income for the year, however, is $300,000. The difference is due to the use of different depreciation methods. Given that the applicable tax rate is 34%, Harbin's net income for the period is likely to be:

a. $132,000.
b. $330,000.
c. $198,000.
d. $170,000.

___ 8. Omaha Company reported income for the first two years of its operation as follows:

	December 31	
	1992	**1993**
Pretax accounting income	$1,000,000	$1,200,000
Taxable income	$ 800,000	$1,400,000

The disparity between pretax accounting income and taxable income is attributable to temporary differences. What should Omaha report as income tax expense for 1993, assuming the applicable tax rate for the year is 40%:

a. $560,000.
b. $280,000.
c. $400,000.
d. $480,000.

____ 9. Using the same data in Question 8 but assume that the differences are permanent, income tax expense for 1993 would be:

a. $560,000.
b. $280,000.
c. $400,000.
d. $480,000.

____ 10. At the end of its first year of operation, Prudent Company reports the following accounting information:

Pretax accounting income	$300,000
Income tax expense	102,000
Net income	$198,000
Tax on taxable income	$119,000
Deferred tax assets	$ 17,000 (Dr.)

Prudent estimates its annual warranty expense as a percentage of sales. The amount charged to warranty expense on its books this year was $65,000. Assuming a 34% income tax rate, what amount was actually paid this year on the corporation's warranty?

a. $15,000.
b. $50,000.
c. $40,000.
d. $42,000.

____ 11. Bell Company reported $10,000 depreciation deduction for tax purposes, while included only $8,000 depreciation expense in its income statement. Furthermore, Bell earned $10,000 of interest on municipal securities and amortized $24,000 of goodwill for the year. What is Bell's reported net income for that period, assuming it has a taxable income of $120,000 and an applicable tax rate of 34%?

a. $40,800
b. $66,520
c. $76,480
d. $80,520

___ 12. Presented below are the reported pretax income (loss) amounts of Hillgard Company for the last five years:

	Pretax income/loss	Tax rate
1989	$20,000	40%
1990	$30,000	35%
1991	$40,000	32%
1992	$(70,000)	34%
1993	$100,000	34%

Assuming that Hillgard did not have any difference between pretax accounting and taxable income, and elected the carryback/carryforward option, what amount of net accounting loss would be reported for 1992?

a. $70,000 loss.
b. $45,100 loss
c. $28,000 loss.
d. $24,900 loss.

___ 13. Use the information from item 12, but assume instead that Hillgard elected to use the carryforward only option and the realization of future tax benefits is more likely than not, what amount of net accounting loss would be reported for 1992?

a. $70,000.
b. $46,200.
c. $89,800.
d. $42,000.

___ 14. For the year ended December 31, 1992, Hannover Company reported pretax accounting income of $2,000,000. Selected information for the year follows:

Interest income on municipal bonds	$ 160,000
ACRS cost recovery claimed on tax return in excess of book depreciation	280,000
Warranty expense reported on income statement	130,000
Actual warranty expenditures in 1992	70,000

Hannover's applicable income tax rate is 40%. Its income tax currently payable should be:

a. $624,000.
b. $648,000.
c. $736,000.
d. $800,000.

SOLUTIONS TO REVIEW QUESTIONS AND EXERCISES

TRUE-FALSE

1.	F	5.	F	9.	T	13.	F
2.	T	6.	T	10.	T	14.	F
3.	F	7.	T	11.	F		
4.	T	8.	F	12.	F		

EXERCISE 1

Step 1. Analyze tax data:

	1992 (Current year)	Future Years	Effect on Future Taxable Income: Deductible	Effect on Future Taxable Income: Taxable
1. Schedule temporary differences.				
Rental revenue	$ 2,400	$(2,400)	$(2,400)	
Depreciation expense	(4,500)	4,500		$ 4,500
Warranty expense	2,000	(2,000)	(2,000)	
Scheduled temporary differences	$ (100)	$ 100	$(4,400)	$ 4,500
2. Determine tax payable.				
Adjusted pretax accounting income ($8,600 - $1,400)	7,200			
Taxable income	$7,100			
Tax rate	30%		30%	30%
Income tax payable	$2,130			
3. Determine deferred taxes.				
Deferred tax asset			$(1,320)	
Deferred tax liability				$1,350

Step 2. Determine income tax expense:

Income tax payable	$2,130
Increase in deferred tax asset	(1,320)
Increase in deferred tax liability	1,350
Income tax expense (before valuation allowance)	$2,160

Step 3. Record income taxes:

Income tax expense	2,160	
Deferred tax asset	1,320	
Deferred tax liability		1,350
Income tax payable		2,130

EXERCISE 2

Year	Straight-line	ACRS	Temporary Differences (Current)	Temporary Differences (Accumulated)	Deferred Tax Liability Current Change	Deferred Tax Liability Ending Balance
1992	$ 5,000	$ 5,000	$ 0	$ 0	$ 0	$ 0
1993	5,000	7,600	2,600	2,600	1,040	1,040
1994	5,000	7,400	2,400	5.000	960	2,000
1995	5,000	0	(5,000)	0	(2,000)	0
	$20,000	$20,000	$ 0			

1992:

Income tax expense	38,000	
Income tax payable [($100,000 - $5,000) x 40%]		38,000

1993:

Income tax expense ($36,960 + $1,040)	38,000	
Deferred tax liability ($2,600 x 40%)		1,040
Income tax payable [($100,000 - $7,600) x 40%]		36,960

1994:

Income tax expense ($37,040 + $960)	38,000	
Deferred tax liability ($2,000 - $1,040)		960
Income tax payable [($100,000 - $7,400) x 40%]		37,040

1995:

Income tax expense ($40,000 - $2,000)	38,000	
Deferred tax liability ($0 - $2,000)	2,000	
Income tax payable ($100,000 - 0) x 40%]		40,000

Exercise 3

December 31, 1994:

a.

Tax refund receivable	91,000*	
Deferred tax asset	9,000**	
Gain, loss reduction due to 1994 NOL carryback		91,000
Gain, loss reduction due to 1994 NOL carryforward		9,000

* $100,000 x 40% + $80,000 x 30% + $90,000 x 30% = $91,000
** ($300,000 - $270,000) x 30% = $9,000

b.

Tax refund receivable	91,000	
Deferred tax asset	9,000	
Gain, loss reduction due to 1994 NOL carryback		91,000
Allowance to reduce deferred tax asset to realizable amount		9,000

MULTIPLE CHOICE:

1.	c	5.	d	9.	a	13.	b
2.	c	6.	a	10.	a	14.	b
3.	d	7.	b	11.	b		
4.	c	8.	d	12.	b		

Computations:

7. (b) Net income = $500,000 x (1 - 34%) = $330,000.

8. (d) Income tax expense (1993) = $1,200,000 x 40% = $480,000

9. (a) Income tax expense (1993) = $1,400,000 x 40% = $560,000

10. (a) Warranty expense paid during the year
= Warranty expense - Temporary difference
= $65,000 - ($17,000 / 34%) = $15,000

11. (b)

Taxable income	$120,000
Add: Temporary difference (depreciation)	2,000
Adjusted accounting income (pretax)	$122,000
Adjust for permanent differences:	
Interest revenue	10,000
Goodwill amortization	(24,000)
Accounting income (pretax)	$108,000
Less: Income tax ($122,000 x 34%)	41,480
Net income	$ 66,520

12. (b) Net loss (1992) = $70,000 - ($20,000 x 40% + $30,000 x 35% + $20,000 x 32%)
= $45,100

13. (b) Net loss (1992) = $70,000 x (1 - 34%) = $46,200.

14. (b) Income tax payable
= Taxable income x Tax rate
= ($2,000,000 - $160,000 - $280,000 + $60,000) x 40%
= $648,000

CHAPTER 18

Accounting for Leases

CHAPTER OBJECTIVES

This chapter is designed to enable students to:

A. Understand the nature of leases.

B. Know how to distinguish between a capital lease and an operating lease.

C. Be able to account for an operating lease for the lessee and lessor.

D. Be able to make the lessee's entries for a capital lease.

E. Be able to make the lessor's entries for a sales-type lease and a financing-type capital lease.

F. Know how to deal with special problems related to the accounting for leases.

G. Know lease disclosure requirements.

CHAPTER OVERVIEW

A. A lease is a contractual agreement between a lessor and a lessee that conveys the lessee the right to use a specific asset such as property, plant or equipment, for a specified period of time. In return for this right, the lessee agrees to make specified periodic cash payments during the term of the lease. Accounting for leases is complicated whenever a transfer of ownership in the leased asset is involved. The purpose of this chapter is mainly to discuss the fundamentals of accounting for **capital leases** and **operating leases** as specified in **FAS 13.**

B. Capital Leases

A lease must be classified as either a **capital lease** or an **operating lease,** depending on whether substantially all risks and benefits of ownership (equity interest) in the leased asset are transferred from the lessor to the lessee. The following criteria are mandatory:

1. **Capital lease to the lessee:** A capital lease to the lessee is a **noncancellable** lease which meets any of the following criteria:

   a. **Criterion 1 -- Title transfer:** The lease agreement specifies that **ownership (title) in the asset transfers** from the lessor to the lessee by the end of the lease term.

   b. **Criterion 2 -- Bargain purchase option (BPO):** The agreement contains an option that allows the lessee to purchase the leased property for a price that is sufficiently lower than the expected fair value of the asset that, on the date of inception of the lease, exercise of the option appears to be assured.

   c. **Criterion 3 -- Lease term test:** The **lease term** is equal to, or more than 75% of the estimated **economic life** (remaining useful life) of the leased asset.

   d. **Criterion 4 -- Present value test:** The present value of the minimum lease payments (to be elaborated later) is at least **90% of the fair value** of the leased asset at inception of the lease.

   Note that **criteria 3 and 4** are applicable only if the beginning of the lease term does not fall within the **last 25%** of the **whole life** of the leased asset.

2. **Capital lease to the lessor:** Besides meeting any one of the four criteria as stated above, a lease must further meet **the following two additional criteria** to be classified as a capital lease by the **lessor:**

   a. **Collectibility** of the minimum lease payments is reasonably assured; and

   b. **No important uncertainties** surround the amount of **unreimbursable costs** yet to be incurred by the lessor.

   Furthermore, the capital leases to the lessor are subclassified as follows:

   a. **Sales-type lease.** A capital lease involving manufacturer's or dealer's profit or loss (i.e., difference between the present value of the minimum lease payments and the book value of the leased asset) is specified as a sales-type lease.

   b. **Direct-financing lease.** A capital lease to the lessor without involving manufacturer's or dealer's profit or loss is called direct-financing lease.

C. Minimum Lease Payments (MLP)

The MLP to the lessee are payments that **the lessee is obligated** to make or **can be required to make** in connection with the leased property. The **MLP** to the lessor, on the other hand, are payments that **the lessor** expects to collect from the lessee or other parties regarding the leased asset over the term of the lease. Executory costs (e.g., maintenance expenses, property taxes and insurance expenses, etc.). are excluded from the MLP. Depending upon the provisions of a lease contract, the components of the MLP vary:

1. Criterion 1 is satisfied:

   MLP = Periodic rental payments.

2. Criterion 2 is satisfied:

   MLP = Periodic rental payments + BPO price.

3. Neither Criterion 1, nor Criterion 2 is satisfied: If either Criterion 1 or 2 is satisfied, both the lessee and the lessor would have the same MLP as presented above. However, if a capital lease meets only Criterion 3 and/or 4, then:

   a. **MLP -- Lessee** includes:

      (1) Periodic rental payments, and
      (2) Residual value of the leased asset guaranteed by the lessee or a third party related to (affiliated with) the lessee.

   b. **MLP -- Lessor** includes:

      (1) Periodic rental payments, and
      (2) Residual value of the leased asset, whether guaranteed or unguaranteed.

   Furthermore, if there is any penalty that the lessee must pay upon failure to renew or extend the lease at the expiration of the lease term, the payment may be included in the MLP to both the lessee and the lessor, in which case, the related renewal period **must not be added** to the lease term.

D. Accounting for capital leases

1. **Lessee accounting.** A capital lease is accounted for as if the leased asset were being purchased and paid for by periodic installment payments. Accordingly, both an asset and liability **must be** recorded by the lessee at inception of the lease. The amount recorded (capitalized) is the present value of

the minimum lease payments (or fair value of the asset, if lower). The effective interest rate used in the present value computation is the **lower** of:

a. The **lessee's incremental borrowing rate:** The rate that the lessee would have incurred to borrow, over a similar term, the funds necessary to purchase the leased property; or

b. The **implicit rate** used by the lessor in determining the amount of the periodic payments, if it is known to the lessee.

The **effective interest method** is used to allocate each payment between interest expense and reduction in the lease obligation.

In addition:

a. The lessee is normally required to incur the **executory costs** of the leased asset.

b. The lessee should **depreciate** the "acquisition cost" of the leased asset in a manner consistent with its normal depreciation policy. The following three variables are required:

   (1) The acquisition cost of the leased asset. This is the present value of the MLP to the lessee, or the fair value of the leased asset at inception, whichever is lower.

   (2) The residual value of the leased asset. A distinction should be made between the residual value used to determine the lessee's MLP, and that used to compute depreciation expense. For depreciation purposes, if a capital lease meets Criterion 1 or 2, the residual value is the estimated market value of the leased asset at the end of **its economic life**. Otherwise, it is limited to the residual value **guaranteed** by the lessee.

   (3) The useful life of the leased asset. If the lease meets either Criterion 1 or 2, the depreciable cost should be allocated over the estimated **economic life** of the asset. Otherwise, it is depreciated over the **lease term**.

c. Upon termination of the lease, both the net carrying value of the leased asset and the lease liability are removed from the books. A gain or loss is recognized in the period of termination for any difference.

ILLUSTRATION 1 -- Capital lease (lessee):

Lessor Company leased a piece of equipment to Lessee Company. The following information is pertinent:

. Fair value of leased asset at inception of lease	\$228,000.00
. Book value of leased asset at inception of lease ...	\$185,000.00
. Residual value at end of lease term, guaranteed by lessee	\$5,000.00
. Lease payment at end of each year	\$65,846.90
. Executory costs per year paid by lessee	\$2,500.00
. Estimated economic life of the asset	4 years
. Lease term	4 years
. Lessee's depreciation method	Straight-line
. Lessor's implicit interest rate (known to lessee)	12%
. Lessee's incremental borrowing rate	14%
. Bargain purchase option	none
. Title transfer at the end of lease term	none
. Date of inception of lease	January 1, 1992

Required: Record the lease transactions for the lessee.

Solution:

(1) **To classify the lease:** The lease is a **capital lease** because the lease term (4 years) is more than 75% of the remaining useful life of the asset (Criterion 3). Note that the lease **does not** meet Criterion 4 since the present value of the MLP is less than 90% of the fair value of the leased asset at inception of the lease as shown below:

Present value of minimum lease payments

$$= \$65,846.90 \times pva_{n=4,i=12\%} + \$5,000 \times pv1_{n=4,i=12\%}$$
$$= \$65,846.90 \times 3.03735 + \$5,000 \times .63552$$
$$= \$200,000 + \$3,177.60$$
$$= \$203,177.60 < 90\% \times \$228,000.$$

(2) To prepare amortization schedule for the lease:

Lease Amortization Schedule (On Ordinary Annuity Basis)

	Periodic Lease Payments	Periodic Interest Expenses (12%)	Reduction in Liability	Carrying Value of Liability
Jan. 1, 1992	-	-	-	$203,177.60
Dec. 31, 1992	$65,846.90	$24,381.31	$41,465.59	161,712.01
Dec. 31, 1993	65,846.90	19,405.44	46,441.46	115,270.55
Dec. 31, 1994	65,846.90	13,832.47	52,014.43	63,256.12
Dec. 31, 1995	65,846.90	7,590.78*	58,256.12*	5,000.00

* Rounded

(3) To record lease transactions:

January 1, 1992

(a) To record capitalization of lease:

Leased equipment	203,177.60	
Lease liability		203,177.60

During 1992

(b) To record executory costs:

Executory expenses	2,500.00	
Cash, payable, etc.		2,500.00

December 31, 1992

(c) To record lease payment:

Lease liability	41,465.59	
Interest expense	24,381.31	
Cash		65,846.90

(d) To record depreciation:

Depreciation expense	49,544.40 *	
Accumulated depreciation		49,544.40

* ($203,177.60 - $5,000) / 4

Entries (b), (c), and (d) are to be repeated each year until December 31, 1995 when the lease term ends.

December 31, 1995

(e) To record termination of the lease and return of leased asset to lessor:

Accumulated depreciation	198,177.60	
Lease liability	5,000.00	
Leased equipment		203,177.60

(4) To present lease asset/liability on the balance sheet:

Balance Sheet
For year ended December 31, 1992

Property plant & equipment:		Current liabilities:	
		Lease liability	$46,441.46
Leased equipment	$203,177.60		
Accumulated depre.	49,544.40	Noncurrent liabilities:	
Net	$153,633.20	Lease liability	$115,270.55

Note that the total carrying value of lease liability of $161,712.01 on December 31, 1992 is broken down into current and noncurrent components based on their relative due dates as indicated in the amortization schedule.

2. Lessor accounting:

a. Sales-type lease. The lease is treated as an installment sale. The pertinent accounting procedure includes:

(1) At inception of the lease, sales revenues and cost of goods sold are recognized, resulting in a manufacturer's or dealer's profit or loss.

(2) As each rental payment is collected, lease receivable is reduced and interest revenue on the lease receivable is recognized.

(3) If the leased asset is returned to the lessor at the termination of the lease, the asset account is reestablished.

ILLUSTRATION 2 -- Sales-type lease (lessor):

Using the same data as in **ILLUSTRATION 1,** and further assume that the two additional criteria are all met.

Required: Record the lease transactions for the lessor.

Solution:

(1) To classify the lease: Since the lease meets Criterion 3, and satisfies the two additional criteria, it is a capital lease to the lessor. In addition, the lease involves a dealer's profit of $18,177.60 ($203,177.60 - $185,000.00), so it is a sales-type.

(2) To prepare amortization schedule: The same amortization schedule as shown under the lessee accounting is applicable to the lessor, except that interest expense is changed to interest revenue, and lease liability is changed to lease (or MLP) receivable.

(3) To record lease transactions:

January 1, 1992

(a) To record the sale:

Lease receivable	203,177.60	
Cost of goods sold	185,000.00	
Sales revenue		203,177.60
Equipment		185,000.00

December 31, 1992

(b) To record receipt of lease payment:

Cash	65,846.90	
Lease receivable		41,465.59
Interest revenue		24,381.31

Entry (b) is to be repeated each year until the end of the lease term.

December 31, 1995

(c) To reestablish the equipment account:

Equipment	5,000.00	
Lease receivable		5,000.00

(4) To present lease receivable on the balance sheet:

Balance Sheet
For year ended December 31, 1992

Current assets:		
Lease receivable	$46,441.46	
Investment and funds:		
Lease receivable	$115,270.55	

Note that the above accounting procedure for the lessor is based on the **net investment method** under which lease receivable is recorded at the present value of the MLP. An alternative is the **gross investment method**, under which the receivable is recorded at the gross amount of the MLP. The excess of the gross amount over the present value of the MLP is credited to the unearned interest account, which is then debited when the revenue is earned.

b. Direct financing lease. Accounting for a direct financing lease is the same as for a sales-type lease, except that there is no sales revenue and cost of goods sold, and the lease transaction is recorded by debiting lease receivable and crediting asset.

E. Residual Value -- A Closer Look

The residual value of a leased asset is the estimated fair value of the asset at the end of lease term. If the lease satisfies Criterion 1 or 2, the residual value belongs to the lessee, and is simply disregarded in the computation of the MLP.

However, if a capital lease meets only Criterion 3 or 4, the leased asset would eventually be returned to the lessor. In that case the lessee will include the residual value in its MLP only to the extent that it is guaranteed by the lessee. The lessor, however, should include the total residual value, guaranteed or not, in its MLP.

If the residual value is unguaranteed and the lease is a sales type, the leased asset is not **entirely** sold, and the lessor should deduct the present value of the unguaranteed residual value from both the cost of goods sold and the sales revenue. This special adjustment is not required for a direct-financing lease because it assumes no sale. In any event, the total present value of the MLP, which includes unguaranteed residual value, is still carried in the lease receivable account. At the termination of the lease, the lessor restores the asset account and removes the residual value of the leased asset from lease receivable.

ILLUSTRATION 4 -- Sales-type Lease with unguaranteed residual value (lessor)

Given the same data as in **ILLUSTRATION 1**, but assume that (1) lease payments are made at the **beginning** of each year, starting 1992, and (2) residual value of the leased asset is unguaranteed.

Required: Record the lease transactions for the lessor.

(1) To classify the lease: The lease still meets Criterion 3. Since the first lease payment is made on January 1, 1992, instead of the year end, the present value of the MLP should be recalculated in order to conduct Criterion 4 test:

Present value of minimum lease payments
= \$65,846.90 x $pvad_{n=4,i=12\%}$ + \$5,000 x $pv1_{n=4,i=12\%}$
= \$65,846.90 x 3.40183 + \$5,000 x .63552
= \$223,999.96 + \$3,177.60
= \$227,177.56 > 90% x \$228,000

The lease also meets Criterion 4.

(2) To prepare amortization schedule:

Lease Amortization Schedule (On Annuity Due Basis)

	Receipts of Lease Payments	Periodic Interest Revenue (12%)	Reduction in Receivable	Carrying Value of Receivable
Jan. 1, 1992	-	-	-	$227,177.56
Jan. 1, 1992	$65,846.90	-	$65,846.90	161,330.66
Dec. 31, 1992	-	$19,359.68	(19,359.68)	180,690.34
Jan. 1, 1993	65,846.90	-	65,846.90	114,843.44
Dec. 31, 1993	-	13,781.21	(13,781.21)	128,624.65
Jan. 1, 1994	65,846.90	-	65,846.90	62,777.75
Dec. 31, 1994	-	7,533.33	(7,533.33)	70,311.08
Jan. 1, 1995	65,846.90	-	65,846.90	4,464.18
Dec. 31, 1995	-	535.82*	(535.82)*	5,000.00

* Rounded

(3) To record lease transactions:

January 1, 1992

(a_1) To record the sale and cost of goods sold:

Lease receivable	227,177.56	
Cost of goods sold	185,000.00	
Sales revenue		227,177.56
Equipment		185,000.00

(a_2) To adjust for the unguaranteed residual value:

Sales	3,177.60	
Cost of goods sold		3,177.60

Note that the present value of unguaranteed residual value is adjusted to both cost of goods sold and sales revenue because it is "unsold." The above two entries may be combined.

(b) To record receipt of lease payment:

Cash	65,846.90	
Lease receivable		65,846.90

December 31, 1992

(c) To accrue interest for 1992:

Lease receivable	19,359.68	
Interest revenue		19,359.68

Entries (b) and (c) are repeated on each January 1 and December 31, respectively, until the end of 1995.

December 31, 1995

(d) To reestablish the asset account:

Equipment	5,000.00
Lease receivable	5,000.00

If the fair value of the equipment is lower than the estimated residual value, a loss is recognized at the termination of the lease.

F. Operating lease.

All leases that do not satisfy capital lease criteria as described above are operating leases:

1. **Lessee accounting.** The lessee simply rents the asset from the lessor, and makes periodic rent payments which are accounted for as current operating expenses. The leased asset is not "acquired" and should be returned to the lessor at the end of the lease term. Depreciation expense of the leased asset is not recognized by the lessee.

2. **Lessor accounting.** The lessor continues to own the leased asset and to provide depreciation expenses. Periodic rentals are accounted for as current operating income.

G. Sale-Leaseback Transactions

A sale-leaseback transaction is one in which the owner of an asset sells and **immediately** leases it back from the purchaser. The use of the particular asset is thus not interrupted by the transaction. The related accounting procedure is summarized below:

1. **Buyer-lessor.** For a sale-leaseback transaction, if the lease otherwise qualifies as a capital lease, the buyer-lessor accounts for the transaction first as a **purchase** and then as a **direct-financing** lease. A sales-type lease is not permitted. If the lease is an operating lease, it is first recorded as a purchase and then as an operating lease.

2. **Seller-lessee.** The seller-lessee should first record the sale and then the capital or operating lease using the criteria indicated earlier. However:

   a. If the fair (market) value of the asset at the time of sale is less than its undepreciated cost, the difference shall be immediately recognized as a loss.

   b. Otherwise, any profit or loss on the sale shall be deferred and amortized in proportion to the amortization of the leased asset, if a capital lease; or in proportion to the related gross rental over the lease term, if an operating lease. Note that, in a sale-leaseback transaction, an artificial loss could incur even if the fair value is above the undepreciated cost of the leased asset.

H. Initial Direct Costs

Initial direct costs are costs incurred by the lessor that are associated directly with negotiating and consummating a completed lease transaction including legal fees, cost of credit investigations, commissions, and clerical costs directly related to initiating the lease. For **operating leases,** such costs are **deferred and amortized** over the lease term to match against rental income. For **direct-financing leases,** the lessor should account for initial direct costs as part of the investment in the leased asset. This means that these costs must be added to the cost of the leased asset to compute the annual rentals. The effect of this treatment is to spread the initial direct costs over the term of the lease and thereby match the expenditures with the related interest revenue. For **sales-type leases,** the initial direct cost is considered as part of selling expenses and should be expensed by the lessor in the year in which the lease is initiated (i.e., the sale is made).

I. Leveraged Leases

In a **leveraged lease,** a third party (i.e., long-term creditor) provides nonrecourse financing for a lease agreement between a lessor and a lessee. Accounting for leveraged leases is similar to that for nonleveraged leases. Lessors record their investment (receivable) **net** of the nonrecourse debt.

J. Real Estate Leases

Leases that involve real estate (land and buildings) are subject to special accounting treatment as summarized below:

1. Lease involving land only.

A lease involving land only is accounted for by the **lessee** as a capital lease if the lease meets Criterion 1 or 2. Otherwise, it is an operating lease. If the lease meets Criterion 1 or 2 and a dealer's profit is involved, the lease is accounted for by the **lessor** as a sales-type lease. The two additional criteria for the lessor are not applicable. The lease is direct financing if it satisfies Criterion 1 or 2 and the two additional criteria but involves no dealer's profit. Note that Criterion 3 is not applicable to land, and that a lease meets Criterion 4 would in all probability also meet Criterion 1.

2. Lease involving both land and building.

For a lease involving both land and building and meeting Criterion 1 or 2, the **lessee**'s accounting is unchanged. The **lessor**, on the other hand, treats the land and building as a single unit, using either a sales-type or direct-financing lease, as appropriate.

If the lease meets only Criterion 3 or 4 and the fair value of the land is less than 25% of the total fair value, both the lessee and the lessor treat the land and the building as one unit and as a capital lease.

If, however, the fair value of the land equals or exceeds 25% of the total fair value, the lessee and the lessor treat each separately. The lessor accounts for the building as a sales-type or direct-financing lease and for the land as an operation lease. The lessee accounts for the land as an operating lease and for the building as a capital lease. If none of the four criteria is met, the lessee uses operating-lease accounting.

K. **FAS 13** requires the following disclosures with respect to leases:

1. For capital leases:

   a. The gross amount of assets recorded under capital leases.
   b. Future minimum lease payments. MLP
   c. Total of contingent rentals actually incurred.

2. For operating leases:

   a. Future minimum rental payments.
   b. Rental expenses with separate amounts for minimum rentals, contingent rentals, and sublease rentals.
   c. The cost and carrying amount of property on lease.

3. For all leases:

   a. The basis on which contingent rental payments are determined.
   b. The existence and terms of renewal or purchase options and escalation clauses.
   c. Restrictions imposed by lease agreements.

KEY CONCEPTS

Bargain purchase option An option that allows the lessee to purchase the leased asset at the end of lease term at a price so low that the exercise of the option is reasonably assured.

Capital lease to the lessee A noncancellable lease that meets any of the following criteria: (1) ownership transfer, (2) a bargain purchase option, (3) term of the lease is at least 75% of the remaining economic life of the leased asset, or (4) the present value of minimum lease payments is at least 90% of the fair value of the leased asset at inception of the lease.

Capital lease to the lessor A noncancellable lease that meets any of the four criteria under the capital lease to the lessee, and both of the additional criteria: (1) the collectibility of the lease is assured, and (2) no important uncertainties surround the amount of unreimbursable costs yet to be incurred.

Direct-financing lease A capital lease to the lessor which does not involve manufacturer's or dealer's profit or loss.

Initial direct costs Costs incurred by the lessor that are directly associated with accomplishing the lease transaction. Under a sales-type lease, it should be expensed as incurred. Under a direct-financing lease, it should be included in the investment in the leased asset. Under an operating lease, it should be deferred and amortized over the term of the lease.

Lease term The fixed noncancellable term of the lease plus any period covered by renewal options, the exercise of which are reasonably assured. The lease term should never exceed the date a bargain purchase option becomes exercisable.

Minimum lease payments--lessee Payments that the lessee is obligated to make in connection with the leased property. They include (1) the amount of periodic rental payments, (2) the amount of bargain purchase option, (3) the residual value guaranteed by the lessee and (4) the amount of penalty for failure to renew the lease. The last two items are considered only if the lease does not meet Criterion 1 or 2.

Minimum lease payments--lessor Payments that the lessor expects to receive from the lessee and other parties related to the lease. They include the lessee's minimum lease payments plus residual value not guaranteed by the lessee.

Residual value The estimated market value of the leased property at the end of the lease term. It is included in the minimum lease payments of a capital lease which does not transfer ownership at the end of lease or contain a bargain purchase option.

Sales-type lease A capital lease to the lessor which involves manufacturer's or dealer's profit or loss.

REVIEW QUESTIONS AND EXERCISES

TRUE-FALSE

Indicate whether each of the following statements is true or false by circling the correct response.

T F 1. Both lessors and lessees should classify lease transactions as either capital leases or operating leases, and lessees should further subclassify capital leases as sales-type or direct-financing leases.

T F 2. One sufficient criterion for classification as a capital lease by a lessee is that the present value of the minimum lease payments is equal to 75% or more of the fair value of the leased asset.

T F 3. In computing the present value of the minimum lease payments, the lessee should use the lower of its incremental borrowing rate or the implicit rate used by the lessor if known to the lessee.

T F 4. For a lessor to classify a lease agreement as a capital lease, the collectibility of the minimum lease payments must be reasonably assured.

T F 5. An asset classified as an operating lease should be depreciated by the lessee over the period of time the lessee expects to use the asset.

T F 6. In a capital lease containing a bargain purchase option, the lessee should depreciate the asset over its economic life even it is beyond the lease term.

T F 7. In accounting for a capital lease, the lessor debits a leased asset account for the present value of the minimum lease payments.

T F 8. If the present value of the minimum lease payments exceeds the carrying value of the leased asset, a capital lease is characterized as a direct-financing lease.

T F 9. The accounting for a capital lease by the lessee is unaffected by whether the lease is a direct-financing or sales-type lease.

T F 10. When a bargain purchase option is present, the bargain purchase option price should be part of the minimum lease payments to both the lessee and the lessor.

T F 11. When a residual value is guaranteed by the lessee, the guaranteed residual value should be included in the minimum lease payments to both the lessee and the lessor.

T F 12. When an unguaranteed residual value is present, the minimum lease payments to both the lessee and the lessor should include the unguaranteed residual value.

T F 13. Initial direct costs should be expensed immediately, regardless of whether the lease is a capital or operating lease.

T F 14. In a sale-leaseback transaction, the seller-lessee should recognize gain or loss from the sale immediately regardless of whether the fair value of the leased asset is less than its book value.

EXERCISE 1

Lewis Company leases a piece of equipment to Johnson Company under a three year lease agreement on January 1, 1992. Payments (excluding executory costs) are $20,000 on January 1 of each year starting 1992. The equipment's carrying value is $42,000.

The expected useful life of the equipment is 3 years, and the expected residual value is zero. The lessor's interest rate implicit in the lease, unknown to the lessee, is 7%. The lessee's incremental borrowing rate is 8%. Assume that the collectibility of the lease payments is reasonably assured and there are no important uncertainties surrounding the lessor's unreimbursable costs yet to be incurred.

Required: Answer the following for the lessee:

1. What is the appropriate classification of the lease? Why?

2. Determine the present value of the lease:

3. Record the lease contract on January 1, 1992:

4. Record payment on January 1, 1992:

5. Record interest accrued for 1992:

6. Record depreciation expense for 1992:

7. Record payment on January 1, 1993:

EXERCISE 2

Based on the information described in **EXERCISE 1.**

Required: Answer the following for the lessor:

1. What is the appropriate classification of the lease? Why?

2. Determine the present value of the lease:

3. Record the lease contract on January 1, 1992:

4. Record receipt of payment on January 1, 1992:

5. Record interest accrued for 1992:

6. Record receipt of payment on January 1, 1993:

EXERCISE 3

Holloway Company leased a computer from Computer Super Store on January 1, 1992. The lease is for a four-year period expiring December 31, 1995. Equal annual payments of $10,000 are due on December 31 of each year. The cost of the computer to Computer Super Store was $30,000. The residual value of $1,000 is not guaranteed by either the lessee or any third parties. The lease is properly classified as a capital lease by both the lessee and the lessor. Both companies use straight-line depreciation. The rate of interest contemplated by both firms is 10%.

Required: Answer the following for the lessee:

1. Determine the present value of the lease:

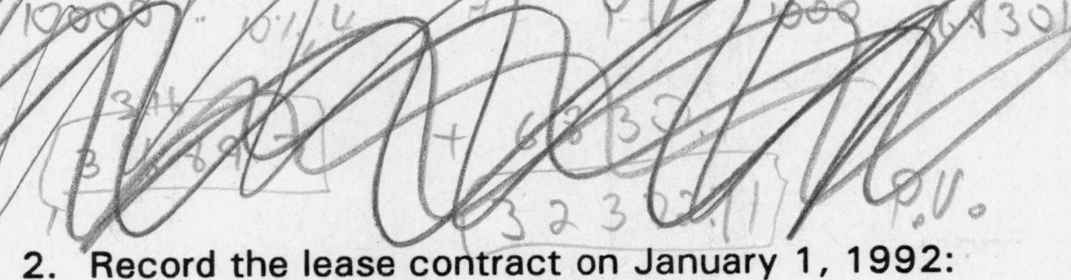

2. Record the lease contract on January 1, 1992:

3. Record payment on December 31, 1992:

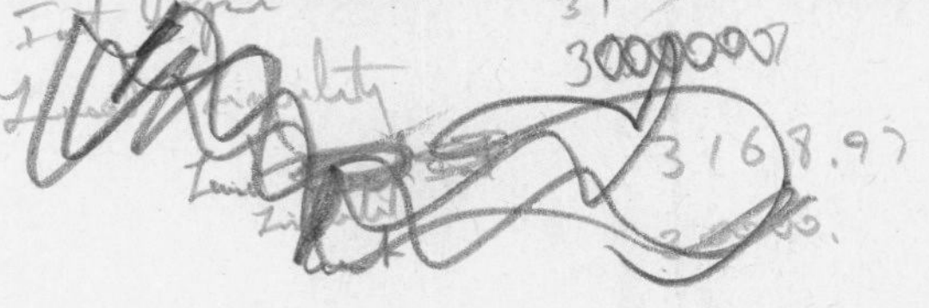

4. Record depreciation expense for 1992:

EXERCISE 4

Based on the same data as in **EXERCISE 3.**

Required: Answer the following for the lessor:

1. Determine the present value of the lease:

2. Record the lease contract on January 1, 1992:

3. Record receipt of payment on December 31, 1992:

4. Record termination of lease on December 31, 1995:

MULTIPLE CHOICE

Enter the letter corresponding to the response which **best** completes each of the following statements or questions.

____ 1. When a lease transaction is accounted for as an operating lease:

a. the leased asset should be depreciated by the lessee over the term of the lease.
b. any advance payment by the lessee should be expensed by the lessee immediately.
c. the lessee would record a leased asset and a related obligation at the present value of the minimum lease payments.
d. the lessor should depreciate the leased asset over its economic life.

____ 2. When a lease is classified as a capital lease and the lease contains a bargain purchase option, the leased asset should be depreciated:

a. over the term of the lease.
b. over the economic life of the leased asset.
c. over the term of the lease or the economic life of the leased asset.
d. by the lessor.

____ 3. Of the following lease arrangements, which would most likely be classified as an operating lease by the lessee?

a. The present value of the minimum lease payments is $15,500, and the fair value of the leased asset is $16,000.
b. The lease contract contains a clause to transfer the title to the leased asset from the lessor to the lessee.
c. The lease contract allows the lessee to buy the leased asset at the market price at the end of the lease term.
d. The economic life of the asset is 10 years, and the lease term is 8 years.

____ 4. In accounting for a lease transaction classified as a capital lease, over the term of the lease:

a. the asset should be depreciated by the lessor in a systematic and rational manner.
b. the lease payments by the lessee constitute a payment for lease liability plus interest.
c. the gross sum of the lease payments equals the dollar amount that would have been paid by the lessee to purchase the property on the date of the inception of the lease.
d. any manufacturer's or dealer's profit or loss should be amortized.

____ 5. Which of the following conditions is **not** a criterion for classifying a lease as a capital lease:

a. The present value of the minimum lease payments is at least 75% of the fair value of the leased asset.
b. The lease transfers ownership in the leased asset to the lessee at the end of the lease term.
c. The lessee has the option of acquiring the asset at the end of the lease term at a bargain price.
d. The lease term is greater than three-fourths of the economic life of the asset.

____ 6. For the lessor to classify a lease agreement as a capital lease, there must be no important uncertainties surrounding the amount of unreimbursable costs yet to be incurred, and:

a. the lease agreement must transfer ownership to the lessee.
b. the lessor must be reasonably certain of the collectibility of the lease payments.
c. the lease term and the economic life of the asset must be approximately the same.
d. the lessee must guarantee the residual value of the leased asset.

____ 7. The primary difference between a direct-financing lease and a sales-type lease is that:

a. in a direct-financing lease, a third party to the transaction supplies a major portion of the financing of the leased asset.
b. the sales-type lease involves a legal transfer of title to the asset.
c. the lessor earns both interest income and a manufacturer's or dealer's profit with a sales-type lease.
d. in a direct-financing lease, the asset is sold by the lessee, who immediately leases the asset back from the purchaser/lessor.

____ 8. In a sale-leaseback transaction, unless the fair (market) value of the asset at the time of sale is less than its undepreciated cost:

a. a loss from the sale should be deferred and amortized, but a gain should be recognized immediately.
b. a gain from the sale should be deferred and amortized, but a loss should be recognized immediately.
c. any gain or loss from the sale should be deferred and amortized over the term of the lease.
d. any gain or loss from the sale should be recognized immediately.

____ 9. Lessee Company leased a computer from Lessor Corporation on January 1, 1992, for a ten-year period, the useful life of the asset. Equal rental payments of $5,000 are due on January 1 of each year. The first payment was made on January 1, 1992. The present value of the minimum lease payments over the lease term discounted at 10% was $33,795. The balance in Lessee's lease liability account (including accrued interest) at december 31, 1992 should be:

a. $26,680
b. $27,256
c. $30,392
d. $31,675

____ 10. Troy Supermarket leased a piece of equipment from Dewolf Leasing Company on July 1, 1992, for an eight-year period. Equal payments under the lease are $12,000, due on July 1 of each year. The first payment was made on July 1, 1992. The rate of interest is 10%. The selling price of the computer is $70,400 and its cost to Dewolf $56,000. If the lease is appropriately recorded as a sales-type lease, the amount of interest income Dewolf should record for the year ended December 31, 1992 is:

a. $0
b. $2,800
c. $2,920
d. $3,200

____ 11. On October 1, 1992 Jacoby Company signed an operating lease for a building with Bear Company for 6 years, at $10,000 per year. At the inception of the lease, Jacoby paid $20,000, covering rent for the first two years. Jacoby closed its books on December 31, and correctly reported $20,000 as rent expense on its 1992 income tax return. How much should Jacoby report in the 1992 income statement as rent expense:

a. $0
b. $2,500
c. $1,667
d. $3,333

____ 12. Escondido Company leased a new piece of equipment to Koestner on January 1, 1992 for a four-year period. Rental payments of $4,000 are due on January 1 of each year. The first payment was made on January 1, 1992. The fair value of the equipment at the inception of the lease is $14,000 and the cost of the equipment to Escondido is $10,000. Escondido properly classified the lease as a sales-type lease. For the year ended December 31, 1992, what amount of profit on the sale and interest income should Escondido record if the applicable interest rate is 10%?

	Gain on Sale	Interest income
a.	$ 0	$ 995
b.	$3,947	$ 995
c.	$ 995	$3,947
d.	$3,947	$ 0

____ 13. Milligan Corporation leased a machine to Longs Company on January 1, 1992, for a five-year lease. The machine has an economic life of ten years, a residual value at the end of lease term of $50,000, and the residual value at the end of economic life of zero. The lease contains a **bargain purchase option** which allows Longs to purchase the leased machine at the end of the lease term for $25,000. Equal lease payments of $15,000 are made on each January 1, and the first payment is made on January 1, 1992. The applicable interest rate to both the lessee and the lessor is 12%. For the year ended December 31, 1992, Longs should report lease liabilities as:

	Current	Noncurrent
a.	$15,000	$51,916
b.	$15,000	$15,916
c.	$51,746	$15,000
d.	$51,916	$15,000

____ 14. Based on the same information as in Question 13, Longs should report the following in its financial statements for the year ended December 31, 1992:

	Interest expense	Depreciation expense
a.	$3,585	$14,950
b.	$7,170	$7,475
c.	$7,475	$7,170
d.	$3,585	$7,475

SOLUTIONS TO REVIEW QUESTIONS AND EXERCISES

TRUE-FALSE

1.	F	5.	F	9.	T	13.	F
2.	F	6.	T	10.	T	14.	F
3.	T	7.	F	11.	T		
4.	T	8.	F	12.	F		

EXERCISE 1

Lessee Accounting:

1. **What is the appropriate classification of the lease? Why?**

   The lessee should classify the lease as a capital lease since Criterion 3 is met, i.e., the term of the lease is greater than 75% of the economic life of the leased asset.

2. **Determine the present value of the lease:**

   Present value of MLP to the lessee
   = $20,000 x $pvad_{n-3,i=8\%}$
   = $20,000 x 2.78326
   = $55,665.20

3. **Record the lease contract on January 1, 1992:**

Leased equipment	55,665.20	
Lease liability		55,665.20

4. **Record payment on January 1, 1992:**

Lease liability	20,000.00	
Cash		20,000.00

5. **Record interest accrued for 1992:**

Interest expense	2,853.22	
Lease liability		2,853.22

   ($55,665.20 - $20,000) x 8% = $2,853.22

6. Record depreciation expense for 1992:

Depreciation expense ($55,665.20 / 3)	18,555,07	
Accumulated depreciation		18,555.07

7. Record payment on January 1, 1993:

Lease liability	20,000.00	
Cash		20,000.00

EXERCISE 2

Lessor Accounting:

1. What is the appropriate classification of the lease? Why?

The lessor should classify the lease as a sales-type lease since Criterion 3 and the two additional criteria are all met, and the lease involves profit.

2. Determine the present value of the lease:

Present value of MLP to the lessor
= $20,000 x $pvad_{n=3,i=7\%}$
= $20,000 x 2.80802
= $56,160.40

2. Record the lease contract on January 1, 1992:

Lease receivable	56,160.40	
Cost of goods sold	42,000.00	
Sales		56,160.40
Equipment		42,000.00

4. Record receipt of payment on January 1, 1992:

Cash	20,000.00	
Lease receivable		20,000.00

5. Record interest accrued for 1992:

Lease receivable [($56,160.40 - $20,000) x 7%]	2,531.23	
Interest revenue		2,531.23

6. Record receipt of payment on January 1, 1993:

	Debit	Credit
Cash	20,000.00	
Lease receivable		20,000.00

EXERCISE 3

Lessee Accounting:

1. Determine the present value of the lease:

Present value of MLP to the lessee
= \$10,000 x $pva_{n\text{-}4,i=10\%}$
= \$10,000 x 3.16987
= \$31,698.70

2. Record the lease contract on January 1, 1992:

	Debit	Credit
Leased equipment	31,698.70	
Lease liability		31,698.70

3. Record payment on December 31, 1992:

	Debit	Credit
Interest expense (\$31,698.70 x 10%)	3,169.87	
Lease liability	6,830.13	
Cash		10,000.00

4. Record depreciation expense for 1992:

	Debit	Credit
Depreciation expense (\$31,698.70 / 4)	7,924.68	
Accumulated depreciation		7,924.68

EXERCISE 4

Lessor Accounting:

1. **Determine the present value of the lessor:**

Present value of MLP to the lessor
= $10,000 x $pva_{n-4,i=10\%}$ + $1,000 x $pv1_{n=4,i=10\%}$
= $10,000 x 3.16987 + $1,000 x .68301
= $31,698.70 + $683.01
= $32,381.71

2. **Record the lease contract on January 1, 1992:**

Lease receivable	32,381.71	
Cost of goods sold	30,000.00	
Sales		32,381.71
Equipment		30,000.00

3. **Record receipt of payment on December 31, 1992:**

Cash	10,000.00	
Lease receivable		6,761.83
Interest revenue		3,238.17

4. **Record termination of lease on December 31, 1995:**

Equipment	1,000.00	
Lease receivable		1,000.00

MULTIPLE CHOICE:

1.	d	5.	a	9.	d	13.	a
2.	b	6.	b	10.	c	14.	b
3.	c	7.	c	11.	b		
4.	b	8.	c	12.	b		

Computations:

9. (d) Lease liability (Dec. 31, 1992)
= Acquisition cost - First lease payment + Interest for 1992
= $33,795 - $5,000 + ($33,795 - $5,000) x 10%
= $28,795 + $2,880
= $ 31,675.

To prove:

Lease Amortization Schedule (On Annuity Due Basis)

	Periodic Lease Payments	Periodic Interest Expense (10%)	Reduction in Liability	Carrying Value of Liability
Jan. 1, 1992	-	-	-	$33,795
Jan. 1, 1992	$5,000.00	-	$5,000	28,795
Dec. 31, 1992		2,880	(2,880)	31,675

10. (c) Interest income for the first six months (July 1 to December 31, 1992):
= ($70,400 - $12,000) x 10% / 2
= $2,920

11. (b) Rent expense for the first three months (October 1 to December 31, 1992):
= $10,000 x 3 / 12
= $2,500

12. (b) Gain on sale = Present value of MLP - Cost
= $4,000 x $pvad_{n=4,i=10\%}$ - $10,000
= $4,000 x 3.48685 - $10,000
= $13,947 - $10,000
= $3,947

Interest income for 1992
= ($13,947 - $4,000) x 10%
= $9,947 x 10%
= $995

13. (a)

Present value of MLP
$= \$15{,}000 \times pvad_{n=5,i=12\%} + \$25{,}000 \times pv1_{n=5,i=12\%}$
$= \$15{,}000 \times 4.03735 + \$25{,}000 \times .56743$
$= \$60{,}560.25 + \$14{,}185.75$
$= \$74{,}746$

Lease Amortization Schedule (On Annuity Due Basis)

	Periodic Lease Payments	Periodic Interest Expense (12%)	Reduction in Liability	Carrying Value of Liability
Jan. 1, 1992	-	-	-	$74,746
Jan. 1, 1992	$15,000	-	$15,000	59,746
Dec. 31, 1992		7,170	(7,170)	66,916
Jan. 1, 1993	15,000	-	15,000	51,916

Total lease liability at Dec. 31, 1992
= $66,916

Current lease liability
= $15,000

Noncurrent lease liability
= $66,916 - $15,000
= $51,916

14. (b) Interest expense (1992)
= $7,170

Depreciation expense
= $74,746 / 10
= $7,475

CHAPTER 19

Accounting for Pensions

CHAPTER OBJECTIVES

This chapter is designed to enable students to:

A. Be familiar with fundamental pension concepts.

B. Understand the basic nature of pension expense and be able to compute the components of pension expense not subject to delayed recognition.

C. Distinguish among pension liability measures: projected benefit obligation, accumulated benefit obligation and vested benefit obligation, and accrued pension cost.

D. Understand unrecognized pension amounts and their effect on pension expense.

E. Understand and be able to compute additional minimum liability.

F. Acquire a basic knowledge of accounting for postretirement benefits other than pensions.

G. Be familiar with pension plan settlements, curtailments and termination benefits.

H. Be conversant with accounting for pension plans.

CHAPTER OVERVIEW

A. A pension plan is an arrangement whereby a company agrees to provide benefits to employees upon retirement or upon termination of employment for reasons other than retirement based on specified formula. In most cases, the company engages a trustee to receive periodic funding payments, to invest those assets, and to disburse payments to retired employees from the pension fund. Basically, there are two types of pension plans:

1. Defined contribution plan: A defined contribution plan specifies the formula used to determine the amount of employer's contributions. No promise is made concerning the future benefits to be received by employees.

   Under a defined contribution plan, the specified (defined) amount of contributions for a period is debited to the pension expense account and credited to the cash account if paid, or to a payable account if accrued. Since this accounting procedure is straight-forward, it will not be elaborated any further.

2. Defined benefit plan: A defined benefit plan, the focus of this chapter, specifies either the amount of benefits to be received by employees upon retirement, or, much more likely, a formula to be used for the determination of these benefits. Note that the defined pension benefits must include **vested benefit**, i.e., the portion of future retirement benefits that an employee is entitled to receive even though that person does not remain an employee of the company until retirement.

B. In 1956, the Committee on Accounting Procedure issued ARB No. 47 recommending accrual basis for pension cost recognition. Ten years later, the accrual basis was imposed by the APB in its Opinion No. 8 with an attempt to assure matching pension expense against revenue. However, the APB still allowed some flexibility in the choice of actuarial cost methods which might impair the comparability of financial statements. In 1987, the FASB issued **FAS 87** which replaces APB Opinion No. 8 as the major source of the GAAP on pension cost accounting. Under **FAS 87**, the following concepts are essential:

1. **Accumulated benefit obligations (ABO)**: The actuarial present value of all the benefits attributed to employee service rendered to date on the basis of **existing salary levels.**

2. **Projected benefit obligation (PBO)**: The actuarial present value of all the benefits attributed to employee service rendered to date on the basis of **projected final salary levels.**

3. **Plan assets (PA)**: Assets that have been segregated from the employer and restricted to providing future benefits to the retired employees. Plan assets are primarily investments in stocks, bonds, real estates, etc. They also include operational assets such as office buildings, equipment, etc.

   Pension plan investments are valued at either **fair value** or the **market-related value** which recognizes changes in fair value in a systematic and rational manner over not more than 5 years. The operational assets of a pension plan, on the other hand, are measured at cost less accumulated depreciation. The market-related value of plan assets is used to compute the expected return on plan assets and to apply the 10% test under the corridor approach as to be explained later in this chapter. For simplicity, however, it is generally assumed that the market-related value of plan assets is the same as their fair value.

Projected benefit obligation and plan assets are used by the employer to measure any **underfunding** or **overfunding** of pension obligations at each measurement date.

C. According to **FAS 87**, periodic pension expense is the net cost of 6 components which may be classified into two groups as follows:

1. **Group 1** -- The entire amount of each component in this group is **immediately** recognized and included in current pension expense:

   a. **Service cost:** The actuarial present value of benefits attributed to services rendered by employees during the current period.

   b. **Interest cost:** The interest cost on projected benefit obligation outstanding during the period, measured by multiplying the beginning balance of projected benefit obligation by the actuary's interest (discount) rate, i.e., the settlement rate at which the pension benefits could be effectively settled. Note that in the year of plan amendment, the resulting prior service cost is added to the beginning PBO for the computation of current interest cost.

   c. **Expected return on plan assets:** The return derived by multiplying the beginning market-related value of the plan assets by an expected long-term rate of return, i.e., the average rate of return expected to be realized from the operation of the pension plan.

2. **Group 2** -- The amount of each component in this group, once determined, is subject to **delayed recognition** and has to be amortized over some number of years:

   a. **Prior service cost:** The cost of retroactive pension benefits caused by either the initial adoption or amendment of a plan attributed to services rendered by employees in periods before the adoption or amendment. In the year of plan adoption or amendment, the related prior service cost should first be deferred and then amortized starting in the same year.

   b. **Unexpected gains or losses:** Pension cost accounting is based on actuarial cost methods, which are, in turn, based on (1) the expected fund earnings, and (2) actuarial assumptions concerning employee turnover rates, mortality ages, compensation levels, retirement ages, etc. Conceivably, the expectation may not be realized, and/or the assumptions may have to be revised. In these cases, the following gain and/or loss would be resulted:

(1) **Asset (or experience) gain or loss**, i.e., the difference between the actual return and the expected return on plan assets, and/or

(2) **Liability (or actuarial) gain or loss**, i.e., an increase or decrease in the amount of projected benefit obligation due to the changes in actuarial assumptions.

All asset and liability gains or losses should be deferred in the year of occurrence and amortized starting in the following year.

c. **Transition cost**

An employer who already had a defined benefit pension plan in effect before the issuance of **FAS 87** must change from the original accounting method to the new GAAP. Transition cost is thus a changeover cost, which can occur only once, and is measured on the changeover date by the difference between the projected benefit obligation and the fair value of the plan assets, with an adjustment for any previously recognized accrued or prepaid pension cost, i.e.:

Transition cost
= PBO - PA - (+) Accrued (Prepaid) pension cost

Based on the above calculation, the resulting transition cost could be either positive or negative. in either case, it shall be amortized over a number of years, starting in the year of changeover.

D. Amortization of Group 2 Components

1. **Amortization methods:** **FAS 87** requires that transition cost be amortized using the straight-line method over the average remaining service life of employees. If the average service life is less than 15 years, the employer may elect to use a 15-year period. For the amortization of prior service cost or unexpected gain or loss, on the other hand, two methods are acceptable, namely, the expected-future-years-of-service method and the straight-line method. Presented below are examples of applying these methods:

Given:

Number of employees participating in plan **(P)**:	100
Average retirement rate per year **(R)**:	20%

a. **Expected-future-years-of-service method**: The basic equation under this method is:

Amortization rate for the year
= Expected service years for the year
/ Total expected future years of service

The following schedule would facilitate the calculation:

Year	Expected Future Years of Service			Amortization Rate (r)
1	100 x (1 - 0%)	=	100	33%
2	100 x (1 - 20%)	=	80	27%
3	100 x (1 - 40%)	=	60	20%
4	100 x (1 - 60%)	=	40	13%
5	100 x (1 - 80%)	=	20	7%
	Total (N)		300	100%

The total expected future years of service, N, can also be computed as follows:

N = P x (1 + R) / (2 x R)
= 100 x (1 + 20%) / (2 x 20%)
= 100 x 1.20 / .40
= 300

b. **Straight-line method**: The annual amortization rate (r) is computed as:

r = Number of participating employees / Expected future years of service
= P / N
= 100 / 300
= 1 / 3

It may also be computed using the following equation:

$$
\begin{aligned}
r &= (2 \times R) / (1 + R) \\
&= .40 / 1.20 \\
&= 1 / 3
\end{aligned}
$$

2. **Corridor approach:** To reduce the wide fluctuation of pension expenses, a corridor approach is applied to the amortization of **unexpected gain or loss**. The main feature of the corridor approach is twofold:

   a. An amortization is required only if, at the beginning of current period, the net unrecognized gain or loss exceeds 10% of the greater of projected benefit obligation or the market-related value of plan assets, and

   b. Only the excessive amount over the 10% limit is required to be amortized over the remaining service life of active employees expected to participate in the plan.

   It should be noted that management has the option to adopt any **rational and systematic** method of amortization as long as the required minimum amount under the corridor approach is observed.

E. For pension cost accounting, the following three entries are generally required:

1. **To record employer's contribution to pension plan:**

Pension liability	xxxx	
Cash		xxxx

2. **To record pension expense:**

Pension expense	xxxx	
Accrued pension cost		xxxx

3. **To record additional pension liability**

Deferred pension cost	xxxx	
Unrealized pension cost	xxxx	
Additional pension liability		xxxx

Note that Entry 3 is needed to comply with **FAS 87** which requires a firm report a minimum liability including the following:

1. **Additional pension liability**
   = Accumulated benefit obligation - Plan assets (fair value)
   - (+) Accrued (Prepaid) pension cost

2. **Deferred pension cost** (an intangible asset)
   = The lesser of additional pension liability or unrecognized prior service cost.

3. **Unrealized pension cost** (a contra stockholders' equity account)
   = Any excess of additional pension liability over deferred pension cost.

F. A Spreadsheet Approach to Pension Cost Analysis

An amortization spreadsheet is prepared to determine pension expense. The spreadsheet is constructed on the basis of the following relationships:

If	Then	Where
1. Plan fully funded	PBO = PA	PBO = projected benefit obligation PA = pension plan assets
2. Plan underfunded	PBO = PA + APC	APC = accrued pension cost
3. Plan overfunded	PBO = PA - PPC	PPC = prepaid pension cost
4. PSC involved	PBO = PA + PSC	PSC = prior service cost
5. Gain involved	PBO = PA - UEG	UEG = unexpected gain (asset & liab.)
6. Loss involved	PBO = PA + UEL	UEL = unexpected loss (asset & liab.)
7. TC involved	PBO = PA + TC	TC = transition cost

The above relationships can be combined and generalized as follows:

PBO = PA + PSC +/- UEL/UEG + TC +/- APC/PPC

Note that for simplicity unexpected gains are combined with unexpected losses and prepaid pension cost is combined with accrued pension cost.

Each of the above elements is represented by a column on the spreadsheet. One more column, representing **pension expense (PE)**, is added to the spreadsheet to determine current pension expense. Once the expense is determined, it is closed (transferred) to the accrued pension cost. Note that the records on those elements on the spreadsheet are maintained respectively by three parties, namely, the actuary (PBO), the trustee (PA), and the company (all the rest).

Spreadsheet entries include the following:

Components of pension expense:

1. **Group 1:**

   a. **Service cost** increases both PBO and PE.

   b. **Interest cost** increases both PBO and PE.

   c. **Expected return** on plan assets increases PA and decreases PE.

2. **Group 2:**

   a. **Prior service cost:**

      (1) PSC arises during the year increases both PBO and PSC.

      (2) PSC amortized for the year decreases PSC and increases PE.

   b. **Unexpected loss and gain:**

      (1) Asset loss arises during the year decreases PA and increases UEL/UEG, whereas asset gain increases PA and decreases UEL/UEG.

      (2) Liability loss arises during the year increases both PBO and UEL/UEG, whereas liability gain decreases both PBO and UEL/UEG.

      (3) Unexpected loss amortized to the year decreases UEL/UEG and increases PE; whereas gain amortization increases UEL/UEG and decreases PE.

   c. **Transition cost** amortized decreases TC and increase PE.

Additional entries:

1. **Employer's contribution** increases PA and decreases APC/PPC.

2. **Benefits paid** decreases both PBO and PA.

3. **Current pension expense** transferred decreases PE and increases APC/PPC.

ILLUSTRATION -- Accounting for pensions

Given the following:

	1992	1993	1994
1. Projected benefit obligation:			
a. Beginning balance	$1,500	$1,550	$1,620
b. Ending balance	1,550	1,620	1,950
2. Accumulated benefit obligation:			
a. Beginning balance	1,400	1,200	1,250
b. Ending balance	1,300	1,450	1,750
3. Plan assets (fair value)			
a. Beginning balance	1,000	1,190	1,350
b. Ending balance	1,190	1,350	1,460
4. Service cost	180	200	240
5. Prior service cost	0	0	180
6. Unexpected losses (gains):			
a. Asset loss (gain) occurred ..	(20)	9	(25)
b. Liability loss (gain) occurred .	(100)	0	130
7. Unamortized transition cost at 1/1/1992	500		
8. Employer's contributions	250	335	350
9. Benefits paid to retirees	180	285	400

10. Additional information:
    a. Interest (settlement) rate 10%
    b. Expected return rate 10%
    c. Amortization policies:
        (1) Prior service cost amortized over .... 9 years
        (2) Unexpected losses (gains):
            (a) Not to apply the corridor approach
            (b) Amortization rate (applied to beginning unamortized balances) .. 10%
        (3) Transition cost amortization rate 10%

1. Prepare amortization spreadsheets for the three-year period:

a. **Amortization Spreadsheet, 1992**

	Actuary	Trustee	Company			
	PBO	PA	Memorandum		Accounts	
	Projected Benefit Obligation	Plan Assets	UEL/UEG Unexpected Loss (Gain)	TC Trans. Cost	PE Pension Expense	APC/PPC Accrued (prepaid) pen. cost
Balance, 1/1/1992	$ 1,500	$ 1,000	$ 0	$ 500	$ 0	$ 0
Service cost	180				180	
Interest cost (10% on PBO)	150				150	
Expected return (10% on PA)		100			(100)	
Asset gain - current		20	(20)			
Liability gain - current	(100)		(100)			
Transition cost amortization ($500 / 10)				(50)	50	
Employer's cash contribution		250				(250)
Benefits paid	(180)	(180)				
Pension expense transferred					$ (280)	280
Balance carried, 12/31/1992	$ 1,550	$1,190	$(120)	$ 450	$ 0	$ 30

Note that a liability gain ($100) reduce PBO, and an asset gain ($20) increases plan assets. Both of these gains, furthermore, are subject to delayed recognition.

b. **Amortization Spreadsheet, 1993**

	Actuary	Trustee	Company			
	PBO	PA	Memorandum		Accounts	
	Projected Benefit Obligation	Plan Assets	UEL/UEG Unexpected Loss (Gain)	TC Trans. Cost	PE Pension Expense	APC/PPC Accrued (prepaid) Pen. Cost
Balance, 1/1/1993	$ 1,550	$1,190	$ (120)	$ 450	$ 0	$ 30
Service cost	200				200	
Interest cost (10% on PBO)	155				155	
Expected return (10% on PA)		119			(119)	
Gain amortization ($120 x 10%)			12		(12)	
Asset loss - current		(9)	9			
Transition cost amortization ($450 / 9)				(50)	50	
Employer's cash contribution		335				(335)
Benefits paid	(285)	(285)				
Pension expense transferred					$ (274)	274
Balance carried, 12/31/1993	$ 1,620	$1,350	$ (99)	$ 400	$ 0	$ (31)

Note that the beginning unexpected gain ($120) is amortized to the current period at 10%, whereas the recognition of current asset gain ($9) is delayed.

c. **Amortization Spreadsheet, 1994**

	Actuary	Trustee	Company				
	PBO	PA	Memorandum			Accounts	
	Projected Benefit Obliga-tion	Plan Assets	PSC Prior Service Cost	UEL/UEG Unexptd Loss (Gain)	TC Trans. Cost	PE Pension Expense	APC/PPC Accrued (Prepaid) Pen. Cost
Balance, 1/1/1994	$ 1,620	$1,350	$ 0	$ (99)	$ 400	$ 0	$(31)
Prior service cost-Addition	180		180				
Adjusted beginning balance	$ 1,800						
Service cost	240					240	
Interest cost (10% on PBO)	180					180	
Expected return (10% on PA)		135				(135)	
PSC Amortization ($180 / 9)			(20)			20	
Gain amortization ($99x10%)				10		(10)	
Asset gain - current		25		(25)			
Liability loss - current	130			130			
TC amortization ($400 / 8)					(50)	50	
Cash contribution		350					(350)
Benefits paid	(400)	(400)					
Pension expense transferred						$(345)	345
Balance carried, 12/31/1994	$ 1,950	$1,460	$ 160	$ 16	$ 350	$ 0	$ (36)

Note that the recognition of current asset gain of $25 and liability loss of $130 are delayed, whereas prior service cost is amortized to the current period. Note also that, as indicated in all the above schedules, PBO equals the sum of all the other columns, e.g., at the end of 1994:

$$\begin{aligned} \text{PBO} &= \text{PA} + \text{PSC} +/- \text{UEL/UEG} + \text{TC} +/- \text{APC/PPC} \\ &= \$1{,}460 + \$160 + \$16 + \$350 - \$36 \\ &= \$1950 \end{aligned}$$

2. Record employer's contributions and pension expenses:

	1992		1993		1994	
Accrued/prepaid pension cost	250		335		350	
Cash		250		335		350
Pension expense	280		274		345	
Accrued/prepaid pension cost		280		274		345

3. **Determine and record additional pension liability:**

a. **Compute the required ending balances of additional pension liability and the related accounts:**

	1992	1993	1994
Accumulated benefit obligation, ending	$1,300	$1,450	$1,750
Less: Plan assets, ending	(1,190)	(1,350)	(1,460)
Unfunded accumulated benefit obligation	**$ 110**	**$ 100**	**$ 290**
Less: Accrued/Prepaid pension cost	(30)	31	36
Additional pension liability	**$ 80**	**$131**	**$326**
Less: **Deferred pension cost** *	**0**	**0**	**160**
Unrealized pension cost	**(80)**	**(131)**	**(166)**

* The lesser of additional pension liability or unamortized (unrecognized) past service cost.

b. **Record (adjust) additional pension liability:**

	1992		1993		1994	
Deferred pension cost	0		0		160	
Unrealized pension cost	80		51		35	
Additional pension liability		80		51		195

Remember that, at the year-end, additional pension liability, deferred pension cost and unrealized pension cost are all adjusted to the **required balances** as indicated in the above schedule.

G. Accounting for Postretirement Benefits other than Pensions

Nonpension postretirement benefits include all benefits an employer promises to provide retirees, other than pension, such as health care coverage, life insurance, tuition assistance, day care, legal services and housing subsidies. **FAS 106** requires the accrual of the cost and obligation under defined benefit plans as employees become fully eligible to receive their benefits.

An employee is fully eligible whenever the employee renders all the service necessary to receive the expected benefits. Service beyond the full eligibility date does not increase future benefits. However, if the employee continues to earn material benefits for each year of service until retirement date, the full eligibility date is the retirement date.

An employer's obligation under a postretirement benefit plan is the actuarial present value of expected future payments to retirees, whereas the postretirement benefit expense is the cost recognized in a reporting period, which has the same six components as the pension expense, although there are some minor differences in measurement.

Accounting for pensions and accounting for postretirement benefits are in essence parallel. Nevertheless their impacts on income may differ. For example, employee turnover can completely erase postretirement benefits whereas pension benefits might only be reduced. In addition, health care costs often increase dramatically with age, whereas pension benefit payments remain constant.

H. Pension Plan Settlement and Curtailment (FAS 88):

1. **Pension plan settlement:** A settlement is a transaction such as making lump-sum cash payment that relieves the employer of primary responsibility for a pension benefit obligation. The employer is required to include in the income statement a gain (or loss) no more than any unrecognized gain (or loss) and any remaining unrecognized net asset existing at transition date (i.e., when FAS 87 is first applied). The following entry is pertinent:

Accrued/prepaid pension cost	xxxx	
Settlement gain		xxxx

2. **Pension plan curtailment:** A curtailment is an event such as closing of a plant that significantly reduces the expected years of future service of present employees or eliminates the accrual of defined benefits of their future services. The employer is required to include in the income statement as a loss the related unrecognized prior service cost associated with years of service no longer expected to be rendered plus any unrecognized net obligation existing at the transition date.

I. Termination Benefits

When **special termination benefits** are offered as an inducement for employees to retire, both a **loss** and a **liability** should be recorded if (1) the employees accept the offer and (b) the amount of the benefits can be **reasonably estimated.** The amount recognized is the present value of the expected benefits.

When the termination benefits are contractual (contingent on a specific event), the loss and liability are recorded if (1) the entitlement to benefits is probable and (2) the amount can be reasonably estimated.

J. **Financial Statement Presentation:**

1. Income statement presentation: Pension expense is presented in the income statement as an operating expense. FAS 87 further requires the disclosure of its components. Gain or loss from a single occurrence not directly related to the operation of the pension plan and not in the ordinary course of the employer's business should be recognized immediately, but not as a pension expense, e.g., the pension related gain or loss due to plant closing should be included in the gain or loss from discontinued operations.

2. Balance sheet presentation: Accrued/prepaid pension cost is either a current liability or a current asset depending on whether its ending balance is a credit or debit. Additional pension liability is presented as a noncurrent liability. Deferred pension cost is considered as an intangible asset, while unrealized pension cost should be included as a stockholders' equity adjustment.

3. Additional disclosure includes:

   a. A description of the plan.
   b. A schedule reconciling the funded status of the plan with the amounts reported in the balance sheet.
   c. The **vested benefit obligation**, i.e., the present value of pension benefits earned by employees that are not subject to continuing service with the company as indicated in the Employee Retirement Income Security Act (ERISA).

KEY CONCEPTS

Accumulated benefit obligation The actuarial present value of all the benefits attributed to employee service rendered to date on the basis of **existing** salary levels.

Defined benefit plan A plan that specifies either the amount of benefits to be received by employees upon retirement, or a formula to be used for the determination of these benefits.

Interest cost Interest cost on the projected benefit obligation, measured by multiplying the actuary's discount rate by the beginning balance of the projected benefit obligation.

Liability gain or loss Gain or loss resulting from changes in actuarial assumptions with respect to a pension plan. This gain or loss is subject to delayed recognition.

Plan assets Assets that have been segregated from the employer and restricted to providing future benefits to the retired employees.

Prior service cost Cost of retroactive benefits attributed to service rendered prior to the initiation or amendment of a pension plan. Prior service cost must be amortized over the expected remaining years of service, starting in the year of plan adoption or amendment.

Projected benefit obligation The actuarial present value of all the benefits attributed to employee service rendered to date on the basis of projected **final** salary levels.

Return on plan asset Return on plan asset investment may be expected or actual. The expected return for a period is fully included in the pension expense of that period, while the recognition of the difference between the expected return and the actual return, known as asset gain or loss, must be delayed.

Service cost The actuarial present value of benefits attributed by the pension benefit formula to services rendered by employees during the current period.

Transition cost The changeover cost from **APB Opinion No. 8** to FAS 87 measured by the difference between projected benefit obligation and plan asset, adjusted for the existing accrued (prepaid) pension cost on the beginning of the changeover year. Transition cost must be amortized using the straight-line method.

REVIEW QUESTIONS AND EXERCISES

TRUE-FALSE

Indicate whether each of the following statements is true or false by circling the correct response.

T F 1. Pension expense is recognized only when pension benefits are paid to retired employees.

T F 2. A defined benefit pension plan is a plan that specifies either the amount of benefits to be paid upon employees' retirement or a formula used for the determination of these benefits.

T F 3. A projected benefit obligation is the actuarial present value of all the benefits attributed to employee's service on the basis of current salary levels.

T F 4. To determine periodic pension expense, all the six components have to be amortized over the expected future service years of participating employees.

T F 5. The interest cost component of pension expense is generally calculated by multiplying the beginning balance of projected benefit obligation by the actuary's discount rate.

T F 6. Unexpected gain or loss must be amortized using the expected-future-years-of-service method, the straight-line method or any other systematic method as long as the required minimum amount under the corridor approach is observed.

T F 7. Transition cost must be amortized over the expected future years of service of participating employees using either the expected-future-years-of-service method or the straight-line method.

T F 8. The difference between actual return and the expected return on plan assets may be combined with gains and losses from assumption changes for possible future amortization to pension expense.

T F 9. In order to reduce the wide fluctuation of pension expenses, it is acceptable that some or all the unexpected gains or losses may be excluded from the computation of periodic pension expense.

T F 10. The employer must recognize as a minimum liability an amount equal to the excess of projected benefit obligation over the fair value of pension plan assets.

T F 11. Amortization of a net gain **increases** pension expense, and amortization of a net loss **decreases** pension expense.

T F 12. Prior service cost is amortized over the average remaining service life of employees, beginning in the year **after** the prior service cost arises.

T F 13. The PBO minus the sum of the fair value of plan assets and unrecognized (unamortized) prior service cost, unexpected loss/gain and transition cost must equal the balance in accrued/prepaid pension cost.

T F 14. In accounting for additional pension liability, if the additional pension liability exceeds the unrecognized prior service cost, the excess should be reported as an unrealized pension cost.

EXERCISE 1

Match the terms with the most appropriate description by entering the corresponding letters in the blanks provided.

ITEMS

D 1. Additional pension liability

G 2. Vested benefit obligation

E 3. Prepaid pension cost

H 4. Accumulated benefit obligation

C 5. Defined contribution plan

I 6. Interest cost

J 7. Pension plan assets

B 8. Projected benefits obligation

F 9. Net periodic pension expense

A 10. Pension benefit formula

DESCRIPTIONS

A. Determines the retirement benefits based on a defined benefit pension plan.

B. Actuarial present value of all future pension benefits on the basis of projected future compensation levels.

C. Formula used to determine the amount of employer's contribution. No promise is made concerning employees' future benefits.

D. A pension liability that may cause a debit to an intangible asset.

E. Cumulative employer's contributions in excess of recognized pension expense.

F. Computed by the employer; comprised of up to six components.

G. Pension obligation that is not contingent on future employment of employees.

H. Actuarial present value of future pension benefits on the basis of existing salary levels.

I. Beginning PBO multiplied by the actuary's discount rate.

J. Funds related to the pension that usually are administered by an independent trustee.

EXERCISE 2

Assume that Aloha Company made the following information available:

1. At beginning of year -- 1/1/1992:

a.	Projected benefit obligation	$800,000
b.	Plan assets (Fair value)	$750,000
c.	Unamortized transition cost	$50
d.	Number of participating employees	200

2. For the year -- 1992:

a.	Service cost	$100,000
b.	Liability gain (due to assumption changes) ...	$ 50,000
c.	Employer's contribution	$190,000
d.	Benefits paid to the retirees	$115,000

3. At the year-end -- 12/31/1992:

a.	Plan assets (Fair value)	$900,000
b.	Accumulated benefit obligation	$890,000

4. Additional information:

a.	Settlement rate	10%
b.	Expected rate of return	10%
c.	Actual rate of return	10%
d.	Estimated employees' retirement rate	20%

Required: **For 1992:**

1. Prepare amortization spreadsheet.
2. Prepare journal entries to record:
   a. Cash contribution to pension plan.
   b. Pension expense.
3. Determine and record additional pension liability.

EXERCISE 3

Camry Company sponsored a defined benefit pension plan for its employees at the beginning of 1992. The following data relate to the operation of the plan for 1992 and 1993:

	1992	1993
Service cost for the year	6,000	7,000
Cash contribution to the plan	5,000	6,000
Benefits paid	1,000	1,250
Liability loss during the year	0	1,200
Beginning balance:		
Projected benefit obligation	0	6,635
Accumulated benefit obligation	0	5,500
Plan assets -- Fair value	0	4,000
Prior service cost	$1,500	$?
Ending balance:		
Projected benefit obligation	6,635	14,182
Accumulated benefit obligation	5,500	11,200
Plan assets -- Fair value	4,000	9,150
Settlement rate	9%	9%
Expected rate of return	10%	10%
Actual rate of return	10%	10%
Prior service cost and unexpected loss amortization rate	12%	12%

Required: **For 1992 and 1993:**

1. Prepare amortization spreadsheet.
2. Prepare journal entries to record:
   a. Cash contribution to pension plan.
   b. Pension expense.
3. Determine and record additional pension liability and related accounts.

MULTIPLE CHOICE

Enter the letter corresponding to the response which **best** completes each of the following statements or questions.

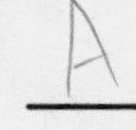
____ 1. Which of the following is not relevant for the calculation of periodic pension expense?

a. Accumulated benefit obligation.
b. Projected benefit obligation.
c. Pension plan asset.
d. Expected rate of return on pension plan asset.

____ 2. Which of the following is not a component of periodic pension expense?

a. Service cost.
b. Interest cost on accumulated benefit obligation.
c. Expected return on pension plan asset.
d. Transition cost.

____ 3. Which of the following is not relevant for the calculation of additional pension liability?

a. Accumulated benefit obligation.
b. Projected benefit obligation.
c. Accrued pension expense.
d. Pension plan asset.

____ 4. Which of the following is allowed to apply the corridor approach?

a. The amortization of prior service cost.
b. The amortization of unexpected gain or loss.
c. The amortization of transition cost.
d. None of the above.

____ 5. The pension expense reported by a company will be increased by **interest cost** when:

a. Projected benefit obligation exists at the beginning of the year.
b. Amounts funded are greater than pension cost accrued.
c. Pension plan asset exists at the beginning of the year.
d. The plan is fully vested.

6. Which of the following is more likely to be a journal entry to recognize the additional pension liability?

a. Pension expense	xxx	
Accrued/prepaid pension expense		xxx
b. Accrued/prepaid pension expense	xxx	
Cash		xxx
c. Pension expense	xxx	
Deferred pension cost		xxx
Additional pension liability		xxx
d. Deferred pension cost	xxx	
Unrealized pension cost	xxx	
Additional pension liability		xxx

7. In the computation of pension expense, which of the following component is likely to be **negative** (i.e., reduce pension expense):

a. service cost.
b. interest cost.
c. amortization of prior service cost.
d. Amortization of net asset gain.

8. Assuming a zero balance in the accrued/prepaid pension cost account, an **additional pension liability** must be recorded if the:

a. accumulated benefit obligation is more than the fair value of pension plan assets.
b. projected benefit obligation is more than the fair value of pension plan assets.
c. vested benefit obligation is more than the fair value of pension plan assets.
d. projected benefit obligation is more than the accumulated benefit obligation. value.

____ 9. The projected benefit obligation on January 1, 1992 was $160,000. During 1992 pension benefits paid by the trustee were $20,000. The actuary's discount rate was 10%. Service cost for 1992 is $60,000. Pension plan assets (at fair value) increased during 1992 by $30,000 as expected. There had been no liability gain or loss. The amount of the PBO at December 31, 1992 was:

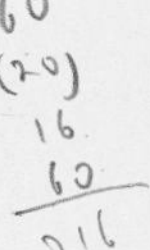

a. $176,000.
b. $196,000.
c. $216,000.
d. $246,000.

____ 10. Divina Company's records revealed the following related to its defined benefit pension plan:

Plan assets at fair value, January 1, 1992	$3,000
Expected return on plan assets during 1992	300
Actual return on plan assets during 1992	200
Contributions to the pension fund during 1992	500
Amortization of unexpected loss for 1992	10
Pension benefits paid during 1992	520
Pension expense, 1992	360

The December 31, 1992 amount of pension plan assets at fair value is:

a. $2,480.
b. $2,980.
c. $3,180.
d. $3,200.

____ 11. Desco Company had $50,000 unrecognized prior service cost when it amended a defined benefit plan on January 1, 1992. The number of employees participating in the plan was 200 with average retirement rate 25% per year.

Based on the above information, what would be the amount of prior service cost amortized for 1992 under each of the two amortization methods?

	Expected-Future-Years-of-Service	Straight-Line
a.	$10,000	$12,500
b.	$10,000	$20,000
c.	$20,000	$12,500
d.	$20,000	$20,000

The following information is pertinent to Items 12 to 14:

Duesedorf Company adopted a defined benefit pension plan on January 1, 1992. Data presented below relate to the operation of the plan for 1992 and 1993:

	1992	1993
Service cost	$600,000	$700,000
Cash contribution to the plan	500,000	500,000
Beginning balance:		
Projected benefit obligation	0	600,000
Accumulated benefit obligation	0	450,000
Plan assets -- Fair value	0	500,000
Ending balance		
Projected benefit obligation	600,000	1,360,000
Accumulated benefit obligation	450,000	1,000,000
Plan assets -- Fair value	500,000	1,045,000
Settlement rate	10%	10%
Rate of return (expected and actual)	9%	9%

____ 12. What is the recognized periodic pension expense for the year?

	1992	1993
a.	$500,000	$700,000
b.	$600,000	$715,000
c.	$500,000	$500,000
d.	$600,000	$700,000

____ 13. What is the balance of the accrued pension cost as of December 31?

	1992	1993
a.	$-0-	$600,000
b.	$600,000	$700,000
c.	$100,000	$150,000
d.	$100,000	$315,000

____ 14. What is the additional pension liability as of December 31?

	1992	1993
a.	$0	$0
b.	$100,000	$200,000
c.	$100,000	$150,000
d.	$100,000	$315,000

SOLUTIONS TO REVIEW QUESTIONS AND EXERCISES

TRUE-FALSE

1.	F	5.	T	9.	T	13.	T
2.	T	6.	T	10.	F	14.	T
3.	F	7.	F	11.	F		
4.	F	8.	T	12.	F		

EXERCISE 1

1.	D	5.	C	9.	F
2.	G	6.	I	10.	A
3.	E	7.	J		
4.	H	8.	B		

EXERCISE 2

1. Prepare amortization spreadsheet:

Amortization Spreadsheet, 1992

	Actuary	Trustee	Company			
	PBO	PA	Memorandum		Accounts	
	Projected Benefit Obliga-tion	Plan Assets	UEL/UEG Unexpected Loss (Gain)	TC Trans. Cost	PE Pension Expense	APC/PPC Accrued (prepaid) Pen. Cost
Balance, 1/1/1992	$ 800	$ 750	$ 0	$ 50	$ 0	$ 0
Service cost	100				100	
Interest cost (10% on PBO)	80				80	
Expected return (10% on PA)		75			(75)	
Liability gain - Current	(50)		(50)			
Transition cost amortization ($50 x 1/3)				(17)	17	
Employer's cash contribution		190				(190)
Benefits paid	(115)	(115)				
Pension expense transferred					$ (122)	122
Balance carried, 12/31/1992	$ 815	$ 900	$ (50)	$ 33	$ 0	$ (68)

Note that the transition cost amortization rate is 1/3 [i.e., r = (2 x R) / (1 + R) = 2 x 20% / (1 + 20%) = 1/3], and the liability gain currently incurred is not amortized until next year.

2. To prepare journal entries:

a. To record cash contribution:

Accrued/prepaid pension cost	190	
Cash		190

b. To record pension expense:

Pension expense	122	
Accrued/prepaid pension cost		122

3. To determine and record additional pension liability:

a. To compute the required balances of additional pension liability and related accounts:

Accumulated benefit obligations, ending	$ 890
Less: Plan asset (fair value), ending	(900)
Add: Prepaid pension cost ($190 - $122)	68
Additional pension liability	$ 58

b. To record additional pension liability:

Unrealized pension cost	58	
Additional pension liability		58

Since there is no unrecognized prior service cost, the additional pension liability is totally debited to unrealized pension cost.

EXERCISE 3

1. Prepare amortization spreadsheets:

Amortization Spreadsheet, 1992

	Actuary	Trustee	Company			
	PBO	PA	Memorandum		Accounts	
	Projected Benefit Obliga-tion	Plan Assets	PSC Prior Service Cost	UEL/UEG Unexpected Loss (Gain)	PE Pension Expense	APC/PPC Accrued (prepaid) Pen. Cost
Balance, 1/1/1992	$ 0	$ 0	$ 0	$ 0	$ 0	$ 0
Prior service cost-Addition	1,500		1,500			
Adjusted beginning balance	$ 1,500					
Service cost	6,000				6,000	
Interest cost (9% on PBO)	135				135	
PSC amortization ($1,500 / 12%)			(180)		180	
Employer's cash contribution		5,000				(5,000)
Benefits paid	(1,000)	(1,000)				
Pension expense transferred					$(6,315)	6,315
Balance carried, 12/31/1992	$ 6,635	$4,000	$ 1,320	$ 0	$ 0	$ 1,315

Amortization Spreadsheet, 1993

	Actuary	Trustee	Company			
	PBO	PA	Memorandum		Accounts	
	Projected Benefit Obliga-tion	Plan Assets	PSC Prior Service Cost	UEL/UEG Unexpected Loss (Gain)	PE Pension Expense	APC/PPC Accrued (prepaid) Pen. Cost
Balance, 1/1/1993	$ 6,635	$ 4,000	$ 1,320	$ 0	$ 0	$ 1,315
Service cost	7,000				7,000	
Interest cost (9% on PBO)	597				597	
Expected return (10% on PA)		400			(400)	
PSC amortization ($1,500 / 12%)			(180)		180	
Liability loss - current	1,200			1,200		
Employer's cash contribution		6,000				(6,000)
Benefits paid	(1,250)	(1,250)				
Pension expense recognized					$(7,377)	7,377
Balance carried, 12/31/1993	$ 14,182	$9,150	$ 1,140	$1,200	$ 0	$ 2,692

2. To prepare journal entries:

a. To record cash contribution:

	1992		1993	
Accrued/prepaid pension cost	5,000		6,000	
Cash		5,000		6,000

b. To record pension expense:

	1992		1993	
Pension expense	6,315		7,377	
Accrued/prepaid pension cost		6,315		7,377

3. To determine and record additional pension liability:

a. To compute required balances of additional pension liability and related accounts:

	1992	1993
Accumulated benefit obligation -- Dec. 31	$ 5,500	$11,200
Less: Plan assets -- Dec. 31	(4,000)	(9,150)
Accrued pension cost -- Dec. 31	(1,315)	(2,692)
Additional pension liability	$ 185	$ 0 *
Deferred pension cost	(185)	
Unrealized pension cost -- Dec. 31	$ 0	

* Since the ABO is less than the sum of plan assets and accrued pension cost, additional pension liability is not required.

b. To record additional pension liability:

	1992		1993	
Deferred pension cost	185			
Additional pension liability		185		
Additional pension liability			185	
Deferred pension cost				185

MULTIPLE CHOICE:

1.	a	5.	a	9.	c	13.	d
2.	b	6.	d	10.	c	14.	a
3.	b	7.	d	11.	d		
4.	b	8.	a	12.	b		

Computations:

9. (c)

PBO -- Beginning balance	$160,000
Interest cost (10%)	16,000
Service cost	60,000
Benefits paid	(20,000)
PBO -- Ending balance	$216,000

10. (c)

PA -- Beginning balance	$3,000
Actual return	200
Cash contribution	500
Benefits paid	(520)
PA -- Ending balance	$3,180

11. (d)

a. Expected-future-years-of-service method:

$$N = P \times (1 + R) / 2R$$
$$= 200 \times 1.25 / .50$$
$$= 500$$

$$r_{1992} = p_{1992} / N$$
$$= 200 / 500$$
$$= 40\%$$

where p_{1992} = Number of active employees during 1992.

PSC amortized = $50,000 x 40% = $20,000

b. Straight-line method:

r = 2R / (1 + R)
= .50 / 1.25
= 40%

PSC amortized = $50,000 x 40% = $20,000

12. (b) The information indicates that there is neither prior service cost, nor transition cost. It is also implied that there is no experience gain/loss. Therefore, pension expense is determined by the three major components as follows:

	1992	1993
Service cost	$600,000	$700,000
Interest cost ($600,000 x 10%)	0	60,000
Expected return ($500,000 x 9%)	0	(45,000)
Pension expense	$600,000	$715,000

13. (d) Accrued pension cost

Beginning balance	$ 0	$100,000
Pension expense	600,000	715,000
Cash contribution	(500,000)	(500,000)
Ending balance	$100,000	$315,000

14. (a)

Accumulated benefit obligation	$450,000	$1,000,000
Plan asset, Fair value	(500,000)	(1,045,000)
Accrued pension cost	(100,000)	(315,000)
Additional pension liability *	0	0

* There is no additional pension liability since the accumulated benefit obligation was overfunded.

CHAPTER 20

Corporations: Contributed Capital

CHAPTER OBJECTIVES

This chapter is designed to enable students to:

A. Be able to describe and appreciate the characteristics, advantages and disadvantages of the corporate form of business organization.

B. Be familiar with different types of investments stockholders make in firms and various rights that attach to each.

C. Be able to describe and demonstrate accounting and reporting practices for the issuance of various forms of capital stock, both for cash and for noncash transactions.

D. Understand the accounting and reporting practices for the issuance of subscription stock.

E. Understand the accounting and reporting practices for treasury stock, including both the cost method and the par value method.

F. Understand the accounting and reporting practices for the retirement of callable and redeemable stock, and for the conversion of convertible preferred stock.

CHAPTER OVERVIEW

A. A **corporation,** which is by far the dominant form of business organization in terms of total capital investment, is characterized by the following:

1. **Limited liability** -- The stockholders (owners) are **not** personally liable for debt of the entity.

2. **Transferability** -- Ownership interest is easily transferable.

3. **Continuity** -- The entity continues when ownership changes.

While the above characteristics are conceived as advantages, there are also disadvantages of a corporation, e.g.:

1. **Double taxation** -- Corporate earnings are first taxed on the corporation as earned, and then taxed on the stockholders when distributed as dividends.

2. **Separation of management** -- Since the ownership of a corporation is separable from its management, small stockholders may lose control.

B. Stockholders' Equity

FAC 6 specifies that in a business enterprise, the **equity** is the ownership interest. It ranks after liabilities as a claim to or interest in the assets of the enterprise, and is thus a **residual** interest measured by the difference between the enterprise's assets and its liabilities, i.e., net assets.

Since the owners of a corporation are stockholders, their equity is generally referred to as the stockholders' equity, which includes contributed (paid-in) capital, retained earnings and unrealized capital. **Unrealized capital** involves both increments and decrements in stockholders' equity. Unrealized capital increment arises when a company (e.g., an insurance or investment company) writes up its investment portfolios based on the **market value method**, an exception allowed under the modification principle known as industry peculiarity. Following **FAS 12**, furthermore, the **LCM rule** is applied to long-term investment in equity securities, and the resulting unrealized loss (capital decrement) should be presented as a contra item in stockholders' equity.

The **contributed capital** is generally divided into:

1. **Capital stock,** representing (a) the minimum initial stock price, (b) the minimum amount of net assets the corporation must maintain, and (c) the basis on which dividends are declared. Since capital stock is legally restricted from being impaired, it is referred to as legal capital.

2. **Other contributed capital**, or **additional paid-in capital**:

   a. **from stockholders** such as paid-in capital in excess of par when the stock is issued, and **other stock transactions** subsequent to the issuance of stock, e.g., the reacquisition and the retirement of stock.

   b. **from other parties** such as land, machinery or building donated to the company by a third party, e.g., the city.

C. Classification of Capital Stock

Capital stock of a corporation may include both **common stock** or **preferred stock**. As determined in the corporate charter and state law, each stock conveys to the stockholders certain rights such as follows:

1. **Common stock** -- the primary issue of shares which normally carries the following rights:

   a. the right to vote for directors.

   b. the right to share profits.

   c. the right to share in the distribution of assets in the event the company is liquidated.

   d. the preemptive right to acquire additional shares in proportion to existing holdings if the total stock outstanding is increased.

2. **Preferred stock.** An issue of stock which confers certain preferences or features not possessed by common stock such as:

   a. The preference to specified amount of **dividends** (stated dollar amount per share or rate of par value of stock). That is, if the board of directors declares dividends, preferred stockholders will receive the stated dividends before any dividends are paid to common stockholders.

   b. The right of conversion which allows preferred stockholders to exchange their shares for common stock at a specified conversion ratio.

   c. A redemption privilege which allows preferred stockholders the option, under specified conditions, to return their shares for a predetermined redemption price.

   d. A preference as to the distribution of assets in the event the corporation is liquidated.

D. Dividend Preference

In terms of dividends distribution, a preferred stock may be:

1. **Cumulative or noncumulative.** Typically, preferred stock is cumulative, which means that if the specified preferred dividends are not paid in a given year, the unpaid dividends, referred to as **dividends in arrears**, accumulate and must be made up in later years before any dividends are paid on common stock. Preferred

dividends in arrears, furthermore, should be paid when the stock is retired or converted into common shares. In any event, however, they are not considered as liabilities, and should only be reported in the notes. If the preferred stock is noncumulative, any unpaid dividends are simply disregarded.

2. **Participating or nonparticipating.** Participating preferred stock allows investors to receive additional dividends **beyond the specified amount**, whereas the dividends on nonparticipating preferred stock are limited to the stated rate. The distribution of additional dividends is a pro rata allocation based on the relative par value amounts of common and preferred stock outstanding. If the stock is fully participating, the pro rata allocation is without upper limit. If the stock is partially participating, on the other hand, there is a ceiling imposed on the participation. Dividends distribution with cumulative and participating preferred stock outstanding is based on the following **priority**:

   a. preferred dividends in arrears.

   b. preferred current dividends.

   c. common dividends at preferred dividend rate, known as current matching.

   d. participation:

      (1) If **fully participating** -- all the remainder is allocated to preferred and common on pro rata basis.

      (2) If **partially participating** -- Allocate the remainder on a pro rata basis to preferred and common **up to** the maximum participation rate, and allocate all the rest to common.

ILLUSTRATION 1 -- Common and preferred dividends

Given: The balance sheet of Young Corporation included the data shown below for 1992. No dividends were declared in 1992. During 1993, Young declared cash dividends of $300,000:

Common stock, 60,000 shares issued, @ $10 par	$600,000
10% Preferred stock, 80,000 shares issued, @ $5 par	400,000

Required: Allocate the declared dividends in each of the following cases:

Case 1: The preferred stock is **noncumulative** and **nonparticipating.**
Case 2: The preferred stock is **cumulative** and **nonparticipating.**
Case 3: The preferred stock is **noncumulative** and **fully participating.**
Case 4: The preferred stock is **cumulative** and **fully participating.**

Case 5: The preferred stock is **cumulative** and **partially participating**, with a maximum participation rate of 5% above the stated rate of 10%.

SOLUTION:

	Preferred	**Common**	**Total**
Case 1	$40,000 [1]	$260,000	$300,000
Case 2	80,000 [2]	220,000	300,000
Case 3	120,000 [3]	180,000	300,000
Case 4	144,000 [4]	156,000	300,000
Case 5	100,000 [5]	200,000	300,000

[1] Preferred dividends (1993) = $400,000 x 10% = $40,000.

[2] Preferred dividends (1992 and 1993) = $400,000 x 10% x 2 = $80,000.

[3] Preferred dividends (1993 including participation) = pro rata allocation based on preferred par value ratio = $300,000 x 40% = $120,000.

where the preferred par value ratio = $400,000 / ($400,000 + $600,000) = 40%.

[4] Preferred dividends (1992 and 1993 including full participation) = preferred dividends in arrears + pro rata allocation based on preferred par value ratio = $40,000 + ($300,000 - $40,000) x 40% = $144,000.

[5] Preferred dividends (1992 and 1993 including participation up to additional 5%) = preferred dividends in arrears + pro rata allocation up to 15% based on preferred par value = $40,000 + $400,000 x 15% = $100,000.

E. Issuance of Stock

1. **Stock issued for cash.** When stock is issued for cash, the capital stock account (common or preferred) is credited for the **par value** of the shares issued. Any proceeds received in excess of the par value amount are credited to contributed (or paid-in) capital in excess of par.

   Many states permit corporations to issue **nopar stock.** If the board of directors is required to assign a value to the nopar stock, the assigned value, known as the **stated value,** is accounted for as a par value. That is, the capital stock is recorded at the stated value, and the excess of issuing price over the stated value is credited to contributed (or paid-in) capital in excess of stated value.

A nopar stock without a stated value is called **true nopar stock**. The entire proceeds from the sale of a true nopar stock are recorded in the capital stock account unless the state of incorporation establishes a minimum amount per share to be maintained separately as the legal capital.

2. **Stock issued for noncash consideration.** If stock shares are issued for considerations other than cash, the transaction is recorded at the fair value of the stock or of the consideration, whichever is more reliably determinable.

3. **Stock issued on subscription basis.** Frequently stock is issued on a subscription basis. That is, prospective stockholders sign a contract to purchase a specified number of shares at a specified price to be paid by installment. Because a legal contract is involved, accounting recognition must be given when these transactions occur. The following entries are typical:

   a. **On date of subscription:**

Subscriptions receivable (at subscription price)	xxxx	
Common stock subscribed (at par value)		xxxx
Contributed capital in excess of par		xxxx

   b. **On date of collection:**

Cash	xxxx	
Subscriptions receivable		xxxx

   c. **On date of issuance of stock:**

Common stock subscribed	xxxx	
Common stock (at par value)		xxxx

Common or preferred stock subscribed is presented on the balance sheet as an addition to the respective capital stock. Subscriptions receivable are generally presented as a contra equity account (i.e., to be deducted from the total stockholders' equity), although some accountants treat it as a current asset like other receivables.

In case a subscriber defaults after partial fulfillment of the subscription contract, the corporation should comply with the state law or follow the contract to (1) return all the collected payments to the subscriber, (2) issue shares proportional to the amount collected, (3) retain all the payments collected from the subscriber, or (4) resell the subscribed shares to a third party under a lien whereby the subscriber is responsible for maintaining the original subscription price.

ILLUSTRATION 2 -- Issue stock on subscription basis

Given: On July 1, 1992, Bamford Corporation sold 1,000 shares of its $10 par common stock to Mr. Marana and another 2,000 shares to Mr. Oranski for $15 per share with 40% down payments. the remainder is due on December 31, 1992. Subscribed shares will be issued upon collection of the subscribed price in full.

On the due date, Mr. Marana paid the additional $9,000 and Bamford issued 1,000 shares to Mr. Marana upon receipt of the payment. Mr. Oranski, however, defaulted the subscription contract.

Required: Record the stock transactions.

Solution:

a. 7/1/1992 -- To record subscription of shares:

Subscriptions receivable (3,000 shares x $15)	45,000	
Common stock subscripted (3,000 x $10)		30,000
Contributed capital in excess of par		15,000

b. 7/1/1992 -- To record collection of down payments:

Cash ($45,000 x 40%)	18,000	
Subscriptions receivable		18,000

c. 12/31/1992 -- To record collection of additional payments made by Mr. Marana:

Cash ($15,000 x 60%)	9,000	
Subscriptions receivable		9,000

d. 12/31/1992 -- To record issuance of shares to Mr. Marana:

Common stock subscribed	10,000	
Common stock, 1,000 shares, par $10		10,000

e. 12/31/1992 -- To record defaulted subscriptions:

Case 1: Return all the amounts collected from Mr. Oranski:

Common stock subscribed	20,000	
Contributed capital in excess of par	10,000	
Subscriptions receivable ($30,000 x 60%)		18,000
Due to defaulting subscriber		12,000

Case 2: Issue shares proportional to the amounts collected, i.e., 40%:

Common stock subscribed	20,000	
Contributed capital in excess of par ($10,000 x 60%)	6,000	
Subscriptions receivable ($30,000 x 60%)		18,000
Common stock, 800 shares, @ $10 par		8,000

Case 3: Retain all payments collected from Mr. Oranski:

Common stock subscribed	20,000	
Contributed capital in excess of par	10,000	
Subscriptions receivable ($30,000 x 60%)		18,000
Contributed capital from defaulted subscriptions		12,000

Case 4: Resell the forfeited shares at Mr. Oranski's cost:

(1) **Cancel the original subscription contract:**

Common stock subscribed	20,000	
Contributed capital in excess of par	10,000	
Subscriptions receivable ($30,000 x 60%)		18,000
Due to defaulting subscriber		12,000

(2) **Resell the forfeited shares,** assuming the shares were sold for **$12.5** per share:

Cash ($12.5 x 2,000 shs.)	25,000	
Due to defaulting subscriber	5,000	
Common stock		20,000
Contributed capital in excess of par		10,000

Note that the defaulting subscriber is responsible for the decline in price as well as resale cost. To avoid the incentive of default, the amount to be refunded to the defaulting subscriber cannot exceed the amount paid to the date of default less resale cost. No resale cost is assumed in the above example.

4. **Stock issue cost.** Costs incurred in connection with the issuance of capital stock are generally treated as a **reduction** in the **proceeds** received and thus reduce contributed capital in excess of par. Some companies, however, record stock issue costs as a deferred charge (e.g., **organization costs**) and amortize the costs over a reasonable period of time.

F. Reacquisition of Stock

Stock previously issued is often reacquired by the issuing corporation. Accounting procedure dealing with such reacquisition depends upon whether the reacquired shares are intended to be reissued:

1. **Formal retirement.** When outstanding stock is reacquired for formal retirement, as with **callable** (at the option of the issuing firm) or **redeemable** (at the option of the investor) stock, the price paid for the retirement represents a return of the original contributed capital by the corporation to its shareholders. The transaction should thus be recorded by debiting capital stock at par value, and contributed capital in excess of par at original issuing price less par value. Then:

   a. Any remaining debit difference is debited to retained earnings as a de facto dividend.

   b. Any remaining credit difference is credited to contributed capital from retirement of stock.

2. **Treasury stock.** When a stock is reacquired with the intention of subsequent reissuance, the reacquired stock is referred to as **treasury stock**. There are two methods to account for treasury stock transactions:

   a. **Cost method.** The **purchase** of treasury stock is viewed as a **temporary** reduction of stockholders' equity. The cost of acquiring the shares is debited to a treasury stock account.

   If some or all of the treasury shares are **reissued**, cash is debited at the resale price and treasury stock is credited at the original reacquisition cost. Then:

   (1) Any debit difference is debited to the existing contributed capital from treasury stock transactions up to the credit balance of the account. Any remainder is debited to retained earnings.

   (2) Any credit difference is credited to contributed capital from treasury stock transactions.

   When treasury stock is formally **retired**, the treasury stock (at cost) is credited and all the related capital accounts, including capital stock and contributed capital in excess of par are debited. Then:

   (1) Any debit difference is debited to retained earnings.
   (2) Any credit difference is credited to contributed capital from stock retirement.

b. **Par value method.** The **purchase** of treasury stock is viewed as **constructive retirement** of the stock. The treasury stock account is debited for the par value of the shares. Any contributed capital in excess of par related to the reacquired shares is removed with a debit. Cash is credited at the reacquisition cost. Then:

(1) Any debit difference is debited to the existing contributed capital from treasury stock transactions up to the credit balance of the account. Any remainder is debited to retained earnings.

(2) Any credit difference is credited to contributed capital from treasury stock transactions.

When treasury stock is subsequently **resold**, the sale is recorded in essentially the same manner as for the issuance of unissued shares. That it, cash is debited at resale price and treasury stock is credited at the par value. Then:

(1) Any debit difference is debited to the existing contributed capital from treasury stock transactions up to the credit balance of the account. Any remainder is debited to retained earnings.

(2) Any credit difference is credited to contributed capital in excess of par.

When treasury stock is **retired**, the treasury stock and the related capital stock, both recorded at par, are removed from the books.

ILLUSTRATION 3 -- Treasury stock transactions

Given: On December 31, 1992, the stockholders' equity section of the balance sheet of Olson Company included the following:

Common stock, 20,000 shares, @$1 par	$20,000
Paid-in capital in excess of par	5,000
Retained earnings	100,000

During 1993:

a. Reacquired 4,000 shares of treasury stock at $2.25 per share.
b. Reacquired 1,000 shares of treasury stock at $1.10 per share.
c. Sold 2,000 shares of treasury stock at $2.50 per share.
d. Sold 1,000 shares of treasury stock at $.50 per share.
e. Retired 1,000 shares of treasury stock.

Required: Record the treasury stock transactions using:

(1) The cost method, and
(2) The par value method.

SOLUTION:

Cost Method			Par Value Method		
a. To record acquisition of treasury stock:					
Treasury stock (at cost)	9,000		Treasury stock (at par)	4,000	
Cash (4,000 shs. x $2.25)		9,000	Paid-in capital in excess of par	1,000	
			Retained earnings	4,000	
			Cash (4,000 shs. x $2.25)		9,000
b. To record acquisition of treasury stock:					
Treasury stock (at cost)	1,100		Treasury stock (at par)	1,000	
Cash (1,000 shs. x $1.10)		1,100	Paid-in capital in excess of par	250	
			Cash (1,000 shs. x $1.10)		1,100
			Paid-in capital from TS trans.		150
c. To record sale of treasury stock (FIFO):					
Cash (2,000 shs. x $2.50)	5,000		Cash (2,000 shs. x $2.50)	5,000	
Treasury stock (at cost)		4,500	Treasury stock, (at par)		2,000
Paid-in capital from TS trans.		500	Paid-in capital in excess of par		3,000
d. To record sale of treasury stock:					
Cash (1,000 shs. x $0.50)	500		Cash (1,000 shs. x $0.50)	500	
Paid-in capital from TS trans.	500		Paid-in capital from TS trans.	150	
Retained earnings	1,250		Retained earnings	350	
Treasury stock (at cost)		2,250	Treasury stock (at par)		1,000
e. To record retirement of treasury stock:					
Common stock (1,000 shs. x $1)	1,000		Common stock	1,000	
Paid-in capital in excess of par	250		Treasury stock (at par)		1,000
Retained earnings	1,000				
Treasury stock (at cost)		2,250			

Under the cost method, treasury stock is presented on the balance sheet as a contra stockholders' equity account. Under the par value method, it is presented as a contra capital stock account. To protect creditors' interests, some states limit the amount of treasury stock that can be held at any one time to the total amount of retained earnings. Therefore, under either the cost method or the par value method, it is required that retained earnings equal to the **cost** of treasury stock should be restricted from being distributed to stockholders. Footnotes are generally used to disclose such a restriction.

3. **Donation.** If treasury stock is acquired by donation, it may be recorded at

either (a) its market value under the cost method, or (b) its par value under the par value method. Alternatively, a memorandum entry may also be appropriate, on the grounds that there was no cost.

4. **Conversion.** When convertible preferred stock is converted by the stockholder into shares of common stock, the converted preferred shares usually are formally retired when received by the corporation. Any dividends in arrears must be paid prior to the conversion.

   To record the conversion, capital stock and paid-in capital in excess of par of the converted shares must be removed and the new shares issued are recorded at their par or stated value. Then:

   a. Any debit difference is debited to retained earnings.

   b. Any credit difference is credited to paid-in capital from conversion.

KEY CONCEPTS

Callable and redeemable preferred stock Preferred stock that the issuing company has the option to retire at a specified price is known as **callable.** Preferred stock that the stockholders have the option to return to the corporation at a specified price is known as **redeemable.**

Common stock Primary issue of shares that entitle the holders of the stock the right to vote, share profit and acquire new shares.

Convertible preferred stock Preferred stock that allows the stockholders to exchange their shares for common stock at a specified conversion ratio.

Cumulative preferred stock Preferred stock on which the undeclared dividends accumulated as dividends in arrears should be paid before any dividends are paid on common stock.

Participating preferred stock Preferred stock that has the right to receive additional dividends on top of the stated amount or rate. A participation with upper limit is known as partially participating, whereas a participation without an upper limit is termed fully participating.

Preferred stock Stock that confers preferences and rights that the common stock does not possess. Typical preferences include dividends distribution, asset distribution and conversion.

Stock subscription A contractual commitment that the prospective stockholders will purchase a specified number of shares at a specified price within a specified time period. The corporation shall issue subscribed shares upon collection of the subscription price in full.

Stockholders' equity Equity of a corporation consisting of contributed capital, retained earnings and unrealized capital. Stockholders' equity represents the residual interest in the business entity measured by the difference between assets and liabilities.

Treasury stock Issued stock is reacquired and temporarily held by the issuing corporation. Treasury stock may be accounted for using either the cost or the par value method.

REVIEW QUESTIONS AND EXERCISES

TRUE-FALSE

Indicate whether each of the following statements is true or false by circling the correct response.

T F 1. An advantage of a corporation over a partnership is that transfer of ownership generally is unrestricted.

T F 2. Legal capital is the portion of stockholders' equity that is legally required to be maintained for the protection of creditors.

T F 3. Owners of common stock are more likely to possess voting rights than owners of preferred stock.

T F 4. The dividend preference of preferred stock generally is a fixed percentage of its market price.

T F 5. If preferred stock is participating, unpaid current dividends must be paid in subsequent years prior to dividend payments to common stockholders.

T F 6. Common stockholders always have a right over preferred stockholders to assets of a corporation in the event of **liquidation**.

T F 7. If preferred stock is callable, preferred stockholders have an option to acquire a specified number of shares of common stock within a specified time period, at a specified call price.

T F 8. At the time a common stock subscription contract is signed, the common stock account is credited for the par value of the shares.

T F 9. When a corporation reacquires shares of its own stock, an asset known as treasury stock is credited.

T F 10. Whether a corporation accounts for treasury stock transactions by the par value method or the cost method, the amount of total stockholders' equity will be the same.

T F 11. When the cost method is used to account for treasury stock, the subsequent resale of treasury shares at a price above the reacquisition cost will be credited to contributed capital from treasury stock transactions.

T F 12. When preferred shares are called and retired, the excess of call price over the original contributed capital of those shares should be debited to retained earnings.

T F 13. The balance sheet presentation of treasury stock is the same under either the cost method or the par value method.

T F 14. Stock issue cost must be recorded as a deferred charge and amortized over 40 years.

EXERCISE 1

The board of directors of Carter Corporation declared cash dividends of $6,000, $21,000, and $90,000 in 1992, 1993 and 1994, respectively. In each of the three years, Carter's capital stock consisted of the following:

Common stock, 20,000 shares, $10 par	$200,000
Contributed capital in excess of par -- common	150,000
8% Preferred stock, 1,000 shares, $100 par	100,000
Contributed capital in excess of par -- preferred	50,000

Determine the amount of dividends to be paid to preferred and common stockholders in each of the three years:

1. The preferred stock is noncumulative and nonparticipating:

	Preferred	**Common**
1992	______	______
1993	______	______
1994	______	______

2. The preferred stock is cumulative and fully participating:

	Preferred	**Common**
1992	______	______
1993	______	______
1994	______	______

EXERCISE 2

Murray Corporation received a charter authorizing the issuance of 100,000 shares of common stock with a par value of $10. Give journal entries to record the following transactions.

a. To record subscriptions of 10,000 shares each for Mr. A and Mr. B, at $20 per share.

Subscription Rec. 400,000
C.S. subscribed A 100000
C.S. Subscribed B 100,000
PIC<PAR 200,000

b. To record collection of 50% of the subscription price.

Cash 200000
Subscription Receivable 200,000

c. To record collection of balance of subscription receivable from Mr. A.

Cash 100,000
Subscription 100,000
C.S. Subsc A 100000
C.S. 100,000

d. To record issuance of the subscribed shares to Mr. A.

e. Mr. B defaulted on the contract. To record the forfeited transaction assuming that Murray refunded the previously collected amount to Mr. B.

C.S. Subscribed 10000
PIC > Par 100,000
Cash 100,000 100000
Loss - Due to Forfeiture 100,000

EXERCISE 3

O'Brien Electrical Company originally issued 40,000 shares of its $10 par common stock at $16 per share. Give the appropriate journal entry for each of the following treasury stock transactions in 1992.

1. assuming that O'Brien uses the cost method:

a. On January 10, O'Brien reacquired 5,000 shares at $20 per share.

b. On April 5, O'Brien sold 1,000 shares of treasury stock at $21 per share.

c. On October 14, O'Brien sold 2,000 shares of treasury stock at $15 per share.

2. Assuming that O'Brien uses the par value method:

a. On January 10, O'Brien reacquired 5,000 shares at $20 per share.

b. On April 5, O'Brien sold 1,000 shares of treasury stock at $21 per share.

c. On October 14, O'Brien sold 2,000 shares of treasury stock at $15 per share.

MULTIPLE CHOICE

Enter the letter corresponding to the response which **best** completes each of the following statements or questions.

____ 1. Which of the following is **not** one of the characteristics of the corporate form of business organization?

a. Income is taxed only when distributed as dividends.
b. Ownership is easily transferable.
c. Liability is limited to resources of the corporate entity.
d. It is not necessary to reorganize the business when ownership changes.

____ 2. The basic rights of common stock ownership generally do **not** include:

a. the right to vote for directors.
b. the right over preferred stock to receive a specified rate or amount of dividends.
c. the right to share in the distribution of assets in the event of liquidation.
d. the right to maintain a proportional share of ownership in the company by purchasing a proportional share of any new stock issued.

____ 3. The excess of the fair value of the consideration received over the par value of common stock issued should be credited to:

a. a liability account.
b. common stock.
c. other contributed capital.
d. retained earnings.

____ 4. A donated operational asset for which the fair value, if known, should be recorded as a debit to operational assets and a credit to:

a. other contributed capital.
b. retained earnings.
c. a deferred charge.
d. other income.

____ 5. The excess of the subscription price over the par value of common stock subscribed should be recorded as:

a. other contributed capital when the subscription price is collected.
b. other contributed capital when the stock is subscribed.
c. retained earnings when the subscribed stock is issued.
d. other contributed capital when the subscribed stock is issued.

____ 6. Dividends in arrears:

a. are reported in a note to the financial statements.
b. arise in connection with fully participating preferred stock.
c. are reported as a current liability.
d. are reported as a noncurrent liability.

____ 7. Treasury stock should be accounted for using:

a. the cost method only.
b. the par value method only.
c. either the cost method or the par value method.
d. none of the above.

____ 8. Treasury stock reacquired by donation and intended to be reissued should be recorded:

a. by debiting treasury stock account at fair value.
b. by debiting treasury stock account at par value.
c. by a memorandum entry.
d. any of the above.

____ 9. A stockholder donated 1,000 shares of Sharpe's $10 par stock to Sharpe Corporation, when the fair value was $16 a share. Assuming that those shares were initially issued at $12 and those donated shares were intended to be reissued, under the par value method, Sharpe's **additional paid-in capital** should be increased by:

a. $5,000
b. $4,000
c. $12,000
d. $10,000

____ 10. Rucker Manufacturing Company has 40,000 shares of $10 par common stock outstanding. All 40,000 shares were issued at $15. If 1,000 of these shares are reacquired at $18 and the par value method is used to account for treasury stock, **stockholders' equity** would **decrease** by:

a. $0.
b. $3,000.
c. $12,000.
d. $18,000.

____ 11. Based on the same data as in Question 10, if the cost method is used to account for treasury stock transactions, stockholders' equity would **decrease** by:

a. $0.
b. $10,000.
c. $12,000.
d. $18,000.

____ 12. Hawks Corporation reported stockholders' equity on its balance sheet at December 31, 1992 as follows:

Common stock, 20,000 shares, $10 par	$200,000
Additional paid-in capital	100,000
Retained earnings	200,000
Total contributed capital	$500,000

In 1993, Hawks earned income of $25,000, declared cash dividends of $15,000 and retired 2,000 shares of its outstanding stock for $20 per share. At the end of 1993, Hawks' additional paid-in capital and retained earnings should have the following balances:

	Additional paid-in capital	Retained earnings
a.	$ 90,000	$200,000
b.	$100,000	$110,000
c.	$ 80,000	$210,000
d.	$ 0	$210,000

____ 13. Based on the same data as in Question 12, except that Hawks intended to reissue those reacquired shares, and the cost method is used to account for treasury stock transactions. Hawks' additional paid-in capital and retained earnings at the end of 1993 should have the following balances:

	Additional paid-in capital	Retained earnings
a.	$ 90,000	$200,000
b.	$100,000	$110,000
c.	$ 80,000	$210,000
d.	$100,000	$210,000

_____ 14. Based on the same data as in Question 13, what is the total amount of stockholders' equity at the end of 1993?

a. $470,000
b. $500,000
c. $510,000
d. $525,000

SOLUTIONS TO REVIEW QUESTIONS AND EXERCISES

TRUE-FALSE

1.	T	5.	F	9.	F	13.	F
2.	T	6.	F	10.	T	14.	F
3.	T	7.	F	11.	T		
4.	F	8.	F	12.	T		

EXERCISE 1

1. **The preferred stock is noncumulative and nonparticipating:**

	Preferred	Common
1992	$ 6,000	$ 0
1993	$ 8,000	$13,000
1994	$ 8,000	$82,000

2. **The preferred stock is cumulative and fully participating:**

	Preferred	Common
1992	$ 6,000	$ 0
1993	$10,000[1]	$11,000
1994	$30,000[2]	$60,000

Notes:

[1] Preferred dividends in arrears ($2,000) and current preferred dividends ($8,000). The remainder ($11,000) was totally distributed to common stock at a rate of 5.5%, which was less than the preferred dividend rate of 8%. There was thus no participation.

[2] Current preferred dividends plus participation = ($90,000 x 1 / 3) = $30,000.

EXERCISE 2

a. **To record subscriptions of 10,000 shares each for Mr. A and Mr. B, at $20 per share.**

Subscriptions receivable (20,000 shs. x $20)	400,000	
Common stock subscribed (20,000 shs. x $10)		200,000
Contributed capital in excess of par		200,000

b. **To record collection of 50% of the subscription price.**

Cash ($400,000 x 50%)	200,000	
Subscriptions receivable		200,000

c. **To record collection of balance of subscription receivable from Mr. A.**

Cash ($200,000 x 50%)	100,000	
Subscriptions receivable		100,000

d. **To record issuance of the subscribed shares to Mr. A.**

Common stock subscribed (10,000 shs. x $10)	100,000	
Common stock		100,000

e. **Mr. B defaulted on the contract. To record the forfeited transaction assuming that Murray refunded the previously collected amount to Mr. B.**

Common stock subscribed (10,000 x $20 x 50%)	100,000	
Contributed capital in excess of par	100,000	
Subscriptions receivable		100,000
Due to defaulting subscriber (Mr. B)		100,000

EXERCISE 3

1. Assuming that O'Brien uses the cost method:

a. On January 10, O'Brien reacquired 5,000 shares at $20 per share.

Treasury stock (5,000 shs. x $20)	100,000	
Cash		100,000

b. On April 5, O'Brien sold 1,000 shares of treasury stock at $21 per share.

Cash (1,000 shs. x $21)	21,000	
Treasury stock (1,000 shs. x $20)		20,000
Paid-in capital from TS trans.		1,000

c. On October 14, O'Brien sold 2,000 shares of treasury stock at $15 per share.

Cash (2,000 shs. x $15)	30,000	
Paid-in capital from TS trans.	1,000	
Retained earnings	9,000	
Treasury stock (2,000 shs. x $20)		40,000

2. Assuming that O'Brien uses the par value method:

a. On January 10, O'Brien reacquired 5,000 shares at $20 per share.

Treasury stock (5,000 shs. x $10)	50,000	
Paid-in capital in excess of par (5,000 shs. x $6)	30,000	
Retained earnings	20,000	
Cash		100,000

b. On April 5, O'Brien sold 1,000 shares of treasury stock at $21 per share.

Cash (1,000 shs. x $21)	21,000	
Treasury stock (1,000 shs. x $10)		10,000
Paid-in capital in excess of par		11,000

c. **On October 14, O'Brien sold 2,000 shares of treasury stock at $15 per share.**

Cash (2,000 shs. x $15)	30,000	
Treasury stock (2,000 shs. x $10)		20,000
Paid-in capital in excess of par		10,000

MULTIPLE CHOICE:

1.	a	5.	b	9.	d	13.	d
2.	b	6.	a	10.	d	14.	a
3.	c	7.	c	11.	d		
4.	a	8.	d	12.	a		

Computations:

9. (d) Increase in additional paid capital
= PIC from donation - PIC in excess of par
= $12,000 - $2,000
= $10,000.

10. (d) Decrease in stockholders' equity
= Cash paid for the reacquisition
= $18,000.

Note that the following entry is pertinent to the reacquisition of stock:

Treasury stock	10,000	
PIC in excess of par	5,000	
Retained earnings	3,000	
Cash		18,000

11. (d) Same as Question 10 above.

Note that the following reacquisition entry is pertinent under the cost method:

Treasury stock	18,000	
Cash		18,000

12. (a) **Additional paid-in capital:**

Beginning balance	$100,000
Less: PIC in excess of par of retired shares	(10,000)
Ending balance	$ 90,000

Retained earnings:

Beginning balance	$200,000
Add: Net income	25,000
Less: Dividends	(15,000)
Less: Reduction due to retirement of stock	(10,000)
Ending balance	$200,000

13. (d) **Additional paid-in capital:**

Beginning balance	$100,000
Current changes	0
Ending balance	$100,000

Retained earnings:

Beginning balance	$200,000
Add: Net income	25,000
Less: Dividends	(15,000)
Ending balance	$210,000

14. (a)

Common stock		$200,000
Paid-in capital in excess of par		100,000
Retained earnings:		
Beginning balance	$200,000	
Add: Net income	25,000	
Less: Dividends	(15,000)	
Ending balance		210,000
Less: Treasury stock (at cost)		(40,000)
Stockholders' equity		$470,000

CHAPTER 21

Corporations: Retained Earnings and Stock Options

CHAPTER OBJECTIVES

This chapter is designed to enable students to:

A. Understand the nature of retained earnings and dividends.

B. Be familiar with the proper accounting for cash dividends, property dividends, liquidating dividends, and scrip dividends.

C. Know how to account for stock dividends and stock splits.

D. Understand what is an appropriation of retained earnings and how it should be reported.

E. Be familiar with the appropriate accounting and reporting standards for a variety of stock option plans, stock rights and warrants.

F. Appreciate what a quasi-reorganization is, when it is appropriate, and the accounting procedures that are applied in a quasi-reorganization.

G. Understand the nature of and accounting treatment for stock appreciation rights.

CHAPTER OVERVIEW

Part I -- Retained Earnings

A. **Retained earnings** represent a corporation's accumulated net income (or net loss) and prior period adjustments, less dividends and other amounts transferred to the contributed capital accounts. The sources and uses of retained earnings are summarized in the following T account:

Retained Earnings

Decreases (debits)	Increases (credits)
Net loss	Net income
Dividends	Prior year adjustments
Prior year adjustments	Removal of deficit by quasi-reorganization
Treasury stock and stock retirement transactions	

A credit balance in this account indicates the amount of net assets previously earned and retained by the firm. A debit balance is referred to as a **deficit.** Note that dividends generally are declared only to the extent of retained earnings available for distribution. In some states, however, dividends may be paid on the basis of contributed capital also.

B. Nature of Dividends

Dividends are distributions of cash, noncash assets, or the corporation's own stock to the stockholders in proportion to the number of outstanding shares of stock held by each of them. The following sequential events are typical:

1. On the **date of declaration**, the board of directors formally announces (declares) the dividends distribution. A declared dividend constitutes an enforceable contract between the corporation and its stockholders. A journal entry is generally required to record the dividend declared on this date.

2. On the **date of record**, a list of **stockholders of record** is prepared to identify those who hold stock at this specified date and are thus entitled to receive the declared dividends. No entry is made.

3. To provide time for transfer of the stock, the stock exchanges advance the effective **ex-dividend date** by three or four days beyond the date of record. In that case, one who holds the stock on the day prior to the stipulated ex-dividend date receives the dividend. No entry is made.

3. On the **date of payment**, cash, noncash asset, or the corporation's stock is distributed to those stockholders who are entitled to the dividend. This date typically follows the declaration date by four to six weeks, and a journal entry is required to record the payment.

C. Forms (Types) of Dividends

Dividends may take the following forms:

1. **Cash dividends.** Cash dividends are the usual form of distributions to

stockholders. The board of directors may declare cash dividends if both retained earnings and cash are available. To record cash dividends:

a. On date of declaration:

Retained earnings	xxxx	
Cash dividends payable		xxxx

b. On date of payment:

Cash dividends payable	xxxx	
Cash		xxxx

Cash dividends are usually reported on the balance sheet as a current liability. In rare situations that a corporation has enough retained earnings but is temporarily short of cash, it may choose to declare a **scrip (or liability) dividend.** In essence, a scrip dividend is also a cash dividend except that a future date longer than ordinary (e.g., one year) is specified as the date of payment. Promissory notes, called scrip, are often issued to stockholders prior to the payment date. Once issued the notes are treated as ordinary notes. Any interest accrued and paid should be debited to interest expense.

2. **Property dividends.** A **property dividend** involves the distribution of noncash assets (property) to stockholders. The dividend is recorded at the fair market value of the property to be distributed. The property should be revalued and a gain or loss on the revaluation should be recognized prior to recording the dividend. The most used property for dividend purpose is investment in equity securities. Note that when a property is revalued, it is limited to that portion of the property that is used for dividends distribution. The remainder should still be maintained at cost. To record a property dividend:

a. On date of declaration:

(1) To record revaluation of the property:

Investment in equity securities	xxxx	
Gain on disposal of security investment		xxxx

(2) To record the dividend:

Retained earnings	xxxx	
Property dividends payable		xxxx

b. On date of payment

To record the payment:

Property dividends payable	xxxx	
Investment in equity securities		xxxx

Like cash dividends, property dividends are usually reported on the balance sheet as current liabilities.

3. **Stock dividends.** A **stock dividend** is a proportional distribution of additional shares of common or preferred stock to the stockholders of the corporation. It is a transfer of certain amount of retained earnings to permanent capital account(s), and the assets, liabilities and the total stockholders' equity of the firm are not affected by the transfer. The primary reasons for the issuance of stock dividends include (a) to retain permanently earnings in the business, and (b) to increase the number of shares outstanding so as to reduce the market price per share and to make it more affordable to small investors.

   The accounting treatment of a stock dividend involves a capitalization (reclassification) of retained earnings. Following **ARB 43,** the amount to be capitalized depends upon the **size** of the stock dividend:

   a. **Small stock dividends.** A stock dividend is small if the dividend rate is **less than 20%** of shares currently outstanding. Based on the presumption that such a small increase in the number of shares does not have any apparent effect on the share market price, an amount equal to the **market price** of those additional shares immediately after their issuance should be capitalized.

   b. **Large stock dividends.** When the proportion of the additional shares issued is **greater than 25%** of shares currently outstanding, the dividend is considered as **large.** Based on the presumption that such a large stock dividend has the effect of materially reducing the share market price, the **par value** or **stated value** of those shares to be distributed is to be capitalized.

   If a stock dividend is in the 20-25% range, judgment is required to capitalize either the market price, or the par value or state value of shares to be issued as dividends. The use of average paid-in capital is also acceptable.

   Most accountants record stock dividends originally on the date of issuance on the grounds that (1) the declaration of a stock dividend is revocable and (2) **ARB 43** specifies that for a small stock dividend the market price at **issuance date** must be used. Some accountants, however, prefer recording stock dividends originally on the date of declaration.

ILLUSTRATION 1 -- Stock dividends

Martinez Industries declared a stock dividend of 10,000 shares of $10 par value common stock. The market price of the stock **at the issuance** of the new shares was $50.

Required:

(1) Recording stock dividends on date of issuance:

ORIGINAL ENTRY AT DATE OF ISSUANCE					
10% stock dividends (small)			**40% stock dividends (large)**		
On dare of declaration:			On date of declaration:		
None			None		
On date of issuance:			On date of issuance:		
Retained earnings	500,000*		Retained earnings	100,000 **	
Common stock (par)		100,000	Common stock (par)		100,000
Paid-in capital in excess of par		400,000			
* 10,000 shs. x $50 = $500,000			** 10,000 shs. x $10 = $100,000		

(2) Recording stock dividend on date of declaration:

ORIGINAL ENTRY AT DATE OF DECLARATION					
10% stock dividends (small)			**40% stock dividends (large)**		
On date of declaration:			On date of declaration:		
Retained earnings	100,000		Retained earnings	100,000	
Stock dividends issuable		100,000	Stock dividends issuable		100,000
On date of issuance:			On date of issuance:		
Stock dividends issuable	100,000		Stock dividends issuable	100,000	
Retained earnings	400,000*		Common stock (par)		100,000
Common stock (par)		100,000			
Paid-in capital in excess of par		400,000			
* The excess of market value over par.					
Note: (1) The par value is used to record initially the dividends. (2) Stock dividends issuable is reported as an increase in contributed capital.					

When a corporation issues stock dividends (e.g., 10% stock dividends), some stockholders may be entitled only to a fractional number of shares (e.g., 3/10 of a share). In this case, the company may either distribute cash for those fractional shares based on current share market price, or issue stock warrants which may be exchanged for stock such as 10 warrants for a share. Stock warrants issued are recorded by crediting stock warrants outstanding at the par value of equivalent number of whole shares. Stock warrants outstanding will then be transferred to common stock when the warrant rights are exercised. As the exercise period is over, any outstanding warrants become unexercisable and are closed to paid-in capital from lapsed warrant rights.

ILLUSTRATION 2 -- Stock dividends with fractional shares

On October 10, 1992 Kinderman Corporation declared 30% stock dividends of 25,000 shares on its $10 par common stock. On November 10, 24,500 shares of common stock and stock warrants equivalent to 500 whole shares were distributed to stockholders. On December 10, 80% of the warrant rights were exercised, and the remaining rights became unexercisable at the year end.

October 10, 1992:

No entry.

November 10, 1992 -- To record stock and warrants distributed:

Retained earnings	250,000	
Common stock (24,500 shs. at par)		245,000
Stock warrants outstanding (500 shs. at par)		5,000

December 10, 1992 -- To record exercise of stock warrants:

Stock warrants outstanding (400 shs. at par)	4,000	
Common stock		4,000

December 31, 1992 -- To record lapse of warrant rights:

Stock warrants outstanding (100 shs. at par)	1,000	
Paid-in capital from lapsed warrants rights		1,000

4. **Liquidating dividends.** A **liquidating dividend** is a return of the contributed capital instead of a distribution of earnings. Liquidating dividends may be either intentional or unintentional. Intentional liquidating dividends occur when the board of directors knowingly declares dividends as returns of investment to the stockholders. In most states, such a dividend is not allowed unless creditors'

claims have been met. Intentional liquidating dividends are recorded by debiting capital and crediting dividends payable.

Unintentional liquidating dividends, on the other hand, occur when retained earnings are improperly overstated, and the board of directors unknowingly declared dividends based on the overstated amount. Unintentional liquidating dividends are recorded as ordinary dividends until the error is discovered. A correcting entry would then be required by debiting contributed capital and crediting retaining earnings.

D. Stock Splits

A **stock split** is similar to a stock dividend in that **additional shares of stock** are distributed. The primary purpose of a stock split is to increase the number of shares, reduce the market price per share, and improve the marketability of the stock. Unlike a stock dividend, a stock split involves no capitalization of retained earnings and does not affect the balance of any account.

E. Appropriations (Restrictions) of Retained Earnings

An **appropriation of retained earnings** restricts a portion of retained earnings from being distributed as dividends. Appropriations may be made (a) to comply with state laws, (b) to satisfy a contractual requirement, or (c) to indicate a specific purpose for a specified portion of retained earnings. A formal journal entry my be used to reclassify retained earnings with a debit to unappropriated retained earnings and a credit to appropriated retained earnings. This entry should be reversed when the need for the restriction no longer exists. Many firms disclose the appropriations in the notes instead of presenting them in the balance sheet.

F. Quasi-Reorganizations

A firm undergoing financial difficulties, but with favorable prospects, may use a quasi-reorganization to write down inflated asset values and eliminate an accumulated deficit (debit balance in retaining earnings). To effect the reorganization the following procedure is pertinent:

1. The firm's assets (and perhaps liabilities) are **revalued** (up or down) to reflect fair market values, with corresponding credits or debits to retained earnings. This process typically increases the deficit.

2. The deficit is eliminated against additional paid-in capital. If additional paid-in capital is not sufficient to absorb the entire deficit, a reduction in capital stock may be necessary (with a reduction in the par value per share).

3. The retained earnings account is **dated** to show the date the deficit was eliminated and when the accumulation of earnings began.

Quasi-reorganization is allowed by the SEC with the following conditions:

1. Retained earnings immediately after the quasi-reorganization must be zero.

2. Upon completion of the quasi-reorganization, no deficit (i.e., debit balance) shall appear in any capital account.

3. The effects of the whole procedure shall be made known to all stockholders entitled to vote and appropriate approval in advance obtained from them.

Part II -- Stock Rights and Options

A. Stock rights allow their holders to acquire a specified number of shares of stock over a specified period of time. There are various circumstances under which stock rights might be issued and the accounting treatment for each varies considerably.

B. **Stock right to Common Shareholders (Preemptive Right).** This right gives **existing** common shareholders the first priority to buy shares of a new stock issue in order to maintain their respective percentages of ownership in the firm. No entry is required at issuance of the right. When it is exercised, record ordinary entry for the sale of new shares. With or without the right makes no difference insofar as accounting treatment is concerned.

C. **Stock Rights to Bondholders or Preferred Stockholders.**

As discussed in Chapter 16, a company may issue bonds with stock rights which may be either nondetachable or detachable from the bonds. If the rights are nondetachable, the bonds are known as convertible bonds, whereas the detachable stock rights are represented by stock warrants. Similarly, a company may issue preferred stock which is convertible to common shares, or stock warrants which are detachable from the preferred stock.

1. **Convertible preferred stock:** When a **convertible preferred stock** is issued, it is treated as ordinary preferred stock. The conversion feature of the stock is not accounted for. When the stock is converted, all account balances of the converted shares (i.e., preferred stock and paid-in capital in excess of par) are removed and the new shares issued are recorded at their par or stated value. Any difference, if credit, is recorded as paid-in capital from conversion of preferred stock, or, if debit, is charged to the retained earnings account.

ILLUSTRATION 3 -- Convertible preferred stock

Assume that on January 1, 1992, Federated R. G. Corporation issued 10,000 shares of 8%, $10 par convertible preferred stock for $15 per share. The conversion privilege specified the issuance of five shares of $1 par common stock for each share of preferred stock. All outstanding preferred shares are converted to common stock on January 1, 1993.

January 1, 1992:

To record issuance of preferred stock:

Account	Debit	Credit
Cash	150,000	
8% Preferred stock		100,000
PIC in excess of par, preferred		50,000

January 1, 1993:

To record conversion of preferred to common:

Account	Debit	Credit
8% Preferred stock	100,000	
PIC in excess of par, preferred	50,000	
Common stock		50,000*
PIC from preferred stock conversion		100,000

* 10,000 shs. x 5 x $1 = $50,000

2. **Preferred stock with detachable warrants.** When a preferred stock is issued with detachable stock warrants, it is accounted for in the same manner as the issuance of bonds with detachable warrants, except that preferred stock and paid-in capital in excess of par are used instead of bonds payable and premium (or discount) on bonds.

D. Stock Rights to Employees -- Stock Option Incentive Plans

1. **Stock option plans** allow employees of a corporation the option of purchasing a specified number of shares of the firm's capital stock at a specified price within a specified period of time. A stock option plan may be **noncompensatory** if it possesses **all** the following characteristics **(APB Opinion No. 25)**:

   (1) Substantially all full-time employees meeting limited employment criteria are included.

   (2) The stock is offered to eligible employees equally, or is based on a uniform percentage of salaries or wages.

(3) The time permitted for exercise of an option is limited to a reasonable period.

(4) The discount from the market price does not exceed 15%.

A noncompensatory plan is not recorded until the option privilege is exercised by the employees. When it is exercised, the following entry is pertinent:

Cash	xxxx	
Common stock		xxxx
Paid-in capital in excess of par, common		xxxx

2. **Compensatory stock option plans.** If a stock option plan does not contain **all** of the four characteristics above, it is classified as **compensatory.** Compensatory plans require the **measurement** of the total compensation and its allocation to compensation expense in the appropriate accounting period. The following dates are essential:

   a. **Date of grant.** This is the date on which a certain option privilege is officially granted to specific employee(s).

   b. **Date of measurement.** This is the first date that (1) the **option price** per share and (2) the **number of shares** obtainable are known, so that the total compensation cost can be measured.

   c. **Date of exercise.** This is the date that the option privilege is exercised and the shares are issued.

   The total compensation cost is measured by multiplying the number of shares obtainable and the difference between the option price and the market price of the stock on the date of measurement. This total cost should be allocated to compensation expense in the period(s) **benefited** by the expected employees' service for which the options are granted.

   a. If the date of measurement is also the date of grant, the total cost is measured on that date and recorded as deferred compensation cost, which is then allocated to the benefited years.

   b. If the date of measurement is subsequent to the date of grant, compensation expense must be accrued each period prior to the date of measurement based on an **estimate** of either the option price, or the number of shares, or both. On the date of measurement, the excess of the measured total compensation cost over the estimated compensation expense recognized to date is to be allocated to the remaining number of benefited years.

When options are exercised, the shares issued are recorded at the sum of the cash received and the recorded value of the stock options tendered.

ILLUSTRATION 4 -- Compensatory stock option plan

On January 1, 1992, Kutlesa Company granted John Kutlesa, the president, an option to purchase 2,000 shares of Kutlesa's $10 par value common stock. The period of expected service, for which the options are being given, is five years. The options were exercised on December 31, 1996.

The quoted market prices of Kutlesa's common stock were as follows:

January 1, 1992	$30
December 31, 1992	$35
December 31, 1994	$40

Case 1: Option price of $20 per share is known at the date of grant:

a. January 1, 1992 (date of grant and also date of measurement):

To record total compensation cost -- [2,000 x ($30 - $20)]:

Deferred compensation cost	20,000	
Stock options outstanding		20,000

b. At the end of each of the five years:

To allocate deferred compensation cost -- ($20,000 / 5):

Compensation expense	4,000	
Deferred compensation cost		4,000

c. December 31, 1996 (date of exercise):

To record issuance of stock:

Cash (2,000 x $20)	40,000	
Stock options outstanding	20,000	
Common stock (2,000 x $10)		20,000
Paid-in capital in excess of par		40,000

Case 2: Option price of $20 per share is not known until the end of 1994. At the end of 1992, the option price is estimated to be $18 per share.

a. January 1, 1992 (date of grant):

No entry.

b. December 31, 1992:

To record compensation cost based on estimated option price:

Deferred compensation cost [2,000 x ($35 - $18)]	34,000	
Stock options outstanding		34,000

c. At the end of each of 1992 and 1993:

To record compensation expense:

Compensation expense ($34,000 / 5)	6,800	
Deferred compensation cost		6,800

d. December 31, 1994 (date of measurement):

To adjust deferred compensation cost:
[2,000 x ($40 - $20) - $34,000]

Deferred compensation cost	6,000	
Stock options outstanding		6,000

e. At the end of each of 1994 to 1996:

To record compensation expense:
{[2,000 x ($40 - $20) - $6,800 x 2] / 3]}

Compensation expense	8,800	
Deferred compensation cost		8,800

f. December 31, 1996 (date of exercise):

To record exercise of stock options:

Cash (2,000 x $20)	40,000	
Stock options outstanding ($34,000 + $6,000)	40,000	
Common stock		20,000
PIC in excess of par		60,000

Specific issues on accounting for compensatory stock option plans:

a. **Service period.** Total compensation cost should be allocated over a service (benefited) period that extends from the date of grant to the date on which the employee has no further option obligations, usually the first date that the option is exercisable. Sometimes, service period is specified in the plan.

b. **Forfeited plan.** Failure of an employee to fulfill the option obligations is treated as a change in estimate. The related stock options outstanding and the unamortized deferred compensation cost should both be removed and the difference accounted for as a reduction in current compensation expense.

c. **Lapsed plan.** If the exercise period lapsed, any outstanding stock options became unexercisable. Then the credit balance of the stock options outstanding may be either transferred to paid-in capital from lapsed stock options, or recognized as compensation expenses for the current and a reasonable number of future periods as a change in estimate.

d. **Disclosure.** On the balance sheet, stock options outstanding, offset by the unamortized deferred compensation cost, is presented as an element of contributed capital.

E. Stock Appreciation Rights

These rights are awards entitling employees to receive cash, stock or a combination of the two in an amount equivalent to any excess of **the market value on the date of exercise** of a stated number of shares of the employer company's stock over a stated price. The form of payment may be specified when the rights are granted or may be determined when they are exercised.

Under a stock appreciation plan, the amount of cash or the number of shares an employee is entitled to receive becomes known only when the employee exercises his (her) appreciation rights. Therefore, prior to the date of exercise, estimates must be used each year to recognize annual compensation expense. If cash is to be paid, the expense should be accrued against a liability account, e.g., "stock appreciation plan liability." If stock is issued, it is accounted for similarly as a stock option plan, except that (1) the date of measurement is the date of exercise, and (2) the number of shares issued is based on their market value equivalent to the amount of share appreciation.

KEY CONCEPTS

Dividends Distributions of earnings of the corporation to its shareholders in proportion to their respective share holdings. A dividend that is a return of the contributed capital is known as a liquidating dividend. Dividends may take various forms such as cash, scrip, property or stock.

Quasi reorganization A special procedure to write down inflated assets and to remove accumulated deficit in order to reestablish a new accounting basis of a company which has a significant deficit but appears to have favorable prospects.

Retained earnings Accumulated, undistributed net income or net loss. It is mainly used to distribute dividends. Appropriations are sometime made to restrict a specified portion of retained earnings from being distributed to the stockholders of the corporation. Such appropriations may be made with or without a journal entry.

Stock appreciation rights A right which allows the employees to receive share appreciation of a certain number of common shares in cash or in stock.

Stock dividends A distribution of additional shares to the stockholders of the corporation. If the stock dividend rate is less than 20% of the outstanding shares, it is specified as small and the market value is used to capitalize retained earnings. If the rate is greater than 25%, it is considered as large and the par value is used for capitalization. Management judgment is required if the rate is in the 20-25% range.

Stock option plans A plan that grants employees the option to purchase a certain number of common shares at a specified option price within a specified period. A stock option plan is **noncompensatory** if (1) substantially all full-time employees are included, (2) the stock is offered to all eligible employees equally, (2) the exercise period is reasonably short, and (4) the discount from the market price is reasonably small. Plans that do not possess all these characteristics are classified as **compensatory**.

Stock split Additional shares distributed to existing stockholders resulting in a reduction in the par value per share. The primary intent is to increase the number of shares outstanding in order to improve the marketability of the stock. A stock split does not require any entry as it does not affect the balance of any account.

Stock warrants Certificates that entitle the holders to purchase a specified number of shares of stock at a specified price within a specified period of time. Stock warrants may be issued for the fractional shares of stock dividends distribution, to attach to bonds or preferred stock issued, or to grant stock option privileges to employees.

REVIEW QUESTIONS AND EXERCISES

TRUE-FALSE

Indicate whether each of the following statements is true or false by circling the correct response.

T F 1. The existence of a credit balance in unappropriated retained earnings indicates that a corporation has cash available for paying dividends.

T F 2. The declaration of a cash dividend creates a legal obligation to pay the dividend which does not exist prior to the declaration.

T F 3. A dividend may involve the distribution of cash, investment in securities, or some other asset.

T F 4. A property dividend is recorded at the carrying value (book value) of the assets to be distributed.

T F 5. A stock dividend does not affect assets, liabilities, or total stockholders' equity.

T F 6. Accounting for a large stock dividend generally involves a reduction of retained earnings and an increase in contributed capital equal to the par value of the shares distributed.

T F 7. In the case of stock split, there is no change in the total par value of the stock, nor in the total amount of the stockholders' equity.

T F 8. A dividend that reduces the contributed capital is a liquidating dividend.

T F 9. An appropriation of retained earnings assures the availability of cash or other assets for some legal, contractual, or discretionary purposes.

T F 10. Generally, a quasi-reorganization results in an adjustment of inflated asset balances and an elimination of a deficit in retained earnings.

T F 11. When a convertible preferred stock is issued, the package price of the issue should be allocated to both the preferred stock and the conversion feature (privilege) of the stock.

T F 12. Stock option plans that require the employees to pay cash as consideration for the stock they receive are referred to as compensatory plans.

T F 13. The measurement date for a compensatory stock option plan is the first date on which both the option price and the market price are known for the shares available under the plan.

T F 14. When the date of grant and the measurement date of a stock option plan differ, no entry is required at the date of grant.

EXERCISE 1

The stockholders' equity of Delman Corporation on June 30, 1992, is presented below:

Common stock, 200,000 shares issued, $10 par	$2,000,000
Contributed capital in excess of par	1,600,000
Retained earnings	9,400,000

On August 15, 1992, the board of directors declared a stock dividend on common stock, to be distributed on October 15, 1992. The market price of Delman's common stock was $30 on August 15, 1992, and $35 on October 15, 1992, respectively. No entry was made on the declaration date.

Required:

1. Assuming the stock dividend was 10%, record the distribution on October 15, 1992:

Retain Earn
C.S.
PIC > Par

2. Assuming the stock dividend was 50%, record the distribution on October 15, 1992:

EXERCISE 2

For each of the transactions below, indicate the effect on **total retained earnings,** using + for increase, - for decrease, or **0** for no effect. Consider each transaction separately.

____ 1. Declaration and distribution of stock dividend.

____ 2. An appropriation for plant expansion.

____ 3. A net loss for the year.

____ 4. Declaration of a property dividend.

____ 5. A sale of treasury stock in excess of cost.

____ 6. A stock split.

____ 7. Acquisition of treasury stock (cost method).

____ 8. Declaration of a cash dividend.

____ 9. Net income for the year.

____ 10. Receipt of land as a donation.

EXERCISE 3

On September 1, 1992, Willie Win Track Shoes declared a property dividend to be paid on October 1, 1992 with 2,000 shares of common stock of Betty Weymer Corporation, currently held as an investment. The investment shares were purchased five years ago at a cost of $15 per share. The market value of the stock on September 1, 1992 was $21 per share.

Required:

Prepare journal entries for Willie Win relative to the declaration and payment of the property dividend.

1. September 1, 1992 (date of declaration):

2. October 1, 1992 (date of payment):

EXERCISE 4

On January 2, 1992, Fablan Sport granted Kee Allen, the president, an option to purchase 10,000 shares of Fablan's $10 par value common stock at $35 per share. The option becomes exercisable on January 2, 1994 after Allen has completed two years of service, for which the options are being granted.

The quoted market price of Fablan's common stock was as follows:

January 2, 1992	$40
December 31, 1992	$45
January 2, 1994	$60

Requires:

Prepare journal entries for Fablan relative to the stock option agreement:

1. January 2, 1992 (date of grant):

2. December 31, 1992:

3. December 31, 1993:

4. January 2, 1994 (date of exercise):

MULTIPLE CHOICE

Enter the letter corresponding to the response which **best** completes each of the following statements or questions.

____ 1. Which of the following does not affect retained earnings?

a. cash dividends.
b. property dividends.
c. stock dividends.
d. intentional liquidating dividends.

____ 2. Which of the following is not affected by stock dividend?

a. contributed capital.
b. retained earnings.
c. total stockholders' equity.
d. number of shares outstanding.

____ 3. Both stock dividend and stock split affect which of the following?

a. contributed capital.
b. retained earnings.
c. total stockholders' equity.
d. number of shares outstanding.

____ 4. Assuming that the market value exceeds the par value of a common stock, both the small and the large stock dividends have the same effect except which of the following?

a. an increase in capital stock.
b. an increase in paid in capital in excess of par.
c. a decrease in retained earnings.
d. an increase in number of shares outstanding.

____ 5. Any compensation cost involved in a compensatory employee stock option plan should be expensed:

a. in the period containing the date of grant.
b. in the period containing the measurement date.
c. in the period(s) benefited by the expected employee's service.
d. in the period in which the options are exercised.

____ 6. The measurement date in accounting for compensatory stock option plans is:

a. The date on which options are granted to employees.
b. The earliest date on which both the number of shares to be issued and option price are known.
c. The date on which the options are exercised.
d. The date the corporation forgoes alternative use of the shares to be sold under option.

____ 7. Under a stock appreciation plan, the date of measurement is also:

a. the adoption date of the plan.
b. the date of grant.
c. the earliest date when the right becomes exercisable.
d. the date of exercise.

____ 8. When a preferred stock is converted into common stock under the book value method, additional paid-in capital increases if the total par of common stock issued is:

a. less than that of the preferred stock converted.
b. greater than that of the preferred stock converted.
c. greater than the market price of the common stock issued.
d. less than the market price of the preferred stock converted.

____ 9. Chambers Corporation had investment in Chavez Company's bonds with a face value of $200,000 and an unamortized discount of $10,000. Eighty percent of the investment bonds is to be distributed as property dividends. On the declaration date, the investment has a total market value of $240,000. How much gain should Chambers recognize as a result of this property dividend:

a. $50,000.
b. $40,000.
c. $30,000.
d. $0.

____ 10. The stockholders' equity section of Ball Corporation as of December 31, 1992, included:

Common stock, 10,000 shs. $5 par	$50,000
Paid-in capital in excess of par	40,000
Retained earnings	70,000

On May 1, 1993, the board of directors declared a 10% stock dividend, and accordingly 1,000 additional shares were issued. The market price of the stock was $10 a share when the dividend was declared. For the year ended December 31, 1993, Ball sustained a net loss of $15,000. Ball's retained earnings at December 31, 1993 should be:

a. $45,000.
b. $50,000.
c. $55,000.
d. $60,000.

____ 11. Based on the same data as in Question 10, except that the board of directors declared a 30% stock dividend. Ball's retained earnings at December 31, 1993 should be:

a. $40,000.
b. $45,000.
c. $50,000.
d. $55,000.

____ 12. On January 2, 1993, the board of directors of Denney Corporation declared a cash dividend of $400,000 to stockholders on record on January 8, 1993, and payable on February 20, 1993. Denney's December 31, 1992 balance sheet reveals the following:

Common stock	$900,000
Paid-in capital in excess of par	500,000
Unappropriated retained earnings	300,000
Appropriate retained earnings	100,000

The $400,000 dividend includes a liquidating dividend of:

a. $400,000.
b. $300,000.
c. $200,000.
d. $100,000.

____ 13. On July 1, 1992, the Tall Corporation granted stock options to certain of its key employees as additional compensation. The options permitted the purchase of 10,000 shares of Tall's common stock at a price of $40 per share. On the date of grant, the market value of the stock was $52 per share. The options were exercisable beginning January 1, 1993, and expire on December 31, 1994. On February 1, 1993, when the stock was selling for $55 per share, the options were exercised. How much total compensation cost should Tall record for these options?

a. $120,000.
b. $150,000.
c. $420,000.
d. $450,000.

____ 14. Based on the same data as in Question 13, except that under the plan adopted by Tall the grantee will receive cash for the difference between the market value and $10 par value per share on the date of exercise. How much total compensation cost should Tall record with respect to the stock appreciation rights plan?

a. $120,000.
b. $150,000.
c. $420,000.
d. $450,000.

SOLUTIONS TO REVIEW QUESTIONS AND EXERCISES

TRUE-FALSE

1.	F	5.	T	9.	F	13.	F
2.	T	6.	T	10.	T	14.	T
3.	T	7.	T	11.	F		
4.	F	8.	T	12.	F		

EXERCISE 1

October 15, 1992 -- To record stock dividends issued:

1. 10% stock dividend (small):

Retained earnings (20,000 shs. x $35)	700,000	
Common stock (20,000 shs. x $10)		200,000
Contributed capital in excess of par		500,000

2. 50% stock dividend (large):

Retained earnings (100,000 shs. x $10)	1,000,000	
Common stock		1,000,000

EXERCISE 2

1.	-	5.	0	9.	+
2.	0	6.	0	10.	0
3.	-	7.	0		
4.	-	8.	-		

EXERCISE 3

1. September 1, 1992 (date of declaration):

Account	Debit	Credit
Investment in equity securities [2,000 shs. x ($21 - $15)]	12,000	
Gain on disposal of investment		12,000
Retained earnings (2,000 shs. x $21)	42,000	
Property dividends payable		42,000

2. October 1, 1992 (date of payment):

Account	Debit	Credit
Property dividends payable	42,000	
Investment in equity securities		42,000

EXERCISE 4

Prepare journal entries for Fablan relative to the stock option agreement:

1. January 2, 1992 (date of grant and also date of measurement):

Account	Debit	Credit
Deferred compensation cost [10,000 shs. ($40 - $35)]	50,000	
Stock options outstanding		50,000

2. December 31, 1992:

Account	Debit	Credit
Compensation expense ($50,000 x 1/2)	25,000	
Deferred compensation cost		25,000

3. December 31, 1993:

Account	Debit	Credit
Compensation expense ($50,000 x 1/2)	25,000	
Deferred compensation cost		25,000

4. January 2, 1994 (date of exercise):

Account	Debit	Credit
Cash (10,000 shs. x $35)	350,000	
Stock options outstanding	50,000	
Common stock		100,000
Paid-in capital in excess of par		300,000

MULTIPLE CHOICE:

1.	d	5.	c	9.	b	13.	a
2.	c	6.	b	10.	a	14.	b
3.	d	7.	d	11.	a		
4.	b	8.	a	12.	d		

Computations:

9. (b)

Market value of investment in bonds		$240,000
Book value of investment in bonds:		
Face value of bonds	$200,000	
Less: Unamortized discount	10,000	
		(190,000)
Excess of market value over book value		$ 50,000
Percentage to be distributed		80%
Gain recognized		$ 40,000

10. (b)

Retained earnings -- December 31, 1992	$ 70,000
Less: Stock dividend (1,000 shs. x $10)	(10,000)
Net loss -- 1993	(15,000)
Retained earnings -- December 31, 1993	$ 45,000

11. (b)

Retained earnings -- December 31, 1992	$ 70,000
Less: Stock dividend (3,000 shs. x $5)	(15,000)
Net loss -- 1993	(15,000)
Retained earnings -- December 31, 1993	$ 40,000

12. (d)

Dividend declared	$400,000
Unappropriated retained earnings	(300,000)
Liquidating dividend	$100,000

13. (a) Compensation cost
= 10,000 shs. ($52 - $40)
= $120,000.

14. (b) Compensation cost
= 10,000 shs. ($55 - $40)
= $150,000.

CHAPTER 22

Earnings per Share

CHAPTER OBJECTIVES

This chapter is designed to enable students to:

A. Understand why financial statement users pay close attention to a company's reported earnings per share (EPS).

B. Know how to calculate EPS for companies with simple capital structures.

C. Be able to define the term primary EPS and know how and when to apply it.

D. Be able to define the term fully diluted EPS and know how and when to apply it.

E. Know how to apply the treasury stock method in conjunction with primary and fully diluted EPS computations.

F. Know how to apply the "if converted" method in conjunction with primary and fully diluted EPS computations.

G. Be able to classify securities as either common stock equivalents or other diluted securities.

H. Know how to apply the dilution/antidilution method in calculating EPS when multiple dilutive/antidilutive securities are present.

CHAPTER OVERVIEW

A. Earnings per share (EPS) is conceived as a primary indicator of a company's success, and a driving force behind common stock market price. Prior to 1960, reporting EPS was left to the discretion of company management. In view of the significance attached by investors and others to EPS data, and the importance of evaluating the data in conjunction with the financial statements, the APB issued **Opinion 15** in 1969 requiring EPS presentation on the income statement. In 1978, the FASB issued **FAS 21** allowing nonpublic enterprises to be exempt from this requirement. For this purpose, a nonpublic enterprise is defined as an enterprise **other than** one (a) whose debt or equity securities trade in a public market on a stock exchange or in the over-the-counter market or (b) that is required to file financial statements with the SEC.

B. Simple Capital Structure

EPS applies only to common stock. For a firm with a simple capital structure (i.e., without potentially dilutive security or right), a single presentation is appropriate. The following formula is applied to the calculation of a **basic EPS (BEPS)**, also known as a **single EPS**:

Let: E = Earnings to common stockholders for the period
S = Weighted average of common shares outstanding during the period

BEPS = E / S

1. To determine E, **preferred dividends** are deducted from net income. If the preferred stock is cumulative, an amount equal to the current-period preferred dividends is deducted, regardless of whether the dividends have been declared. If the preferred stock is noncumulative, only declared dividends are deducted. Note that the deduction must be made even if there is a net loss.

2. To calculate **S,** any increases (e.g., issued new shares) or decreases (e.g., purchased treasury stock) are weighted by the fraction of the period from the date of increase/decrease to the end of period and then added to or subtracted from those shares outstanding for the entire period. Stock dividends and splits should be retroactively applied to those shares previously issued or reacquired.

ILLUSTRATION 1 -- Simple capital structure and basic earnings per share

At the end of 1992 the records of Helmen Corporation reflect the following:

Common stock, par $10, authorized 100,000 shares:

1/1/1992	Outstanding	30,000 shs.
4/1/1992	Sold and issued	6,000 shs.
6/1/1992	Declared stock dividends	10%
7/1/1992	Purchased treasury stock	(1,000) shs.
8/5/1992	Declared stock split	2 for 1
10/1/1992	Sold and issued	2,000 shs.

10% Preferred stock, cumulative and nonconvertible par $10, 10,000 shs. outstanding for the whole year	$500,000
Net income	$120,000

Required:

1. To identify capital structure:

The capital structure is simple because the preferred stock is nonconvertible and there is no dilutive stock rights outstanding during the period.

2. To compute earnings to common:

E = Net income - Preferred dividends
= $120,000 - $500,000 x 10%
= $70,000

3. To compute weighted average outstanding common shares:

			Retroactive Restatement							
Date	No. of Shs.		Stk Div.		Stk Split		WA factors		WA No. of shs.
1/1/1992	30,000	x	1.1*	x	2**	x	12/12	=	66,000
4/1/1992	6,000	x	1.1*	x	2**	x	9/12	=	9,900
7/1/1992	(1,000)			x	2**	x	6/12	=	(1,000)
10/1/1992	2,000					x	3/12	=	500
S (Weighted average number of outstanding common shares)									75,400

* Retroactive adjustment for 10% stock dividends declared on 6/1/1992.
** Retroactive adjustment for 2 for 1 stock split declared on 8/5/1992.

4. To compute EPS:

EPS = E / S
= $70,000 / 75,400 shs.
= $.93

5. To present earnings per share:

To comply with **APB Opinion No. 15**, earnings per share should be calculated and presented for (a) income before extraordinary items and (b) net income. To extend the above illustration, assume the following:

Income before extraordinary loss	$140,000
Extraordinary loss (net of tax)	(20,000)
Net income	$120,000

EPS figures are presented as follows:

Earnings per common share:

Income before extra. loss ($90,000* / 75,400 shs.)	$1.19
Extraordinary loss ($20,000 / 75,400 shs.)	(.26)
Net income	$ .93

*Income before extraordinary loss to common
= Income before extraordinary loss - Preferred dividends
= $140,000 - $50,000
= $90,000.

C. Complex Capital Structures

A capital structure that includes securities and rights that upon conversion or exercise could in the aggregate dilute earnings per share is specified as a complex capital structure. Under the substance over form concept, **APB Opinion No. 15** requires corporations with complex capital structures present two types of EPS data (referred to as dual presentation) including **primary earnings per share (PEPS)** and **fully diluted earnings per share (FDEPS). PEPS** includes the dilutive effects of **common stock equivalents (CSEs)**, i.e., potentially dilutive convertible securities or common stock rights which are highly likely to be converted or exercised. **FDEPS**, on the other hand, incorporates the dilutive effects of not only **CSEs**, but also **all** the other potentially dilutive securities and stock rights in order to reflect the maximum effect of dilution. Note that those outstanding securities or rights which are not exercisable within five years are not qualified as CSEs, and those securities or rights which are not exercisable within 10 years should be simply ignored. Unless it is otherwise stated, however, all the securities and rights discussed in this chapter are assumed to be exercisable within 5 years.

Potentially dilutive securities and rights are generally classified into three categories, namely, equity contracts, convertible securities, and contingent issues. These securities and rights should be separately identified and individually analyzed.

Before analyzing individual securities and rights, it is often convenient to calculate the **BEPS** as if the capital structure were simple.

D. Equity Contracts

Equity contracts include common stock rights, options, warrants, other common stock purchase contracts, and subscribed common stock. These contracts give the holders the right to purchase stock at a specified price for a specified number of shares. The following procedure is applicable to the analysis of such contracts:

1. **Dilution test.** An equity contract is dilutive if the average market price of the common stock for the period is greater than the option price.

2. **CSE test.** If dilutive, an equity contract is always common stock equivalent.

3. **Determine the effects:** Assuming that the specific stock right were exercised, determine its effect on earnings (^E) and on shares (^S):

   a. **Effect on earnings (^E).** Except for the 20% reacquisition limit as discussed later, the exercise of an equity contract does not affect the earnings to common, i.e.:

      ^E = 0

   b. **Effect on shares (^S).** Based on the if-exercised method, the shares are assumed to have been issued, and the purchase (exercise or option) price collected. Then the "collected" amount is further assumed to be used concurrently to repurchase outstanding shares at the existing market price (known as the **treasury stock method**). The excess of shares "issued" over the shares "repurchased" determines the effect on shares. The following equation is pertinent:

      ^S = Common shares x $(P_m - P_o) / P_m$

      where:

      Common shares = Number of shares related to the specific contract
      P_m = Market price per common share
      P_o = Option price per common share

      In computing the **PEPS,** The average market price during the period is used to determine the effect on shares. In the computation of **FDEPS,** on the other hand, the average market price or the closing market price, **whichever is higher,** should be used.

Note that the assumed repurchase of treasury stock is limited to 20% of the outstanding common shares at the end of the period. Any unused cash proceeds are further assumed to be applied first to (a) an "as if" reduction of debt so that the related interest expenses are to be saved, and then to (b) an "as if" acquisition of government securities so that a certain amount of interest revenue is to be earned. Both interest expense saved and interest revenue earned, net of tax, are considered as an effect on earnings to common stockholders.

E. Convertible Securities

Convertible securities include both convertible bonds and convertible preferred stock. Because these stock rights involve different assumptions and require different testing procedures from those of equity contracts, they are analyzed in the following order:

1. **Determine the effects.** Assuming that the specific security had been converted at the earliest possible date during the period, determine its effects on earnings (^E) and on shares (^S):

   a. **Convertible bonds:**

      (1) **Effect on earnings (^E).** If the bonds had been converted into common stock, current interest on bonds would have been saved. Since the interest is tax deductible, the net effect on earnings is:

      ^E = Interest savings net of taxes
      = Interest expense (1 - Tax rate)

      (2) **Effect on shares (^S).** If the bonds had been converted, the additional shares of common stock would have been issued:

      ^S = Number of bonds outstanding x Conversion rate

   b. **Convertible preferred stock:**

      (1) **Effect on earnings (^E).** If the preferred stock had been converted into common stock, current preferred dividends (as discussed under the basic EPS) would have been saved. Note that preferred dividends are not tax deductible, so the effect on earnings is:

      ^E = Preferred dividends savings

      (2) **Effect on shares (^S).** If the preferred stock had been converted, the additional shares of common stock would have been issued:

      ^S = Number of preferred shares outstanding x Conversion ratio

2. **Dilution test:** An earnings rate (i.e., **ER** = ^E / ^S), also known as the Dilution/Antidilution (D/A) ratio, is computed for each convertible security, which is then compared with basic earnings per share, **BEPS:**

   If ER > = BEPS, the security is not **dilutive** and should be ignored. Otherwise, the analysis should continue.

3. **CSE test** (also known as **yield rate test**). An effective yield rate test is

conducted to determine whether the convertible security is a **CSE**. As discussed in Chapter 16, an effective yield is the market interest rate at the time of issuance. This rate is compared with the then current average interest rate of Aa corporate bonds:

If the effective interest rate of a convertible security < 2 / 3 of Average Aa corporate bond interest rate, the security is a CSE.

Note that if a bond was issued at its face value, the effective interest rate is its stated interest rate. Note also that if the security does not have a stated maturity date, the effective interest rate is the security's annual interest or dividend payment divided by its market price at issuance.

F. Contingent Common Stock Issue

In conjunction with corporate acquisitions, buy-outs and business combinations, the acquiring company may offer the equivalent of bonus shares to be issued at some point in the future, contingent on the profit performance of the acquired company. If contingent issue shares are offered to the acquired company's stockholders gratis, they are dilutive and must be included in EPS computation. If the target net income level is set at or below the acquired company's current period net income level, the contingent stock issue is treated as a CSE. If the target level is set above the acquired company's current period net income level, the contingent stock issue is treated as "other dilutive securities" and is used in computing FDEPS only.

G. Overall Dilution/Antidilution test. When multiple dilutive securities and rights are present, an overall D/A test such as follows is applied in order to report the maximum dilution effect:

1. Obtain **ER** for each of the securities and rights.

   Note that ER = 0, if ^E = 0.

2. Rank the ERs from the lowest to the highest.

3. Recompute EPS by including BEPS and the effects of the security with the lowest ER (i.e., ranked 1).

4. If the recomputed EPS is greater than the next higher ER, recompute EPS by including that item.

5. Repeat "4" until the recomputed EPS is smaller than the next higher ER. Ignore all the remaining items because they are antidilutive.

The above procedure is applied to PEPS and FDEPS computations, respectively. The obtained lowest possible EPS is presented in the income statement.

H. **Materiality Test** (also known as **3% test**). This is the last test conducted to determine whether the difference between the FDEPS and the BEPS is material. If their difference is at least 3% of the BEPS (i.e., **FDEPS = < 97% x BEPS**), it is considered material and the dual presentation is called for.

I. **Presentation of PEPS and FDEPS**

Similar to the simple capital structure, EPS figures are required for both net income and income before extraordinary items. In cases where an extraordinary item is present and a common stock equivalent results in dilution only on income before extraordinary items per share, or net income per share, but not both, the common stock equivalent should still be recognized for all computations even though it has an antidilutive effect of one of the per share amounts.

ILLUSTRATION 2 -- Complex capital structure and dual presentation

At the end of 1992, the record of the Hall Corporation reflected the following:

Common stock, nopar, authorized 100,000 shares

Outstanding at beginning of year, 20,000 shares	$200,000
Sold and issued on April 1, 1992, 5,000 shares	$60,6000

9% Preferred stock, cumulative, $100 Par, 1,000 shares

Issued on January 1, 1991 at 120	
Each share convertible into 4 shares of common	$100,000

10% Convertible bonds, due Dec. 31, 1996,
Interest payable on June 30 and Dec. 31
Each $1,000 par bond convertible into 50 shares of common
200 bonds issued on January 1, 1992:

Face value	$200,000
Initial discount on bonds	$14,720
Effective yield	12%

Stock options, 12,000 shares granted on September 30, 1991:

Option price per share	$40
Exercisable in	1992

Stock warrants, 5,000 shares issued on October 31, 1992

Stated purchase price per share	0
Exercisable in	1998

Additional information:

1.	Net income reported for 1992	$45,000
2.	Applicable tax rate	34%
3.	Average Aa corporate bond yield rates:	
	On January 1, 1991	12%
	On January 1, 1992	20%
4.	Market price of common stock per share:	
	Average for 1992	$50
	Closing at end of 1992	$60

Required: Determine and present primary and fully diluted earnings per share.

Solutions:

Step 1 -- Compute basic earnings per share (BEPS):

E = Net income - Current preferred dividends
= \$45,000 - \$100,000 x 9%
= **\$36,000**

S = 20,000 + 5,000 x 9/12
= **23,750 shs.**

BEPS = \$36,000 / 23,750 shs.
= **\$1.52**

Step 2 -- Equity contract analysis:

1. **Stock options:**

a. **Dilution test:**

Average price per share (P_m) = \$50
Option price per share (P_o) = \$40

Since $P_m > P_o$, the options were **dilutive.**

b. **CSE test:**

Since the options were exercisable within 5 years, they were **CSEs.**

c. **Determine the effects:**

(1) **^E = 0**

(2) **Applying the treasury stock method:**

[Since the closing price ($P_{m'}$) was greater than the average price (P_m), ^S should be separately computed for PEPS and FDEPS].

^S (PEPS) = Common shares x (P_m - P_o) / P_m
= 12,000 shs. x (\$50 - \$40) / \$50
= **2,400 shs.**

^S (FDEPS) = Common shares x ($P_{m'}$ - P_o) / $P_{m'}$
= 12,000 shs. x (\$60 - \$40) / \$60
= **4,000 shs.**

2. **Stock warrants:**

   a. **Dilution test:**

   Average price (P_m) = \$50
   Option price (P_o) = 0

   Since $P_m > P_o$, the warrants were **dilutive**.

   b. **CSE test:**

   Since the warrants were exercisable beyond 5-year period, but within 10 years, they were **not CSEs,** but **included in the computation of FDEPS.**

   c. **Determine the effects:**

   ^E = 0

   ^S = 5,000 shs.

Step 3 -- Convertible security analysis:

1. **Convertible preferred stock:**

   a. **Determine the effects:**

   ^E = Preferred dividends which would have been saved
   = Current preferred dividends
   = **\$9,000**

   ^S = Additional common shares assumed to have been issued
   = Shares of preferred stock x conversion ratio
   = 1,000 shs. x 4
   = **4,000 shs.**

   b. **Dilution test:**

   ER = ^E / ^S
   = \$9,000 / 4,000 shs.
   = **\$2.25**

   Since ER > BEPS, the convertible preferred stock was **antidilutive,** and should thus be ignored.

2. Convertible bonds:

a. **Determine the effects:**

^E = Bond interest expense (net of tax) which would have been saved.
= Beginning carrying value x effective yield x (1 - Tax rate)
= ($200,000 - $14,720) x 12% x (1 - 34%)
= **$14,674**

^S = Additional common shares assumed to have been issued
= Number of bonds x conversion rate
= 200 shs. x 50
= **10,000 shs.**

b. **Dilution test:**

ER = ^E / ^S
= $14,674 / 10,000 shs.
= **$1.47**

Since ER < BEPS, the convertible preferred stock was **dilutive**, and the analysis should continue.

c. **CSE test (Yield rate test):**

Yield rate of bond = 12%
Average Aa bonds rate = 20%

Since 12% < 2/3 x 20%, the bonds were **CSEs.**

Step 4 -- Overall Dilution/Antidilution Test:

1. Determine PEPS:

a. Ranking -- Common stock equivalents:

	^E	^S	ER(^E/^S)	Rank
(1) Stock options	$ 0	2,400	$ 0	1
(2) Convertible bonds	14,674	10,000	1.47	2

b. Recompute earnings per share based on the basic earnings per share:

BEPS (E = $36,000, S = 23,750) $1.52

(1) Include the No. 1 ranked stock options in the computation:

PEPS (1)
= [E + ^E(1)] / [S + ^S(1)]
= ($36,000 + 0) / (23,750 + 2,400)
= $36,000 / 26,150
= $1.38

(2) Since the ER of No. 2 ranked convertible bonds ($1.47) was greater than the recomputed EPS(1), the bonds, the last ranked CSE, should be excluded, and:

PEPS = $1.38

2. Determine FDEPS:

a. Ranking -- Common stock equivalents and other stock rights:

	^E	^S	ER(^E/^S)	Rank
(1) Stock options	$ 0	4,000	$ 0	1
(2) Stock warrants	0	5,000	0	1
(3) Convertible bonds	14,674	10,000	1.47	3

b. Recompute earnings per share based on basic earnings per share:

BEPS (E = $36,000, S = 23,750) $1.52

(1) Include the No. 1 ranked stock options and stock warrants in the computation:

FDEPS (1)
= [E + ^E(1) + ^E(2)] / [S + ^S(1) + ^S(2)]
= ($36,000 + 0 + 0) / (23,750 + 4,000 + 5,000)
= $36,000 / 32,750
= **$1.10**

(2) Since the ER of No. 3 ranked convertible bonds ($1.47) was greater than the recomputed EPS(1), the bonds should be ignored and:

FDEPS (final) = $1.10

Step 5 -- Overall materiality (3%) test:

FDEPS = \$1.10
BEPS = \$1.52

Since \$1.10 < 97% x 1.52, dual presentation is required.

Step 6 -- Financial statement presentation (partial income statement):

Earnings per share:

	Primary	**Fully diluted**
Net income	\$1.38	\$1.10

KEY CONCEPTS

Antidilutive securities and stock rights A convertible security or a common stock right that would increase earnings per share if it is converted, or exercised. Antidilutive securities and common stock rights should be ignored in the calculation of earnings per share.

Common stock equivalents A common stock right for which the exercise of the right appears probable, or a convertible security for which the eventual conversion appears highly likely. Based on the substance over form principle, common stock equivalents should be included in the computation of both primary and fully diluted earnings per share.

Complex capital structure A capital structure that consists of common stock and potentially dilutive securities and stock rights. A complex capital structure is required to report two types of earnings per share (i.e., the primary and the fully diluted earnings per share), known as dual presentation.

Dilutive securities and stock rights A convertible security, equity contract or other common stock right that would reduce earnings per share if converted or exercised. Dilutive securities and stock rights should be included in the computation of earnings per share.

Earnings per share A primary indicator of a company's success measured by dividing earnings to common stockholders by the weighted average common shares outstanding.

Fully diluted earnings per share Earnings per share figures that are calculated as if all the **common stock equivalents and other dilutive securities** had already been converted and/or exercised, and the related common shares issued.

Primary earnings per share Earnings per share figures that are calculated as if all the **common stock equivalents** had already been converted, and/or exercised, and the related common shares issued.

Simple capital structure A capital structure that does not involve convertible securities or stock rights that would materially dilute the reported earnings per share. A simple capital structure is required to report single (or basic) earnings per share.

REVIEW QUESTIONS AND EXERCISES

TRUE-FALSE

Indicate whether each of the following statements is true or false by circling the correct response.

T F 1. When a firm's capital structure includes securities **other than common stock** the firms is said to have a complex capital structure.

T F 2. The Gelvin Company began the calendar-year accounting period with 100,000 shares of common stock outstanding and on October 1 sold 10,000 additional shares. Its weighted average number of shares outstanding would be 105,000.

T F 3. In computing the weighted average number of common shares outstanding, shares issued as **stock dividends** are weighted by the fraction of the period that these additional shares are outstanding.

T F 4. A stock warrant or option is considered to be a **common stock equivalent** if, at the time of issuance, its cash yield is significantly below what would be a comparable rate for a similar security.

T F 5. If a firm declares no dividends on cumulative preferred stock, no adjustment of the earnings to common is required in earnings per share calculations.

T F 6. Securities not considered to be common stock equivalents are not considered in the calculation of primary earnings per share.

T F 7. In computing primary earnings per share, the treasury stock method requires the assumption that proceeds obtained from the exercise of stock options are used to reacquire shares at the average market price.

T F 8. For nonpublic enterprises, reporting earnings per share is not required.

T F 9. A convertible bond is a common stock equivalent if it is potentially dilutive and its effective yield is greater than 2/3 of the average Aa corporate bond yield rate at the end of the reporting period.

T F 10. A stock option is dilutive if its option price is smaller than 2/3 of the average market price of the common stock during the period.

T F 11. The current dividends of a cumulative preferred stock should be ignored in computing earnings per share if the company incurred a net loss for the period and no dividend was declared during the period.

T F 12. If the capital structure is simple, neither stock dividends, nor stock splits, would be considered in the computation of earnings per share.

T F 13. All the outstanding stock rights should be included in EPS computations, regardless of when the rights are exercisable.

T F 14. All the dilutive securities and stock rights should be included in EPS computation, regardless of whether the overall dilution effect is material.

EXERCISE 1

Cormier Company is authorized to issue 500,000 shares of $10 par common stock. Stock activities during 1992 are listed as follows:

January 1 -- Outstanding	....	100,000 shs.
April 1 -- Sold and issued	....	20,000 shs.
May 1 -- Issued 20% stock dividends	....	24,000 shs.
July 1 -- Reacquired treasury stock	....	5,000 shs.
August 1 -- Declared stock split	....	2 to 1
October 1 -- Sold treasury stock	....	4,000 shs.

Required:

1. Compute the weighted average common shares outstanding during 1992:

2. Further assume that Cormier declared and issued another 20% stock dividend on May 1, 1993. Determine the weighted average common shares to be used in computing earnings per share for 1992 and 1993 on the 1993 **comparative income statement.**

EXERCISE 2

On January 1, 1992, Murphy of Leisure had outstanding 220,000 shares of common stock (par $10) that was sold originally at $20, and 10,000 shares of 7% nonconvertible, cumulative preferred stock (par $20). The preferred stock was sold originally at $28 at a time when the average yield on Aa corporate bonds was 9%. No dividends had been declared since 1990.

On October 1, 1992, Murphy sold and issued an additional 80,000 shares of common stock at $80.

Net income for 1992 was $254,000. The tax rate for the year was 40%.

Required: Compute BEPS for the year ended December 31, 1992:

EXERCISE 3

Extend **EXERCISE 2** and further assume that on January 1, 1992, Murphy issued common stock options for 20,000 shares of common stock, exercisable two years after the date of issuance. The option price was $30. The market price of the common stock at year-end was $60. During the year the price of the stock had averaged $50.

Required: For the year ended December 31, 1992:

1. To compute PEPS:

2. To compute FDEPS:

EXERCISE 4

Gordon Company's net income for 1992 is $260,000. At the end of 1992, Gordon reported 200,000 common shares, outstanding for the entire year, and 8% bonds payable of $100,000. The bonds were convertible into 20,000 shares of common stock. The bonds were issued at par, and at the date of issuance, the average yield of Aa rated corporate bond was 14%. The applicable tax rate was 30%.

Required: Compute PEPS and FDEPS:

MULTIPLE CHOICE

Enter the letter corresponding to the response which **best** completes each of the following statements or questions.

____ 1. In computing the weighted average number of shares outstanding, the number of shares should be weighted by the fraction of the period they are (are not) outstanding for each of the following **except:**

a. new shares of common stock sold during the period.
b. shares reacquired as treasury stock.
c. shares represented by a stock option plan initiated in mid-year.
d. shares of common stock issued during the period pursuant to a stock dividend.

____ 2. A firm is considered to have a complex capital structure if it has outstanding:

a. nonconvertible cumulative preferred stock.
b. a compensatory employee stock option plan.
c. nonconvertible bonds whose effective yield is significantly less than the average for such securities of other firms.
d. more than five types of securities.

____ 3. In applying the treasury stock method of including the effect of outstanding stock options in the calculation of **fully diluted earnings per share:**

a. generally accepted accounting principles would be violated because the treasury stock method is applicable only in the calculation of primary earnings per share.
b. the effect on shares (^S) should be based on the average price of common shares.
c. shares are assumed to be repurchased at the average or year-end market price, whichever is lower.
d. it is assumed that the options had been exercised.

____ 4. When calculating EPS for a complex capital structure, which of the following is generally considered a common stock equivalent?

	Nonconvertible preferred stock	Stock warrants
a.	Yes	No
b.	Yes	Yes
c.	No	Yes
d.	No	No

____ 5. In determining basic earnings per share (BEPS), dividends on nonconvertible cumulative preferred stock should be:

a. deducted from net income whether declared or not.
b. deducted from net income only if declared.
c. added back to net income whether declared or not.
d. disregarded.

____ 6. When computing primary earnings per share, common stock equivalents are:

a. recognized only if they are dilutive.
b. recognized only if they are antidilutive.
c. recognized whether they are dilutive or antidilutive.
d. ignored.

____ 7. When determining earnings per share, interest expense, net of income taxes, on convertible bonds that are both a common stock equivalent and dilutive should be:

a. deducted from net income for both PEPS and FDEPS calculation.
b. deducted from net income for PEPS, but not for FDEPS calculation.
c. added back to net income for both PEPS and FDEPS calculation.
d. added back to net income for PEPS, but not for FDEPS calculation.

____ 8. Common stock equivalents that are antidilutive generally are used in the computation of:

	Primary earnings per share	Fully diluted earnings per share
a.	Yes	Yes
b.	Yes	No
c.	No	No
d.	No	Yes

____ 9. At December 31, 1991, Foster Corp. had outstanding 200,000 shares of common stock and 2,000 shares of 10%, $100 par value nonconvertible but cumulative preferred stock. No dividends were declared on either the preferred or the common stock in 1992. Net income for 1992 was $100,000. For 1992, EPS was:

a. $.40.
b. $.50.
c. $.60.
d. $2.00.

_____ 10. Greene Company's balance sheet at December 31, 1992 included the following:

	Shares issued and outstanding
Common stock, $5 par	400,000
Preferred stock, $10 par noncumulative and nonconvertible	200,000

On October 1, 1993, Greene issued a 25% stock dividend on its common stock and paid $500,000 cash dividends on preferred stock. Net income for the year ended December 31, 1993 was $2,000,000. Greene's 1993 EPS should be:

a. $3.00.
b. $3.53.
c. $4.00.
d. $5.00.

_____ 11. Stock options exercisable at $25 each to obtain 6,000 shares of common stock were outstanding during a period when the average market price of the common stock was $30 and the ending market price was $28. In computing fully diluted earnings per share, the assumed exercise of these options will increase the weighted average number of shares outstanding by:

a. 643.
b. 1,000.
c. 5,000.
d. 6.000.

_____ 12. On December 31, 1992, White, Inc., had 600,000 shares of common stock issued and outstanding. White issued a 10% stock dividend on July 1, 1993 and on October 1, 1993, purchased 48,000 shares of its common stock. The number of shares that White should use in computing earnings per share for the year ended December 31, 1993 is:

a. 612,000.
b. 618,000.
c. 648,000.
d. 660,000.

____ 13. Basic earnings per share is $15. Including a stock option will result in a PEPS of $14.86. Including the stock option and other dilutive securities will result in a PEPS of $14.80 and a FDEPS of $14.62. The EPS data should be presented as:

	BEPS	PEPS	FDEPS
a.	$15.00	$ -	$ -
b.	$ -	$14,86	$14.86
c.	$ -	$14.80	$14.62
d.	$14.62	$ -	$ -

____ 14. Epperson Company had 100,000 shares of common stock outstanding at the beginning of 1992. On July 1, 1992, Epperson issued 20% bonds at face value of $500,000. The bonds were convertible into 20,000 shs. of common stock, but were not qualified as common stock equivalent. Assuming net income of $185,000 and a tax rate of 30%, what should be Epperson's fully diluted earnings per share for 1992?

a. $2.00.
b. $1.00.
c. $1.50.
d. $1.85.

SOLUTIONS TO REVIEW QUESTIONS AND EXERCISES

TRUE-FALSE

1.	F	5.	F	9.	F	13.	F
2.	F	6.	T	10.	F	14.	F
3.	F	7.	T	11.	F		
4.	F	8.	T	12.	F		

EXERCISE 1

1. Compute the weighted average common shares outstanding during 1992:

Date	No. of Shs.		Retroactive Restatement Stk Div.		Stk Split		WA factors		WA No. of shs.
1/1/1992	100,000	x	1.2*	x	2**	x	12/12	=	240,000
4/1/1992	20,000	x	1.2*	x	2**	x	9/12	=	36,000
7/1/1992	(5,000)			x	2**	x	6/12	=	(5,000)
10/1/1992	4,000					x	3/12	=	1,000
S (Weighted average common shares outstanding)									272,000

* Retroactive adjustment for 20% stock dividends declared on 5/1/1992.
** Retroactive adjustment for 2 to 1 stock split declared on 8/1/1992.

2. Compute weighted average common shares outstanding for 1993 comparative EPS reporting:

Weighted average common shares outstanding (1992) adjusted for 1993 stock dividends
= 272,000 x 1.2
= 326,400 shs.

Weighted average common shares outstanding (1993):
= 282,000* x 1.2
= 338,400 shs.

* Number of shares outstanding at January 1, 1993:

1/1/1992	100,000 x 1.2 x 2	240,000
4/1/1992	20,000 x 1.2 x 2	48,000
7/1/1992	(5,000) x 2	(10,000)
10/1/1992	4,000	4,000
1/1/1993		282,000

EXERCISE 2

BEPS = E / S
= (Net income - Preferred dividends) / Weighted average common shares outstanding
= ($254,000 - $200,000 X 7%) / (220,000 shs. + 80,000 shs. x 3/12)
= $240,000 / 240,000
= $1

EXERCISE 3

Data analysis:

1. **Dilution test:**

   Given: P_m = **$50**
   P_o = **$30**

   Since $P_m > P_o$

   The stock options were dilutive.

2. **CSE test:**

   Since the options are exercisable within 5 years, they are **CSEs.**

3. **Determine the effects:**

   a. **^E = 0**

   b. Since the closing market price ($P_{m'}$ = **$60**) is greater than the average market price (P_m = **$50**), the effects on shares should be separately calculated for the computations of PEPS and FDEPS:

      (1) **^S (PEPS)**
      = 20,000 x ($50 - $30) / $50
      = **8,000 shs.**

      (2) **^S (FDEPS)**
      = 20,000 x ($60 - $30) / $60
      = 10,000 shs.

So:

1. **PEPS** (Primary earnings per share)
   = ($240,000 + 0) / (240,000 shs. + 8,000 shs.)
   = **$.97**

2. **FDEPS** (Fully diluted earnings per share)
   = ($240,000 + 0) / (240,000 shs. + 10,000 shs.)
   = **$.96**

Note that the FDEPS ($.96) is less than 97% of BEPS ($1), the dilution effect is material and a dual presentation of EPS figures is justified.

EXERCISE 4

Data analysis:

Step 1. Compute BEPS:

BEPS
= E / S
= $260,000 / 200,000
= **$1.30**

Step 2. Convertible bonds analysis:

a. Determine the effects:

^E = $100,000 x 8% x (1 - 30%)
= **$5,600**

^S = 20,000 shs.

b. Dilution test:

ER = ^E / ^S
= $5,600 / 20,000 shs.
= **$.28**

Since **ER < BEPS**
The bonds were dilutive

c. **CSE test:**

Effective yield of bonds = 8%
Average Aa bond yield = 14%

Effective yield < 2 / 3 x 14%

The bonds were CSEs.

So:

PEPS (= FDEPS)
= (E + ^E) / (S + ^S)
= ($260,000 + $5,600) / (200,000 + 20,000)
= $265,600 / 220,000
= **$1.21**

Note that the PEPS and the FDEPS are identical because there is only one dilutive security which is a CSE.

MULTIPLE CHOICE:

1.	d	5.	a	9.	a	13.	a
2.	b	6.	a	10.	a	14.	a
3.	d	7.	c	11.	b		
4.	c	8.	c	12.	c		

Computations:

9. (a) EPS = E / S = ($100,000 - $200,000 x 10%) / 200,000 shs.
= $.40

10. (a) EPS = E / S = ($2,000,000 - $500,000) / 400,000 shs. x 1.25
= $1,500,000 / 500,000 shs.
= $3

11. (b) Given: P_m = $30
P_o = $25

^**S** = 6,000 shs. x ($30 - $25) / $30
= **1,000 shs.**

12. (c) Weighted average common shares outstanding
= 600,000 x 1.1 - 48,000 shs. x 3 / 12
= 648,000 shs.

13. (a) Single presentation (i.e., BEPS) is justified because the dilution effect is not material:

BEPS = $15
FDEPS = $14.62

$14.62 > 97% x $15

14. (a) FDEPS = [$185,000 + ($500,000 x 20% x 6 / 12) x (1 - 30%)] / (100,000 shs. + 20,000 shs. x 6 / 12)
= $220,000 / 110,000 shs.
= $2

CHAPTER 23

Statement of Cash Flows

CHAPTER OBJECTIVES

This chapter is designed to enable students to:

A. Recognize the usefulness of the statement of cash flows.

B. Know the main provisions of **FAS 95**, "Statement of Cash Flows."

C. Be able to analyze transactions to identify disclosures in the statement of cash flows.

D. Know how to prepare a statement of cash flows by analyzing transactions.

E. Be familiar with the spreadsheet approach to preparing a statement of cash flows.

F. Be familiar with the T-account approach to preparing a statement of cash flows.

CHAPTER OVERVIEW

A. Following **FAS 95**, a business enterprise that provides a set of financial statements that reports both financial position and results of operations shall also provide a statement of cash flows (**SCF**) for each period for which results of operations are provided. The primary purpose of this requirement is to provide relevant information about cash receipts and payments of the enterprise during the period in order to help investors and creditors to:

1. assess the enterprise's ability to generate positive future net cash flows from operations;

2. assess the enterprise's ability to meet obligations and to pay dividends, and its needs for external financing;

3. assess the reasons for the difference between net income and net cash flow from operating activities; and

4. assess the effects of investing and financing transactions on the enterprise's financial position.

B. Cash and Cash Equivalents Basis

FAS 95 requires the statement of cash flows be prepared on a cash plus cash equivalents basis. Cash includes currency on hand and demand deposits with financial institutions. Cash equivalents are defined as short-term and highly liquid investments such as debt securities with remaining maturities of three months or less at the time of acquisition.

If cash equivalents are present, only the net change in the cash equivalents is to be reported in the statement of cash flows, because purchases and sales of cash equivalent items are considered as part of a company's cash management activities which are not the focus of the SCF.

C. Classifications on the SCF:

FAS 95 requires companies to report cash flows in terms of **operating, investing,** and **financing activities,** and, if applicable, to report the effect of exchange rate changes as summarized below:

1. **Operating activities:**

   a. Cash receipts and payments related to the operating cycle.

   b. Receipts of interest and dividends from investments in debt and equity securities of other enterprises, and payments for interest and tax expenses.

   c. Other cash flows such as amounts received or paid to settle lawsuits, proceeds of insurance settlements not pertaining directly to investing or financing activities, and cash contributions to charities.

2. **Investing activities:**

   a. Making and collecting loans.

   b. Acquiring and disposing of investments in debt or equity securities of other enterprises.

   c. Acquiring and disposing of property, plant, equipment and other productive assets.

3. **Financing activities:**

   a. Issuing and reacquiring equity securities, and paying dividends.

   b. Borrowing money and repaying money borrowed.

c. Obtaining and paying for other resources provided by creditors on long-term basis.

4. **Effect of foreign exchange rate changes.** This effect is reported only for companies having operations in foreign countries or foreign currency transactions, and is measured by the increase or decrease in cash balance (US dollars) resulting from changes in exchange rate.

D. Presentation Methods and the SCF

1. **Cash flows from operating activities:** The following two methods are both allowed:

   a. **Direct method:** This method involves presenting the major classes of operating cash receipts and payments such as:

      (1) Operating cash inflows -- cash received from:

      Customers.
      Interest on receivables.
      Dividends from investments.
      All other sources of cash that do not stem from investing and financing activities.

      (2) Operating cash outflows -- cash paid for:

      Purchase of goods for resale.
      Interest on liabilities.
      Income taxes, duties, and fines.
      Salaries and wages.
      All other uses of cash that do not stem from investing and financing activities.

   To determine cash flows from operating activities under the direct method, it may be necessary to convert accounting data from the accrual basis to the cash basis. The following equations are usually used:

   (1) **Cash received from customers**
   = Sales revenue
   +/- Decrease/Increase in accounts receivable

   (2) **Cash received from interest, dividends or other revenues**
   = Interest revenue, dividend revenue, etc.
   +/- Decrease/Increase in the respective receivable account
   +/- Increase/Decrease in the respective unearned revenue account

(3) **Cash paid for purchase of goods for resale**
= Cost of goods sold
+/- Increase/decrease in inventory
+/- Decrease/Increase in accounts payable

(4) **Cash paid for salaries and wages, interest, taxes or other expenses**
= Salaries and wages, interest, income taxes, and other expenses
+/- Decrease/Increase in the respective payable accounts
+/- Increase/Decrease in the respective prepaid expense accounts

b. **Indirect method:** This method starts with the reported net income and converts it to the cash basis with the following adjustments:

(1) **Revenues.** **Remove** from net income those revenues that did not generate cash, e.g., credit sales, income from equity security investments under the equity method and current revenues collected in prior period(s). **Add back** to income those revenues collected but not yet earned.

(2) **Expenses.** **Add back** to net income those expenses that did not use cash, e.g., bad debt expenses, depreciation expenses, amortization expenses including the amortization of goodwill, bonds discounts. **Reduce** from net income those expenses paid but not yet incurred and the amortization of bonds premiums.

(3) **Gains/Losses.** **Remove** from net income those incidental gains, and **add back** to net income those incidental losses directly pertaining to investing or financing activities, e.g., gains or losses from disposal of operational assets, discontinued operations, and extraordinary items.

2. **Cash flows from investing and financing activities:**

a. All investing and financing activities affecting cash flows should be presented using the direct method. Note that:

(1) Changes in marketable security investments, either current or noncurrent, should be treated as investment activities.

(2) Changes in long-term debt reclassified as short-term should be included in the financing activities.

(3) Cash proceeds or payments arose from investing or financing activities giving rise to the incidental gains or losses, before taxes, should be reported in its **entirety** as investing or financing activities, as appropriate.

(4) All income taxes should be classified as operating cash flow, even though some portion of the taxes may be directly related to investing or financing activities.

b. **Noncash investing and financing activities** that do not result in cash receipts or cash payments **in the period** should not be presented on the **SCF**. Rather, they should be disclosed separately in a supplementary schedule or elsewhere in the financial report. Examples are:

(1) Obtaining plant assets by issuing debt or equity securities.

(2) Settlement of debt by issuing new debt or equity securities.

(3) Cash or other dividends declared but remaining unpaid.

(4) Granted stock options under a compensatory option plan.

(5) Converted preferred stock to common shares.

(6) Appropriation of retained earnings.

Noncash transactions involving **related accounts**, e.g., declared stock dividends, write off fully depreciated plant assets and noncollectible accounts receivable, are not required to be disclosed on the **SCF**.

Note further that an investing or financing transaction may involve part cash and part noncash items, such as paying cash and issuing a long-term note for the acquisition of a piece of equipment. In this case, the cash amount would be reported under the caption "Cash flow from investing activities" and the noncash amount would be separately reported as a noncash investing or financing transaction.

E. Preparing the Statement of Cash Flows

1. **Schedule approach.** This approach is neither systematic nor comprehensive. Nevertheless, it is appropriate for companies with small number of transactions and accounts. Accounting data are analyzed to identify transactions during the period and determine their effects on cash flows. These effects are then organized using a schedule as presented below. For demonstration purposes, both the direct method and the indirect method are presented on the same schedule.

Schedule to Prepare a Statement of Cash Flows

	Cash Flows	
	Direct Method	Indirect Method
Operating activities:		
Cash basis:		
Revenues received	+	
Expenses paid	-	
Accrual basis:		
Net income/loss		+ (-)
Adjustments to income/loss:		
Estimated expenses		+
Gains (Losses)		- (+)
Increase/Decrease in current assets (excluding marketable securities)		- (+)
Increase/Decrease in current debt (excluding reclassified long-term debt)		+ (-)
Investing activities:		
Cash acquisition of investment items	-	
Cash received from disposal of investment	+	
Financing activities:		
Issuance of debt or equity securities	+	
Retired debt or equity securities	-	
Distribution of cash dividends	-	
Increase (Decrease) in cash (current)	+ (-)	
Beginning cash balance	+	
Ending cash balance	+	

ILLUSTRATION 1 -- The schedule approach to preparing a SCF:

To illustrate, given the following accounting records of the Illustration Company at the end of 1992:

Statement of income:

Sales	$ 60,000
Cost of sales	(22,000)
Depreciation expenses	(14,000)
Other expenses	(8,000)
Loss on sale of plant assets	(1,000)
Net income	$15,000

Comparative balance sheet:

	December 31		
	1991	1992	Increase (decrease)
Debits			
Cash	$ 20,000	$ 26,000	$ 6,000
Accounts receivable	28,000	41,000	13,000
Inventory	22,000	43,000	21,000
Plant assets	120,000	150,000	30,000
Total debits	$190,000	$260,000	$ 70,000
Credits			
Accumulated depreciation	$ 40,000	$ 50,000	$ 10,000
Accounts payable	25,000	30,000	5,000
Accrued expenses	60,000	65,000	5,000
Notes payable	0	10,000	10,000
Common stock	50,000	80,000	30,000
Retained earnings	15,000	25,000	10,000
Total credits	$190,000	$260,000	$ 70,000

Additional information:

a. A machine with a cost of $10,000 and accumulated depreciation of $4,000, was disposed of for $5,000.
b. A note was issued for the acquisition of plant assets of $10,000.

A schedule to prepare a statement of cash flows is presented as follows:

Schedule to Prepare a Statement of Cash Flows

	Cash Flows	
Operating activities:	Direct Method	Indirect Method
Cash basis:		
Cash received from customers	$ 47,000 (1)	
Cash paid for purchase of goods	(38,000) (2)	
Cash paid for other expenses	(3,000) (3)	
Accrual basis:		
Net income		$15,000
Adjustments to reconcile net income with cash flows:		
Depreciation expenses		14,000
Loss on sale of plant assets		1,000
Increase in accounts receivable		(13,000)
Increase in inventory		(21,000)
Increase in accounts payable		5,000
Increase in accrued expenses		5,000
Net cash inflow from operating activities	$ 6,000	$ 6,000
Investing activities:		
Cash acquisition of plant assets	$ (30,000)	
Cash received from disposal of plant assets	5,000	
Net cash outflow from investing activities	$ (25,000)	
Financing activities:		
Issued common stock for cash	$ 30,000	
Paid cash dividends	(5,000) (4)	
Net cash inflow from financing activities	$ 25,000	
Net increase in cash ($6,000 - $25,000 + $25,000)	$ 6,000	
Beginning cash balance	20,000	
Ending cash balance	$ 26,000	

(1) **Cash received from customers**
= Sales revenue - increase in accounts receivable
= $60,000 - $13,000 = $47,000.

(2) **Cash paid for purchase of goods for sale**
= Cost of sales + Increase in inventory - Increase in accounts payable
= $22,000 + $21,000 - $5,000 = $38,000.

(3) **Cash paid for other expenses**
= Other expenses - Increase in accrued expenses
= $8,000 - $5,000 = $3,000.

(4) **Cash dividends paid**
= Net income - Increase in retained earnings
= $15,000 - $10,000 = $5,000.

As indicated in the above schedule, under the indirect method, the adjustments consist of (1) amortization items, (2) gains and losses, and (3) changes in current assets and current liabilities **not** directly pertaining to investing and financing activities. It is noted that these current item changes reflect the leads and lags between income and cash flows from operating activities.

Based on the above schedule, a statement of cash flows is prepared as follows:

Illustration Company
Statement of Cash Flows
For the Year Ended December 31, 1992
(in $000s)

Cash Flows From Operating Activities: (Direct method)		
Received from customers	$ 47	
Paid for purchase of goods	(38)	
Paid for other expenses	(3)	
Net cash inflow from operating activities		$ 6
Cash Flows From Investing Activities:		
Acquisition of plant assets	$(30)	
Disposal of plant assets	5	
Net cash outflow from investing activities		(25)
Cash Flows from Financing Activities:		
Issuance of common stock	$ 30	
Paid cash dividends	(5)	
Net cash inflow from financing activities		$ 25
Net increase in cash, 1992		$ 6
Cash balance, January 1, 1992		20
Cash balance, December 31, 1992		$ 26

Note A: Noncash Investing and Financing Activities:

Acquired $10,000 of plant assets by issuing a 10%, 5-year note.

If the **indirect method** is applied, cash flows from operating activities would be presented differently as follows:

Cash Flows From Operating Activities: (Indirect method)		
Net income	$ 15	
Adjustments to reconcile net income with cash flows:		
Depreciation expenses	14	
Loss on disposal of plant assets	1	
Increase in accounts receivable	(13)	
Increase in inventory	(21)	
Increase in accounts payable	5	
Increase in accrued expenses	5	
Net cash inflow from operating activities		$ 6

2. **Spreadsheet (or work sheet) approach.** This approach offers a more systematic method of analyzing the changes in **all account balances** (in the income statement and balance sheet) for evidence of cash inflows and outflows. The following steps are pertinent:

   a. Set up a spreadsheet with the upper section presenting the comparative balance sheet, and the lower section showing the effects of changes in balance sheet accounts on cash flows.

   b. For each balance sheet account other than cash, construct debit = credit entries to (1) explain the changes in the account during the year, and (2) determine the effects of these changes on cash flows.

   c. To construct spreadsheet entries, it is preferable to follow a sequential order such as:

      (1) Starting with the **additional information items;**

      (2) Analyze the **income statement accounts**, enter first the reported net income, and then search for, from top to bottom, (a) items not affecting cash flows and (b) gains and losses; and

      (3) Complete the explanation for the change in each of the balance sheet account starting with the account next to cash.

   d. After the changes in all balance sheet accounts other than cash and cash equivalents are fully explained, the net cash flow from the three business activities should be identical with the net increase (or decrease) in cash and cash equivalent accounts. Enter these changes and complete the spreadsheet.

ILLUSTRATION 2 -- The spreadsheet approach to preparing a SCF (indirect method):

Using the same data as in **ILLUSTRATION 1**, a typical spreadsheet under the indirect method is presented below:

Illustration Company

Spreadsheet to Prepare the Statement of Cash Flows

For the year ended December 31, 1992
(Indirect method)

Comparative Balance Sheet	12/31/1991	Analysis of Changes Debit		Credit		12/31/1992
Cash	$ 20,000	(l)	6,000			$ 26,000
Accounts receivable	28,000	(e)	13,000			41,000
Inventory	22,000	(f)	21,000			43,000
Plant assets	120,000	(b)	10,000	(a)	10,000	
		(g)	30,000			150,000
Less: Accumulated depreciation	(40,000)	(a)	4,000	(d)	14,000	(50,000)
Total assets	$150,000					$210,000
Accounts payable	$ 25,000			(h)	5,000	$ 30,000
Accrued expenses	60,000			(i)	5,000	65,000
Notes payable	0			(b)	10,000	10,000
Common stock	50,000			(j)	30,000	80,000
Retained earnings	15,000	(k)	5,000	(c)	15,000	25,000
Total Liabilities and OE	$150,000		$ 89,000		$ 89,000	$210,000
Statement of Cash Flows		Inflows (Dr.)		Outflows (Cr.)		Sub total
Cash flows from operating activities:						
Net income		(c)	15,000			
Adjustment to net income:						
Loss on disposal of plant assets		(a)	1,000			
Increase in accounts receivable				(e)	13,000	
Increase in inventory				(f)	21,000	
Depreciation expenses		(d)	14,000			
Increase in accounts payable		(h)	5,000			
Increase in accrued expenses		(i)	5,000			$ 6,000
Cash flows from investing activities:						
Disposal of plant assets		(a)	5,000			
Acquisition of plant assets				(g)	30,000	(25,000)
Cash flows from financing activities:						
Issued common stock for cash		(j)	30,000			
Paid cash dividends				(k)	5,000	25,000
Net increase in cash during 1992				(l)	6,000	$ 6,000
Total			$ 75,000		$ 75,000	

Explanation of spreadsheet entries:

Spreadsheet entries based on the additional information:

a. **Disposal of assets.** The cost of the assets which were disposed of and the related accumulated depreciation are removed from the accounts, the recognized loss is added back (debit) to cash flow from operating activities, and the **entire proceeds** are included in the cash inflows from investing activities (debit):

Cash flow from investing activities	5,000	
Cash flow from operating activities	1,000	
Accumulated depreciation	4,000	
Plant assets		10,000

b. **Noncash investing and financing transaction.** A noncash investing and financing transaction is debited and credited to the appropriate balance sheet accounts without affecting cash flows:

Plant assets	10,000	
Notes payable		10,000

Spreadsheet entries based on the income statement:

c. **Net income.** Net income is entered as an increase in retained earnings (credit) and an increase in cash flows from operating activities (debit):

Cash flow from operating activities	15,000	
Retained earnings		15,000

d. **Depreciation expenses.** The net change of $10,000 in the accumulated depreciation account reflects a reduction of the $4,000 accumulated depreciation associated with the disposed of plant assets, and a current increase in depreciation of $14,000, which is debited to cash flows from operating activities.

Cash flows from operating activities	14,000	
Accumulated depreciation		14,000

Spreadsheet entries based on the balance sheet:

e. **Accounts receivable.** An increase in accounts receivable implies a credit sale during the period. Accounts receivable is debited, and cash flows from operating activities is credited for the increase:

Accounts receivable	13,000	
Cash flow from operating activities		13,000

f. **Inventory.** Inventory changes are resulted from operating activities and an inventory increase implies a cash outflow exceeding cost of goods sold. The inventory account is debited, and cash flows from operating activities is credited:

Inventory	21,000	
Cash flows from operating activities		21,000

g. **Acquisition of plant asset.** The net change of $30,000 in plant assets reflects a deduction of $10,000 for the assets disposed of, an addition of $10,000 new assets acquired through a noncash exchange transaction, and another addition of $30,000 new assets currently acquired for cash:

Plant assets	30,000	
Cash flows from investing activities		30,000

h. **Accounts payable.** Increase in accounts payable implies an excess of current merchandise purchases over payments. Accounts payable is credited, and cash flows from operating activities is debited:

Cash flows from operating activities	5,000	
Accounts payable		5,000

i. **Accrued expenses.** An increase in accrued expenses indicates an excess of the recognized expenses over cash payments. The amount is thus credited to accrued expenses, and debited to cash flows from operating activities:

Cash flows from operating activities	5,000	
Accrued expenses		5,000

j. **Common stock.** Increase in common stock indicates the issuance of new shares for cash, a financing activity:

Cash flows from financing activities	30,000	
Common stock		30,000

k. **Dividends.** The $10,000 net increase in retained earnings reflects the $15,000 current net income and a cash dividends of $5,000. Paying cash dividends reduces retained earning and increase cash outflow from financing activity:

Retained earnings	5,000	
Cash flows from financing activities		5,000

l. **Cash account.** As the final entry, $6,000 is entered to explain the net change in cash account on the one hand, and to balance the total cash inflows and outflows on the other hand:

Cash	6,000	
Net increase in cash (balancing factor)		6,000

After all the changes in the balance sheet accounts are fully explained and the spreadsheet completed, a **SCF** can be prepared using the information provided in the lower section of the spreadsheet.

ILLUSTRATION 3 -- The spreadsheet approach to preparing a SCF (direct method):

If the direct method is desired, the spreadsheet may be modified to include income statement items. As an alternative, a reconciliation schedule such as follows may be used to convert income components under the accrual basis to cash flows from operating activities under the cash basis, i.e., the direct method:

Reconciliation Schedule to Determine
Cash Flows from Operating Activities
Direct Method

	Income Statement	Reconciliation Adjustments Dr.	Reconciliation Adjustments Cr.	Cash Flows from Operating Activities
Sales (Cash received from customers)[1]	$ 60,000		$ 13,000 (1)	$ 47,000
Cost of sales (Cash paid to suppliers)[2]	(22,000)	$ 5,000 (2)	21,000 (3)	(38,000)
Depreciation expenses[3]	14,000	14,000 (4)		0
Other expenses (Cash paid for expenses)[4]	(8,000)	5,000 (5)		(3,000)
Loss on sale of plant assets[5]	(1,000)	1,000 (6)		0
Net income	$ 15,000	$ 25,000	$ 34,000	$ 6,000

Notes:

[1] Cash received from customers = Sales revenue - Increase in accounts receivable.
[2] Cash paid to suppliers = Cost of goods sold + increase in inventory - increase in accounts payable.
[3] Depreciation expenses are removed under the direct method.
[4] Cash paid for other expenses = Other expenses - Increase in accrued expenses.
[5] Loss is removed from operating activities.

3. **The T-account approach.** The T-account approach is similar to the spreadsheet approach. The constructed entries are directly entered into a complete set of T-accounts, which replace the columnar format of the spreadsheet. This approach is particularly efficient for simple problems. T-accounts may also be established selectively and used in conjunction with any other approaches under either the direct or the indirect method. A T-account to summarize cash transactions as indicated in **ILLUSTRATION 2** is presented below:

Cash

Inflows			Outflows		
1/1/1992		20,000			
Operating activities					
(a)	Loss on disposal of assets	1,000	(e)	Increase in accounts receivable	13,000
(b)	Net income	15,000	(f)	Increase in inventory	21,000
(d)	Depreciation expenses	14,000			
(h)	Increase in accounts payable	5,000			
(i)	Increase in accrued expenses	5,000			
		40,000			34,000
Investing activities					
(a)	Disposal of plant assets	5,000	(g)	Acquisition of plant assets	30,000
		5,000			30,000
Financing activities					
(j)	Issuance of common stock	30,000	(k)	Paid cash dividends	5,000
		30,000			5,000
12/31/1991		26,000*			

* Ending cash balance
= $20,000 + ($40,000 - $34,000) + ($5,000 - $30,000)
+ ($30,000 - $5,000)
= $26,000.

F. Statement of Cash Flows and Additional Disclosure. Whichever approach is used, the statement of cash flows is the same as presented earlier in this chapter (see **ILLUSTRATION 1**). In addition to the statement, the following disclosures are also required:

1. Separately disclose the noncash investing and financing activities.
2. Disclose the policy for determining which items are treated as cash equivalents.
3. Reconciliation of net income with net cash flows from operating activities unless included in the SCF.
4. The amount of cash paid for interest and income taxes.
5. Changes during the period in receivables, inventory, and accounts payable.

Note that disclosing **cash flow per share** in the financial reports is not allowed.

KEY CONCEPTS

Statement of cash flows A required primary financial statement designed to help users to assess an entity's ability to generate positive future cash flows, to pay dividends, and to meet obligations, and to project the entity's needs for external financing. In the statement, cash flows are classified in terms of business activities, including operating, investing and financing.

Operating activities All transactions and other events that are not defined as investing or financing activities. They generally involve producing and delivering goods and providing services. Cash flows from operating activities are generally measured by the cash effects of transactions and other events that enter into the determination of income.

Investing activities Making and collecting loans, and acquiring and disposing of investments and operational assets.

Financing activities Obtaining resources from owners and providing them with a return on their investment; borrowing money and repaying amounts borrowed, and obtaining and paying for other resources obtained from creditors on long-term basis.

Cash equivalents Short-term and highly liquid investments which are (a) readily convertible to cash, and (b) so near their maturity that they present insignificant risk of changes in value because of changes in interest rates. Generally, an investment with original maturities of three months or less would qualify under that definition.

Noncash investing and financing transactions Investing or financing transactions not affecting cash flows are noncash exchanges which are not required to be presented on the statement of cash flows. Rather, they should be disclosed separately in a schedule or somewhere else.

Direct method and indirect method The net cash flow from operating activities may be calculated **directly** or **indirectly.** Under the direct method, the calculation involves a listing of major classes of cash receipts and cash payments. Under the indirect method, the calculation starts with net income and then making adjustments to net income for those items not affecting cash in order to reconcile net income to net cash flow from operating activities.

REVIEW QUESTIONS AND EXERCISES

TRUE-FALSE

Indicate whether each of the following statements is true or false by circling the correct response.

T **F** 1. One of the objectives of the Statement of Cash Flows is to determine and present the cash flow per share.

T **F** 2. Cash flows from investing and financing activities include both inflows and outflows of cash that are directly related to transactions and events reported in the income statement.

T **F** 3. The full cash effect of a transaction involving an **extraordinary gain or loss**, pretax, is reported in the statement of cash flows as either an investing or financing activity.

T **F** 4. The payment of cash to acquire treasury stock is reported as an investing activity in a statement of cash flows.

T **F** 5. Investing (or financing) activities that include both cash and noncash components, such as the purchase of equipment by paying partially cash and issuing a note for the difference, should be reported with either cash flows from investing (financing) activities or noncash investing (financing) activities, depending on whether the cash or noncash component is dominant.

T **F** 6. Cash dividends declared but not yet paid should be reported on a statement of cash flows as a noncash investing and financing activity.

T **F** 7. The appropriation of retaining earnings for future plant expansion should be reported on a statement of cash flows as a noncash financing and investing activity.

T **F** 8. The net increase or decrease in cash as reported in a statement of cash flows must be identical with the difference between the beginning and the ending cash balances as indicated in the comparative balance sheet.

T **F** 9. An increase in accounts receivable for the period means that the cash collected from customers is more than the reported sales amount.

T **F** 10. A decrease in inventory should be a deduction from net income in deriving cash flows from operating activities (indirect method).

T F 11. Amortization of bond payable premium should be added to net income in deriving cash flows from operating activities (indirect method).

T F 12. When a current liability, directly related to an operating expense, decreases during a reporting period, the cash outflow related to the expense exceeds the expense as reported on the income statement.

T F 13. Cash payments for interest or taxes should be classified in a **SCF** as an operating, investing, or financing activity depending upon the classification of the item that caused the interest or tax.

T F 14. When reporting cash flows from operating activities by the indirect method, net income should be (a) reduced by increases in current assets and (b) increased by increases in current liabilities, if those current accounts are directly related to activities reported on the income statement.

Exercises 1 through 6 are based on the following data provided by the accounting record of Everready Company at December 31, 1992:

Statement of income

Sales	$ 280
Cost of sales	(168)
Depreciation expenses	(20)
Other expenses	(72)
Gain on sale of investment	12
Loss on sale of plant assets	(4)
Net income	$ 28

Comparative balance sheet:

	December 31		
	1991	1992	Increase (decrease)
Debits			
Cash	$ 136	$ 138	$ 2
Accounts receivable (net) .	48	64	16
Inventory	64	56	(8)
Long-term investments . .	24	0	(24)
Plant assets	320	392	72
Treasury stock	0	46	46
Total debits	$ 592	$ 696	$ 104
Credits			
Accumulated depreciation	$ 192	$ 156	$ (36)
Accounts payable	76	48	(28)
Long-term notes payable .	40	120	80
Common stock	200	260	60
Retained earnings	84	112	28
Total credits	$ 592	$ 696	$ 104

Additional information:

a. Purchased plant assets for cash, $36.
b. Sold plant assets for $24 cash; cost, $84, and two thirds depreciated.
c. Purchased plant assets by issuing a note payable of $120 in payment.
d. Sold the long-term investments for $36 cash.
e. Purchased treasury stock for cash, $46.
f. Retired notes payable at maturity date by issuing common stock, $40.
g. Sold unissued common stock for cash, $20.

EXERCISE 1

Complete the following schedule to compute cash flows from operating activities using (a) the direct method and (b) the indirect method:

Schedule to Prepare the Statement of Cash Flows -- 1992		
Operating activities:	a. Direct method	b. Indirect method
Cash basis:		
Cash received from customers		
Cash paid for purchase of goods		
Cash paid for other expenses		
Accrual basis:		
Net income		
Adjustments to reconcile net income with cash flow:		
Depreciation expenses		
Gain on sale of investments		
Loss on sale of plant assets		
Increase in accounts receivable		
Decrease in inventory		
Decrease in accounts payable		
Net cash inflow from operating activities		

(1) **Cash received from customers**
= Sales revenue - increase in accounts receivable
=

(2) **Cash paid for purchase of goods for sale**
= Cost of sales - Decrease in inventory + Decrease in accounts payable
=

(3) **Cash paid for other expenses**
= Other expenses - Increase in accrued expenses
=

EXERCISE 2

Complete the following schedule to compute cash flows from investing activities:

Investing activities:	
Cash received from:	
Sale of plant assets	
Sale of long term investments	
Cash paid for:	
Purchase of plant asset	
Net cash inflow from investing activities	

EXERCISE 3

Complete the following schedule to compute cash flows from financing activities:

Financing activities:	
Cash received from:	
Issuing common stock for cash	
Cash paid for:	
Purchasing treasury stock for cash	
Net cash outflow from financing activities	

EXERCISE 4

Complete the following abbreviated statement of cash flows using your answers from the previous exercises:

Statement of Cash Flows For year ended 12/31/1992	
Cash flow from operating activities	
Cash flow from investing activities	
Cash flow from financing activities	
Net increase in cash	
Beginning cash balance	
Ending cash balance	

EXERCISE 5

Complete the following disclosure note concerning noncash investing and financing activities.

Note: Noncash investing and financing activities:

1.

2.

EXERCISE 6

Complete the following spreadsheet (indirect method) for Everready Company.

Everready Company

Spreadsheet to Prepare the Statement of Cash Flows

For the year ended December 31, 1992
(Indirect method)

Comparative Balance Sheet	12/31/1991	Analysis of Changes Debit	Credit	12/31/1992
Cash	$ 136			$ 138
Accounts receivable	48			64
Inventory	64			56
Investments, long-term	24			0
Plant assets	320			392
Less: Accumulated depreciation	(192)			(156)
Total assets	$ 400			$ 494
Accounts payable	$ 76			$ 48
Notes payable, long-term	40			120
Common stock	200			260
Retained earnings	84			112
Treasury stock	0			(46)
Total Liabilities and OE	$ 400			$ 494

Statement of Cash Flows	Inflows (dr.)	Outflows (Cr.)	Sub total
Cash flow from operating activities:			
Net income			
Adjustment to net income:			
Loss on sale of plant assets			
Gain on sale of investments			
Depreciation expenses			
Increase in accounts receivable			
Decrease in inventory			
Decrease in accounts payable			
Cash flow from investing activities:			
Acquisition of plant assets			
Sale of plant assets			
Sale of long-term investments			
Cash flow from financing activities:			
Purchased treasury stock			
Issued common stock for cash			
Net increase in cash during 1992			
Total			

MULTIPLE CHOICE

Enter the letter corresponding to the response which **best** completes each of the following statements or questions.

____ 1. Which of the following is not a primary objective of the statement of cash flows?

a. to provide alternative to net income as an indicator of the firm's overall performance.
b. to help investors and creditors assess the firm's ability to generate positive future cash flows.
c. to help investors and creditors assess the firm's ability to meet its obligations.
d. to help investors and creditors assess the reasons for differences between net income and associated cash flows.

____ 2. Which of the following is **not** an appropriate adjustment to reconcile net income with net cash flow from operating activities (indirect method):

a. an addition for patent amortization.
b. a deduction for bonds payable discount amortization.
c. an addition for a loss on sale of land.
d. an addition for depreciation expense.

____ 3. Which of the following is a cash transaction and would be presented as an inflow (or outflow) of cash in a statement of cash flows:

a. an acquisition of treasury stock.
b. an acquisition of a building with a long-term note.
c. a property dividend.
d. common stock issued for a tract of land.

____ 4. A statement of cash flows is required to be presented:

a. as supplemental information in reports filed with SEC.
b. whenever a set of financial statements including balance sheet and income statement are provided.
c. as an alternative to comparative balance sheet.
d. as an alternative to a statement of retained earnings.

____ 5. Receipts from sale of equity securities of other enterprises should be reported as cash inflow from which of the following business activities:

a. operating activities.
b. investing activities.
c. financing activities.
d. some other activities.

____ 6. A stock dividend declared in the period should be reported as which of the following:

a. a cash outflow from investing activities.
b. a cash outflow from financing activities.
c. a cash outflow from operating activities.
d. none of the above.

____ 7. When using the indirect method, an increase in inventory for 1992 should be reported in the 1992 SCF as:

a. an addition to net income in the computation of cash flows from operating activities.
b. a deduction from net income in the computation of cash flows from operating activities.
c. a financing activity.
d. an investing activity.

____ 8. Which of the following is **not** an adjustment to net income to determine the net cash flow from operating activities under the indirect method:

a. Increase in accounts receivable.
b. Increase in inventory.
c. Increase in investment in marketable securities.
d. Increase in prepaid expenses.

____ 9. If sales revenue was $100,000, accounts receivable decreased by $4,000, and inventory increased by $3,000, cash received from customers should be:

a. $98,000.
b. $100,000.
c. $104,000.
d. $101,000.

____ 10. The following entry was recorded by Fantasy Morgan Company:

Cash	30,000	
Loss on sale of plant assets	4,000	
Accumulated depreciation	11,000	
Plant assets		45,000

Fantasy Morgan's statement of cash flows would include which of the following:

a. a cash inflow from investing activities of $26,000.
b. a cash inflow from investing activities of $30,000.
c. a cash inflow from operating activities of $26,000.
d. deduction of $4,000 from net income in using the indirect method of determining cash flows from operating activities.

____ 11. Selected information from Bulldog Inc.'s accounting records and financial statements for 1992 is as follows:

Cash paid to acquire treasury stock	$ 4,000
Cash dividends paid	1,500
Proceeds from sale of land (cost $6,000)	7,000
Issued bonds payable	10,000
Interest paid on bonds	1,000

On the statement of cash flows for the year ended December 31, 1992, Bulldog should report net cash inflow from financing activities in the amount of:

a. $4,500.
b. $5,000.
c. $10,000.
d. $12,000.

____ 12. Assume the following data from the accounting records of Castle Day Care Center:

Cost of goods sold	$84,000
Accounts receivable decrease	6,000
Accounts payable decrease	8,000
Inventory increase	14,000

The cash paid to suppliers of goods should be:

a. $64,000.
b. $90,000.
c. $100,000.
d. $106,000.

____ 13. The net income for the L. G. McCool Company for the year ended December 31, 1992 was $80,000. Additional information follows:

Depreciation expense	$16,000
Decrease in notes payable	2,000
Decrease in accounts receivable	3,000
Increase in bonds payable	10,000
Sale of capital stock for cash	25,000
Amortization of discount on bonds payable	200
Dividend paid	10,000

The net cash flow from operating activities for 1992 should be reported as:

a. $96,000.
b. $96,800.
c. $97,000.
d. $97,200.

____ 14. Selected information from G. L. Kemmer Company's accounting records and financial statements for 1992 is as follows:

Net cash flow from operating activities	$1,500
Cash paid to acquire land and building	1,800
Common stock issued for cash	500
Proceeds from sale of equipment	400
Cost of office equipment purchased	200

Kemmer's statement of cash flows would present net cash outflow from investing activities of:

a. $1,600.
b. $1,800.
c. $2,000.
d. $2,400.

SOLUTIONS TO REVIEW QUESTIONS AND EXERCISES

TRUE-FALSE

1.	F	5.	F	9.	F	13.	F
2.	F	6.	T	10.	F	14.	T
3.	T	7.	T	11.	F		
4.	F	8.	T	12.	T		

EXERCISE 1

Schedule to Prepare the Statement of Cash Flows -- 1992		
Operating activities:	a. Direct method	b. Indirect method
Cash basis:		
Cash received from customers	$ 264 (1)	
Cash paid for purchase of goods	(188) (2)	
Cash paid for other expenses	(72) (3)	
Accrual basis:		
Net income		$ 28
Adjustments to reconcile net income with cash flow:		
Depreciation expenses		20
Gain on sale of investments		(12)
Loss on sale of plant assets		4
Increase in accounts receivable		(16)
Decrease in inventory		8
Decrease in accounts payable		(28)
Net cash inflow from operating activities	$ 4	$ 4

(1)**Cash received from customers**
= Sales revenue - increase in accounts receivable
= $280 - $16
= $264.

(2)**Cash paid for purchase of goods for sale**
= Cost of sales - Decrease in inventory + Decrease in accounts payable
= $168 - $8 + $28
= $188.

(3)**Cash paid for other expenses**
= Other expenses - Increase in accrued expenses
= $72 - 0
= $72.

EXERCISE 2

Investing activities:	
Cash received from:	
Sale of plant assets	$ 24
Sale of long term investments	36
Cash paid for:	
Purchase of plant asset	(36)
Net cash inflow from investing activities	$ 24

EXERCISE 3

Financing activities:	
Cash received from:	
Issuing common stock for cash	$ 20
Cash paid for:	
Purchasing treasury stock for cash	(46)
Net cash outflow from financing activities	$ (26)

EXERCISE 4

Statement of Cash Flows For year ended 12/31/1992	
Cash flow from operating activities	$ 4
Cash flow from investing activities	24
Cash flow from financing activities	(26)
Net increase in cash	$ 2
Beginning cash balance	136
Ending cash balance	$ 138

EXERCISE 5

Note: Noncash investing and financing activities:

1. Plant assets were acquired by issuing a long-term note payable of $120.

2. Common stock was issued to retire notes payable of $40.

EXERCISE 6

Illustration Company

Spreadsheet to Prepare the Statement of Cash Flows

For the year ended December 31, 1992
(Indirect method)

Comparative Balance Sheet	12/31/1991	Analysis of Changes Debit		Analysis of Changes Credit		12/31/1992
Cash	$ 136	(m)	2			$ 138
Accounts receivable	48	(j)	16			64
Inventory	64			(k)	8	56
Investments, long-term	24			(d)	24	0
Plant assets	320	(a)	36	(b)	84	
		(c)	120			392
Less: Accumulated depreciation	(192)	(b)	56	(i)	20	(156)
Total assets	$ 400					$ 494
Accounts payable	$ 76	(l)	28			$ 48
Notes payable, long-term	40	(f)	40	(c)	120	120
Common stock	200			(f)	40	
				(g)	20	260
Retained earnings	84			(h)	28	112
Treasury stock	0	(e)	46			(46)
Total Liabilities and OE	$ 400		$ 344		$ 344	$ 494

Statement of Cash Flows	Inflows (dr.)		Outflows (Cr.)		Sub total
Cash flow from operating activities:					
Net income	(h)	28			
Adjustment to net income:					
Loss on sale of plant assets	(b)	4			
Gain on sale of investments			(d)	12	
Depreciation expenses	(i)	20			
Increase in accounts receivable			(j)	16	
Decrease in inventory	(k)	8			
Decrease in accounts payable			(l)	28	$ 4
Cash flow from investing activities:					
Acquisition of plant assets			(a)	36	
Sale of plant assets	(b)	24			
Sale of long-term investments	(d)	36			24
Cash flow from financing activities:					
Purchased treasure stock			(e)	46	
Issued common stock for cash	(g)	20			(26)
Net increase in cash during 1992			(m)	2	$ 2
Total		$ 140		$ 140	

MULTIPLE CHOICE:

1.	a	5.	b	9.	c	13.	d
2.	b	6.	d	10.	b	14.	a
3.	a	7.	b	11.	a		
4.	b	8.	c	12.	d		

Computations:

9. (c) Cash received from customers
= Sales revenues + Decrease in accounts receivable
= $100,000 + $4,000
= $104,000.

11. (a)

Acquisition of treasury stock	$(4,000)
Cash dividends paid	(1,500)
Bonds issued	10,000
Net cash inflow from financing activities	$ 4,500

12. (d)

Cost of goods sold	$ 84,000
Decrease in accounts payable	8,000
Increase in inventory	14,000
Cash paid to suppliers	$106,000

13. (d)

Net income	$80,000
Depreciation expenses	16,000
Decrease in notes payable	(2,000)
Decrease in accounts receivable	3,000
Amortization of bonds payable discount	200
Net cash inflow from operating activities	$97,200

14. (a)

Acquisition of land and building	$(1,800)
Disposal of equipment	400
Acquisition of office equipment	(200)
Net cash outflow from investing activities	$(1,600)

CHAPTER 24

Accounting Changes and Error Corrections

CHAPTER OBJECTIVES

This chapter is designed to enable students to:

A. Recognize the issues in reporting for accounting changes.

B. Know how to distinguish the three types of accounting changes, and accounting errors.

C. Understand the three approaches to reporting for accounting changes, and when to apply each.

D. Be able to prepare the required entries and disclosures for the current approach to reporting for accounting changes.

E. Be able to prepare the required entries and disclosures for the retroactive approach to reporting for accounting changes.

F. Be able to prepare the required entries and disclosures for the prospective approach to reporting for accounting changes.

G. Recognize several types of accounting errors, and know when to record a prior period adjustment.

CHAPTER OVERVIEW

A. As a response to the changing economic conditions and accounting standards, firms often make accounting changes. In order to enhance consistency and comparability of the financial statements of those firms making such changes, **APB Opinion No. 20** specifies the following:

1. **Types of accounting changes:**

   Accounting changes are classified into three categories as follows:

   a. **A change in accounting principle** occurs when a reporting entity changes from one generally accepted accounting principle to another generally accepted accounting principle (e.g., a change from FIFO to the weighted-average method of inventory costing).

   b. **A change in estimate** occurs when estimates are revised on the basis of new information or new experience (e.g., a revision of the estimate of the useful life of a building).

   c. **A change in reporting entity** occurs when there is a change in affiliated firms reporting as a single entity (e.g., a change in the composition of a group of companies for which consolidated financial statements are prepared).

2. **Approaches to reporting accounting changes:**

   Three approaches to reporting accounting changes are provided. These approaches vary in the extent to which they achieve financial statement comparability and financial statement integrity:

   a. **The current approach** requires that the cumulative effect of the change on prior years' income be determined and that the cumulative effect be included as a separate component of income in **the year of the change.** Since prior years' financial statements are not restated under this approach, financial statement integrity is better maintained, but the degree of comparability is reduced.

   b. **The prospective approach** requires neither a restatement of prior year' financial statements nor a determination of the cumulative effect of the change. Instead, the change is implemented currently and its effects are reflected in the financial statements of the current and future years only. Just like the current approach, this treatment maintains the statement integrity at the expense of comparability.

   c. **The retroactive approach** requires that financial statements issued in previous years be **restated** (when issued again for comparative purposes) to reflect the impact of the change. Comparability among financial statements is achieved by this approach, but public confidence in the integrity of financial data may be sacrificed.

B. Change in Accounting Principle

1. **General rule.** A change in accounting principle is generally accounted for by the **current approach** using the following steps:

   a. **Determine the cumulative effect.** The cumulative effect of the change is the difference between application of each of the two (old and new) principles for all periods affected by the change up to the beginning of the period in which the change is made. Note that the new principle is then applied as of the beginning of the year of change.

   b. **Record the cumulative effect.** The cumulative effect, net of tax, is recorded in a nominal account entitled **adjustment due to change in accounting principle**, which is then closed to income summary.

   c. **Report the change.** The recorded cumulative effect is reported on the income statement for the year of change as a special item between extraordinary items and net income.

   When the financial statements of those prior years affected by the change are reported **again** for comparative purpose, these statements are not restated. However, they should include as supplementary information **pro forma** (as if) presentation of (a) income before extraordinary items, (b) net income and (c) earnings per share, computed as if the new principle had been in effect in those prior years. If only the current period is presented, the actual and **pro forma** amounts for the immediately preceding period and the current period are disclosed.

   Additionally, financial statements should include a **footnote** that explains (a) the nature and effect of the change, and (b) the justification for the change.

ILLUSTRATION 1 -- Change in accounting principle

Apollo, Inc. purchases a piece of equipment on January 1, 1990 with a cost of $10,000, a useful life of 5 years and an estimated salvage value of $1,000. During 1992, Apollo decided to change from the straight-line method to the sum-of-the-years-digit method of depreciation. The applicable income tax rate is 40%.

Required:

(1) Determine the cumulative effect:

Depreciation expenses up to January 1, 1992:

New method (SYD) ($10,000 - $1,000) x (5 + 4) / 15	$5,400
Old method (SL) ($10,000 - $1,000) x 2 / 5	3,600
Cumulative effect before tax	$1,800
Tax effect (40%)	720
Cumulative effect, net of tax	$1,080

(2) Record the cumulative effect:

Cumulative effect on accounting principle changes	1,080	
Deferred income taxes	720	
Accumulated depreciation		1,800

(3) Record current depreciation expense based on the new method:

Depreciation expense ($10,000 - $1,000) x 3 / 15	900	
Accumulated depreciation		900

2. **Exceptions.** A departure from the current approach is required for the following exceptions:

   a. A change from LIFO to another inventory method.

   b. A change in the method of accounting for long-term construction-type contracts.

   c. A change to or from the **full cost** method in extractive industries.

   d. A change in conjunction with a forthcoming issuance of capital stock by a closely held company.

e. A change from retirement/replacement accounting to depreciation accounting.

f. A change required by a new accounting standard.

g. A change to the equity method.

For these exceptions, the retroactive approach is required. That is, the cumulative effect of the change, net of taxes, is adjusted to retained earnings, the financial statements of prior years affected by the change are restated, and footnote disclosure about the change is provided.

3. **Exclusions** Although the following appear similar to accounting changes, they are not so considered under **APB Opinion No. 20:**

a. **Initial adoption** of an accounting principle for new transactions. No cumulative effect is considered.

b. Adopting **a new accounting principle** to a new group of assets or liabilities. No cumulative effect is considered.

c. A **planned** change to straight-line depreciation from accelerated depreciation to fully depreciated plant assets. No cumulative effect is considered.

d. A change in accounting principle which cannot be distinguished from a change in **accounting estimate**, It is generally treated as a change in estimates.

c. A change from an **inappropriate accounting principle** to an allowed method [e.g., from variable (or direct) costing to full (or absorption) costing]. It is treated as a correction of accounting error.

C. Change in Estimates

A change in estimates is accounted for **prospectively**. When a firm revises a previous estimate (e.g., of useful life or salvage value of assets, of the percentage used to estimate bad debt, etc.), prior financial statements are not restated, nor is a cumulative effect on prior years' income to be determined. Instead, the firm merely incorporates the new estimate in any related accounting determination **thereafter**.

ILLUSTRATION 2 -- Change in estimate

A piece of equipment with a cost of $10,000, and an estimated useful life of 10 years, without salvage value, was acquired on January 1, 1990. During 1992, the estimated useful life is revised from 10 years to 7 years. The straight-line method of depreciation is used.

Requires:

(1) Determine the book value of the equipment at January 1, 1992:

Cost		$10,000
Accumulated depreciation, 1990 and 1991,	$10,000 x 2 / 10	2,000
Book value, January 1, 1992		$ 8,000

(2) Determine annual depreciation expense based on the new estimate for the remaining life of the equipment:

Annual depreciation expense
= $8,000 / (7 - 2)
= $1,600

(3) Record depreciation expense for 1992:

Depreciation expense	1,600	
Accumulated depreciation		1,600

D. Change in Reporting Entity

A change in reporting entity requires that financial statements of all prior periods be **retroactively** restated to report the financial information for the new entity in all periods. This type of change is discussed in detail in the advanced accounting textbook.

E. Correction of Accounting Errors

APB Opinion No. 20 and **FAS 16** provide guidelines for the correction of accounting errors in financial statements on their discovery date. An accounting error occurs when a transaction or event is recorded incorrectly or is not recorded. Material errors are not a common occurrence. Larger firms discover most material errors before completing the financial statements. Smaller firms cannot afford the internal control found in large companies and are more prone to errors.

1. **Major causes of accounting errors:** The major causes of accounting errors include the following:

    a. Mathematical mistakes.

    b. Misapplication of accounting principles.

    c. Failure to recognize accruals and/or deferrals.

    d. Misclassification of an account.

    e. Intentional use of an unrealistic accounting estimates.

2. **Analysis of accounting errors:** Accounting errors may be classified in terms of whether the errors affect prior year's financial statements when they are discovered:

    a. **Errors not affecting prior year's financial statements:** These types of errors are **discovered in the same accounting period** when they occur, and the books for the period of discovery are still open. As such, they do not affect retained earnings and can be easily corrected by either (1) reversing the erroneous entry and then recording the correct entry, or (2) making a single correcting entry designed to correct the account balances.

    b. **Errors affecting prior year's financial statements:** These types of errors **occur in one accounting period and are discovered in a later period.** Fundamentally, correction of an error of this type is based on the **retroactive approach.** The application of this approach, however, depends on whether the specific error affects prior years' income:

        (1) **Errors affecting prior financial statements but not income**: This error involves incorrect classification of real or nominal accounts, such as neglecting to classify the current portion of a long-term debt as current. An entry to reclassify the accounts would correct the error.

        (2) **Errors affecting prior financial statements and income**: This type can be further classified on the basis of the effect of the error on retained earnings:

            (a) **Self-corrected (counterbalanced) errors.** An accounting error counterbalances if it self-corrects over a two year period, i.e., the income for the period of error is misstated, as is the income of the second period, with the same amount but in the opposite direction. Examples of this type of errors include:

* Over- or understated ending inventory.
* Unrecognized accruals
* Unadjusted deferrals

A counterbalancing error is **self corrected** if the error is discovered more than two years after it was made, and the books of the second year of the two-year cycle have been closed. In this case, the beginning retained earnings do not contain the error, and no correcting entry is required. However, the financial statements for those years affected by the error should still be retroactively restated if presented, and the cause and effect of the error disclosed.

(b) Errors not yet corrected when discovered. Noncounterbalancing errors do not correct themselves over a two-year cycle, whereas the counterbalancing errors misstate account balances if they are discovered while the books of the second year are still open. In either case, the correction of these errors involves the following:

(i) Compute the cumulative effect of the error up to the beginning of the period of discovery, which is affected by whether the books are closed when the error is discovered. Assume that an accounting error occurred in 1991, and is discovered at the beginning of 1993. If the 1992 books remain open, the year of discovery is 1992. If the 1992 books are already closed, it would be 1993.

(ii) adjust the beginning balance of retained earning (i.e., prior year adjustment) and all other accounts affected by the error, and

(iii) restate prior years' financial statements, and

(iv) disclose the nature of the error and the effect of its correction on income before extraordinary items, net income and the related per share amounts in the period in which the error was discovered and corrected.

ILLUSTRATION 3 -- Correction of accounting errors

An examination of Gray Company's books at the beginning of 1993 reveals the following errors:

(1) A piece of equipment acquired on January 1, 1989 for $50,000 was charged to other expenses. The equipment should have a 5-year useful life with a salvage value of $5,000. Gray used the straight-line method to depreciate its plant assets.

(2) The merchandise inventory at December 31, 1991 was overstated by $4,000.

(3) In January 1991, Gray purchased a two-year insurance policy costing $1,000 and debited the total amount to prepaid insurance expense. No adjusting entry has been made for the insurance.

(4) At the end of 1991, Gray failed to accrue an interest expense of $2,000. This amount was expensed when paid in 1992.

Required: Prepare appropriate correcting entries for the above errors assuming that the 1992 books are (1) open, and (2) closed. Ignore income taxes.

Solution:

			Journal Entries			
			1992 books open		1992 books closed	
Equipment						
1. Determine cumulative effect:						
	Up to Jan. 1					
	1992	1993				
Cost of equipment	$50,000	$50,000				
Accumulated depreciation	27,000	36,000				
Retained earnings understated	$23,000	$14,000				
2. Prepare adjusting entry:						
Equipment			50,000		50,000	
Accumulated depreciation				27,000		36,000
Prior year adjustment				23,000		14,000
3. Record current depreciation expense:						
Depreciation expenses			9,000		9,000	
Accumulated depreciation				9,000		9,000

Merchandise inventory: 1. Determine cumulative effect: Up to Jan. 1 — 1992: ; 1993: Beginning inventory overstated — 1992: $ 4,000; 1993: $ 0 2. Prepare adjusting entry: Prior year adjustment Inventory	4,000 4,000	None.
Prepaid insurance: 1. Determine cumulative effect: Up to Jan. 1 — 1992: ; 1993: Prepaid insurance overstated — 1992: $ 500; 1993: $ 1,000 2. Prepare adjusting entry: Prior year adjustment Prepaid insurance 3. Record current insurance expense: Insurance expense Prepaid insurance	500 500 500 500	1,000 1,000 None
Accrued interest expense: 1. Determine cumulative effect: Up to Jan. 1 — 1992: ; 1993: Retained earnings overstated — 1992: $ 2,000; 1993: $ 0 2. Prepare adjusting entry: Prior year adjustment Interest expense	2,000 2,000	None

KEY CONCEPTS

Change in accounting estimate A change in the estimated accounting figures such as the useful life or the salvage value of a depreciable plant asset. To account for such a change, the prospective approach should be applied.

Change in accounting principle A change from one generally accepted accounting principle to another generally accepted accounting principle. In general, the current approach should be applied to account for such a change, and management is required to justify the change on the grounds that the newly adopted principle is preferable than the old one.

Change in reporting entity This is a change in the group of companies comprising a reporting entity. Such a change should be accounted for retroactively, and the financial statements of all prior years presented should be restated.

Counterbalancing errors An accounting error caused a misstatement of income in one period leads to another error in the following period with the same amount but in the opposite direction. The error is self-corrected over a two-year cycle.

Correction of accounting errors Accounting errors in prior years' financial statement should be corrected using the retroactive approach. Cumulative effect of the error, if any, is adjusted to retained earnings, and the prior years' financial statements, if presented, are restated.

Current approach The cumulative effect of the change in accounting principle, net of taxes, should be determined, and reported in the income statement of the year of change. Prior years' financial statements are not restated. However, a proforma net income and earnings per share should be presented for those prior years affected by the change.

Prospective approach Cumulative effect is not determined, prior years' financial statements are not restated, and the pro forma presentation is not required. The effect of the change is reflected in the current and future periods.

Retroactive approach The cumulative effect of the change is adjusted to retained earnings, and prior years' financial statements presented are restated to reflect the change. This approach is applied to the correction of accounting errors, to the change in reporting entity, and to changes in certain specified accounting principles.

REVIEW QUESTIONS AND EXERCISES

TRUE-FALSE

Indicate whether each of the following statements is true or false by circling the correct response.

T F 1. The retroactive approach requires that prior years' financial statements be restated in order to enhance comparability.

T F 2. The prospective approach requires that the cumulative effect of an accounting change be reported in the current period as a separate component of income.

T F 3. When a firm changes from the weighted-average method of inventory costing to the first-in, first-out method, a change in an accounting principle occurs.

T F 4. The cumulative effect of a change in accounting principle is determined by comparing the balance in retained earnings at the beginning and the end of the year of the change.

T F 5. The cumulative effect of a change in accounting principle is reported net of its tax effect as an extraordinary item in the income statement for the year of the change.

T F 6. In addition to reporting the cumulative effect of a change in accounting principle as a component of current income, prior years' financial statements are restated to reflect the new accounting principle.

T F 7. The cumulative effect of a change from the LIFO method to the FIFO method of inventory pricing is reported as a prior year adjustment instead of a component of income in the year of the change.

T F 8. When a previous estimate of the useful life of a building is revised in the third year of an asset's depreciable life, depreciation expenses for the first two years should be restated using the new estimate.

T F 9. A change in reporting entity requires retroactive restatement of prior years' financial statements to reflect financial information of the new reporting entity in those prior years.

T F 10. If an erroneous entry is made and discovered in the same accounting period, the original entry may be reversed and the correct entry recorded to correct the error.

T F 11. If merchandise inventory is overstated at the end of 1991 and the error is not discovered, net income in 1992 will be overstated.

T F 12. If it is discovered that a major repair in the previous year was incorrectly debited to repair expense and the books of that year were closed, the current year's statement of retained earnings should report an addition to the beginning balance of retained earnings.

T F 13. The discovery of an error in a previous year's income statement may not require a correcting journal entry.

T F 14. A change to a new accounting principle must be justified as a change to a preferable accounting principle.

EXERCISE 1

Indicate with the appropriate letter the nature of each adjustment below:

Type of Adjustments	Reporting approach
A. Change in accounting principle	Current
B. Change in accounting principle	Retroactive
C. Change in estimate	Prospective
D. Change in reporting entity	Retroactive
E. Correction of accounting error	Retroactive

____ 1. Change from the SYD method to the DDB method of depreciation..

____ 2. Change in the composition of firms reporting on a consolidated basis.

____ 3. Change in the residual value of plant equipment.

____ 4. Change in the percentage used to determine bad debts.

____ 5. Change from LIFO to weighted average method of inventory pricing.

____ 6. Change from the market value method to the LCM method of accounting for long-term investments in marketable equity securities by a manufacturing firm.

____ 7. Change from FIFO to LIFO.

____ 8. Change from the percentage-of-completion method in long-term construction.

____ 9. Change from retirement method to SL method of depreciation.

____ 10. Change from direct costing to full (absorption) costing.

EXERCISE 2

Arcaria Corporation acquired a machine at a total cost of $220,000 (no residual value) on January 1, 1991. The machine was being depreciated over a 10-year life using the sum-of-the-years-digits method. At the beginning of 1994 it was decided to change to straight-line. The applicable tax rate was 40%.

Required:

a. Determine the cumulative effect:

Depreciation expense up to January 1, 1994:

New method (SL)
Old method (SYD)

Cumulative effect before tax
Tax effect (40%)

Cumulative effect, net of tax

b. Record the cumulative effect:

Accumulated depreciation
    Cumulative effect on accounting principle changes
    Deferred income taxes

c. Record current depreciation expense based on the new method:

Depreciation expense
    Accumulated depreciation

EXERCISE 3

At the beginning of 1994, it was discovered that Healton Company had debited expense account for the full cost of a piece of equipment purchased on January 1, 1991. The cost was $60,000; useful life 5 years; and straight-line depreciation was used by the company. The residual value was zero, and the income tax was 40%.

Required:

a. **Prepare the correcting entry assuming the error was discovered before the 1993 books were closed.**

Equipment
    Accumulated depreciation (1991 and 1992)
    Deferred tax liability
    Prior year adjustment (plug)

Depreciation expense (1993)
    Accumulated depreciation

b. **Prepare the correcting entry assuming the error was discovered after the 1993 books were closed.**

Equipment
    Accumulated depreciation (1991 to 1993)
    Deferred tax liability
    Prior year adjustment (plug)

EXERCISE 4

On January 1, 1991, Marina Company acquired a piece of equipment for $46,000. The equipment had an estimated life of 8 years and a salvage value of $10,000. On January 1, 1995, Marina revised the useful life to 6 years and the salvage value to zero. The straight-line method was used by Marina.

Required: **Complete the following entries related to the equipment:**

a. **At the end of 1994:**

Depreciation expense
    Accumulated depreciation

b. **At the end of 1995:**

Depreciation expense
    Accumulated depreciation

MULTIPLE CHOICE

Enter the letter corresponding to the response which **best** completes each of the following statements or questions.

____ 1. Which of the following is true concerning the current approach for a change in accounting principle?

a. It offers the advantage that users will not be confused by changes in prior statements.
b. This is the required treatment of **all** changes in accounting principle.
c. It offers the advantage of comparability among financial statements of past and subsequent years.
d. Pro forma data is not required in addition to reporting the cumulative effect.

____ 2. An example of a change in accounting principle requiring the current approach is:

a. a change from LIFO to weighted average inventory pricing.
b. a revision in the percentage used in determining uncollectible accounts.
c. a change in the number of firms to be included in the combined (consolidated) financial statements.
d. the change to declining balance depreciation when sum-of-the-years'-digits method was previously used.

____ 3. The prospective approach is required for:

a. a change in accounting estimate.
b. a change in reporting entity.
c. a change in accounting principle.
d. a correction of accounting error.

____ 4. The cumulative effect of a change in accounting principle:

a. is determined by comparing the amount in the retained earnings account at the beginning and end of the year.
b. is reported as a separate component of income, net of tax, as an extraordinary item.
c. is reported as an adjustment to the beginning balance of retained earnings in a statement of retained earnings.
d. is the cumulative effect of the change on income of prior years.

____ 5. Which of the following is **not** true concerning a change in accounting principle?

a. The new principle must be justified as being preferable.
b. Proforma net income of prior years should be presented as **supplementary information** on the basis of the new principle.
c. Footnote disclosure is required.
d. The cumulative effect due to a change from the percentage of completion method to the completed contract method should be reported in the current income statement.

____ 6. Which of the following is **not** appropriate when it is discovered that a five-year insurance premium payment two years ago was debited to insurance expense?

a. a credit to prepaid insurance.
b. a retroactive restatement of the income statement of the previous year.
c. a retroactive restatement of the balance sheet of the previous year.
d. a footnote explaining the impact of the error on net income and earnings per share of the current year.

____ 7. Proforma data would usually be reported on the face of the income statement for a change:

a. from LIFO to FIFO.
b. in the residual value of a building.
c. from the straight-line method of depreciation to the double-declining-balance method.
d. in the service life of equipment.

____ 8. A change in accounting principle that should be reported by restating the financial statements of prior periods is a change from the:

a. straight-line method of depreciating plant equipment to the declining-balance method.
b. sum-of-the-years'-digits method to the straight-line method.
c. FIFO method of inventory pricing to the LIFO method.
d. LIFO method of inventory pricing to weighted-average method.

_____ 9. Goldman Corporation has amortized a patent on a straight-line basis since it was acquired at a cost of $17,000 on January 1, 1991. During 1994 it was decided that the benefits from the patent would be received over a total period of 10 years rather than the 17-year life being used to amortize the cost. On the basis of the revised estimate, Goldman's 1994 financial statements should reflect:

a. a cumulative effect adjustment of $2,100.
b. a balance in the patent account of $11,900.
c. an amortization expense of $1,400.
d. a reduction in the carrying value of the patent of $2,000.

_____ 10. Hartman Company understated its inventory by $5,000 at the end of 1991. If the error was discovered in 1992 after the 1991 books are closed, which of the following would be appropriate to correct the error?

a. a debit to inventory of $5,000.
b. a $5,000 adjustment in the income statement of 1992.
c. a deduction of $5,000 from the beginning balance of retained earnings in a statement of retained earnings.
d. none of the above.

_____ 11. If the error described in Question 10 is discovered after the 1992 books are closed, the discovery of the error would require:

a. a debit to inventory of $5,000.
b. a $5,000 adjustment in the 1993 income statement.
c. a debit to prior year adjustment.
d. none of the above.

_____ 12. In 1992 McMurgrie Corporation changed its inventory method to the FIFO cost method from the LIFO cost method. McMurgrie's inventories totaled $800,000 on the LIFO bases at December 31, 1991. Records maintained by McMurgrie showed that the inventories would have totaled $960,000 at December 31, 1991, on the FIFO basis. Ignoring income taxes, the adjustment for the effect of the change should be reported in the 1992:

a. income statement as a $160,000 decrease in income.
b. income statement as a $160,000 increase in income.
c. statement of retained earnings as a $160,000 decrease in the beginning balance.
d. statement of retained earnings as a $160,000 increase in beginning balance.

____ 13. During 1992, Gamma Company discovered that its inventories were overstated by \$10,000 and \$20,000 at the end of 1991 and 1992, respectively. If the 1992 books were still open, these errors would be corrected by debiting prior year adjustment and crediting inventory at:

a. \$0.
b. \$10,000.
c. \$20,000.
d. \$30,000.

____ 14. Based on the same data as in Question 13, except that those errors were discovered after the 1992 books were closed. These errors would be corrected by debiting prior year adjustment and crediting inventory account at:

a. \$0.
b. \$10,000.
c. \$20,000.
d. \$30,000.

SOLUTIONS TO REVIEW QUESTIONS AND EXERCISES

TRUE-FALSE

1.	T	5.	F	9.	T	13.	T
2.	F	6.	F	10.	T	14.	T
3.	T	7.	T	11.	F		
4.	F	8.	F	12.	T		

EXERCISE 1

1.	A	4.	C	7.	A	10.	E
2.	D	5.	B	8.	B		
3.	C	6.	E	9.	B		

EXERCISE 2

a. Determine the cumulative effect:

Depreciation expenses up to January 1, 1994:

New method (SL) -- \$220,000 x 3 / 10	\$ 66,000
Old method (SYD) -- \$220,000 x (10 + 9 + 8) / 55	108,000
Cumulative effect before tax	\$(42,000)
Tax effect (40%)	16,800
Cumulative effect, net of tax	\$(25,200)

b. Record the cumulative effect:

Accumulated depreciation	42,000	
Cumulative effect on accounting principle changes		25,200
Deferred income taxes		16,800

c. Record current depreciation expense based on the new method:

Depreciation expense (\$220,000 / 10)	22,000	
Accumulated depreciation		22,000

EXERCISE 3

a. **Prepare the correcting entry assuming the error was discovered before the 1993 books were closed.**

Equipment	60,000	
Accumulated depreciation ($60,000 x 2 / 5)		24,000
Deferred tax liability ($60,000 - $24,000) x 40%		14,400
Prior year adjustment (plug)		21,600
Depreciation expense (1993)	12,000	
Accumulated depreciation		12,000

b. **Prepare the correcting entry assuming the error was discovered after the 1993 books were closed.**

Equipment	60,000	
Accumulated depreciation ($60,000 x 3 / 5)		36,000
Deferred tax liability ($60,000 - $36,000) x 40%		9,600
Prior year adjustment (plug)		14,400

EXERCISE 4

a. **At the end of 1994:**

Depreciation expense ($46,000 - $10,000) / 8	4,500	
Accumulated depreciation		4,500

b. **At the end of 1995:**

Depreciation expense ($46,000 - 4 x $4,500) / (6 - 4)	14,000	
Accumulated depreciation		14,000

MULTIPLE CHOICE

1.	a	5.	d	9.	d	13.	b
2.	d	6.	a	10.	a	14.	c
3.	a	7.	c	11.	d		
4.	d	8.	d	12.	d		

Computations:

9. (d) Book value of patent at beginning of 1994
= \$17,000 x (17 - 3) / 17
= \$14,000

Annual amortization of patent after change in estimate
= \$14,000 / (10 - 3)
= \$2,000

CHAPTER 25

Financial Statement Analysis and Changing Prices

CHAPTER OBJECTIVES

This chapter is designed to enable students to:

A. Understand the importance and limitations of financial statement information in the evaluation of investment opportunities.

B. Be able to perform vertical (within year) and horizontal (across years) comparative percentage analyses.

C. Know how to calculate a number of ratios used in financial statement analysis and interpret the results.

D. Understand the limitations of ratio analysis.

E. Be aware of the effects of price-level changes on historical cost financial statements.

F. Understand the advantages and disadvantages of general and specific price-level adjusted financial statements.

G. Be able to adjust financial statements for general price-level changes (historical cost-constant dollar model).

H. Know how to adjust financial statements for specific price-level changes (current cost/nominal dollar, and current cost/constant dollar models).

CHAPTER OVERVIEW

PART A: Financial Statement Analysis

A. The general purpose financial statements issued by a firm are an important, but not the only, source of financial information about the firm. Other sources include periodic reports filed with the Securities and Exchange Commissions, and financial publications of the Wall Street Journal, Barron's, Dun and Bradstreet, and various advisory services and security brokerage firms. All these and other financial data should be carefully analyzed and interpreted for making investment and credit decisions.

Three steps are generally applied to the use of financial statements. The first step is to examine the accompanying **auditors' report**. This report provides an independent and professional opinion about the fairness of the representations and calls attention to major concerns of the auditors during their examination of the statements. The next step is the analysis of their **footnotes** and **supplementary schedules** as to be discussed in Chapter 26. The third step is to transform financial data into **percentages** or **ratios** in order to gain an overall perspective and to identify major strength and weaknesses of the firm.

B. Financial Percentage Analysis

The corporate annual report typically includes detailed comparative financial statements for the current and preceding year(s). These comparative data facilitate an analysis of trends over a period of time. The following percentage analyses are common:

1. **Vertical analysis.** This analysis involves expressing each item on a financial statement in a given period as a percentage of a base amount (e.g., inventory as a percentage of total assets, salaries expense as a percentage of revenues, etc.). This analysis reveals the composition of items on the specific common-size financial statement, i.e., the percentages of items on the statement always add up to 100%.

2. **Horizontal analysis.** Each item is expressed as a percentage of that same item in the financial statements of another year (base year) in order to more easily see year-to-year changes. This analysis involves scrutiny of not only the resulting percentages but also the relative importance of the items being analyzed.

C. Financial Ratio Analysis

For accounting numbers to be most meaningful, they are usually studied in appropriate perspective. Ratio analysis provides that perspective by expressing accounting numbers as fractions or percentages of other numbers. This analysis is useful when the proportional relationship between the selected factors sheds additional light on the interpretation of the individual absolute amounts. For example, the fact that a firm's net income of $25,000 was earned on total assets of $100,000 is more meaningful information than the absolute amount of net income alone.

Depending on the characteristics they attempt to capture and the specific user needs they are intended to satisfy, financial ratios can be classified into the following four categories:

1. **Current position (or liquidity) ratios.** This set of financial ratios measures the firm's ability to pay short-term obligations when mature. Three ratios are generally used:

   a. **Current ratio**
   = Current assets / Current liabilities

   The current ratio is only one measure of ability to meet short-term obligations and must be interpreted carefully. In general, a high current ratio indicates a strong liquidity position. However, a firm may have a high current ratio even though it has a cash deficit. A high current ratio may also indicate excess funds that should be invested or used for other purposes.

   b. **Quick (or acid-test) ratio**
   = Quick assets / Current liabilities
   = (Current assets - Inventory - Prepaid expenses) / Current liabilities

   This ratio is used as a test of immediate liquidity. An acid-test ratio of 1 to 1 is generally considered satisfactory.

   c. **Working capital ratio to total assets**
   = Working capital / Total assets
   = (Current assets - Current liabilities) / Total assets

   This ratio is a generalized expression of the distribution and liquidity of the assets employed after current liabilities are deducted from current assets. A low ratio may indicate a weakness in the current position.

   d. **Defensive-interval ratio**
   = Defensive assets / Projected daily operational expenditures
   = (Current assets - Inventory - Prepaid expenses) / Projected daily operating expenditures

   This ratio provides a measure of how long a firm can operate on its present defensive or quick assets.

2. **Efficiency (activity) ratios:** These ratios provide information about how efficiently the firm is using its assets. The most used efficiency ratios include:

   a. **Accounts receivable turnover**
   = Net credit sales / Average accounts receivable (net)

   This ratio indicates how quickly a firm is able to collect accounts and short-term notes receivable, where the average accounts receivable is obtained by dividing the total of beginning and ending balances by 2. The age of accounts receivable (i.e., the average number of days required to collect receivables) can be found as follows:

   Age of accounts receivable
   = 365 / Accounts receivable turnover

   b. **Inventory turnover**
   = Cost of goods sold / Average inventory

   This ratio indicates how quickly inventory typically is sold. A high inventory turnover generally reflects efficient inventory management. The average number of days' supply in the average inventory, indicating general condition of over- or understocking, can be found as follows:

   Days' supply in inventory
   = 365 / Inventory turnover

   c. **Working capital turnover**
   = Net sales revenue / Average working capital

   This ratio indicates the effectiveness with which average working capital was used to generate sales.

   d. **Asset turnover**
   = Net sales revenue / Average total assets

   This ratio extends the idea of efficient use of working capital to all assets. Note that the ratio is larger for firms using older, more depreciated assets.

3. **Equity Position Ratios** Long-term creditors are primarily concerned with a firm's long-term solvency and stability. Ratios that measure equity position are designed to provide indications of these aspects of a company's outlook.

   a. **Debt to equity ratio**
   = Total liabilities / Stockholders' equity

This ratio measures the balance between resources provided by creditors and resources provided by owners including retained earnings.

b. **Debt to total assets ratio**
= Total liabilities / Total assets

This ratio measures essentially the same facet of a firm's capital structure as the debt to equity ratio.

c. **Book value per share of common stock**
= Common stock equity / Number of outstanding common shares

This ratio indicates what stockholders might expect to receive in the event of liquidation. Although still popularly used, it is useful only to the extent that book values mirror market values.

4. **Profitability ratios** These ratios are intended to measure various aspects of a firm's profit-making activities.

a. **Profit margin on sales**
= Net income / Net sales revenue

This ratio is useful as a measure of a firm's efficiency in controlling expenses. A low profit margin can be compensated for by a high investment turnover rate, and vice versa.

b. **Return on investment** The broad concept of return on investment has two important applications for a single business entity: evaluating proposed capital addition and other investment decisions on the basis of projected cash flows, and measuring the annual rate of return earned relative to the total assets employed or the average investment of stockholders:

(1) **Return on total assets**
= [Income + Interest expense (after tax)] / Average total assets

(2) **Return on owners' equity**
= Net income / Average stockholders' equity

c. **Earnings per share on common stock**
= Earnings to common / Weighted-average common shares outstanding

Discussed in detail in Chapter 22.

d. **Price earnings ratio**
= Market price per share / Earnings per share

This ratio is widely used as a measure of the market's perception of the quality of a firm's earnings including its growth potential, stability, and relative risk.

e. **Dividend payout ratios.** These ratios indicate the percentage of earnings that is distributed to stockholders as dividends:

(1) **Dividend payout on income to common**
= Cash dividends to common / Income less preferred dividends

(2) **Dividend payout on market price of common**
= Cash dividends per common share / Market price per common share

5. Ratio analysis of financial statements is used widely along with more sophisticated techniques for making investment and credit decisions. However, they must be interpreted with care because of some important limitations such as follows:

a. Ratios represent average conditions that existed in the past.

b. When the data on which ratios are based are historical book values, they do not reflect market values.

c. The method of computing each ratio is not standardized.

d. The use of alternative accounting methods may have an effect on ratios.

e. Change in accounting estimates and principles may affect the ratios for the year of change.

f. Comparison among companies are difficult if each company has different operating characteristics and uses different accounting methods.

PART B: Changing Prices

A. Following GAAP, accounting measurements are based upon the historical cost principle using dollars as the measurement unit. With the basic assumption that the magnitude of changes in the value of the measurement unit is not material, the originally recorded historical data are not adjusted for price-level changes, general or specific. The resulting measurement system is thus referred to as **historical cost/nominal dollar accounting (HC/ND).**

To counter the effects of inflation on financial statements, three alternative systems have been proposed:

1. **Historical cost/constant dollar accounting (HC/CD);**

2. **Current cost accounting (CC or CC/ND); and**

3. **Current cost/constant dollar accounting (CC/CD).**

None of these alternative systems is presently required. Nevertheless, **FAS 89** encourages business enterprises to disclose supplementary information on the effects of price-level changes.

B. Historical Cost/Constant Dollar Accounting (HC/CD)

Under this system, the historical cost model is maintained, but the accounting data based on nominal dollar are adjusted for the general price-level changes using a **general price-level index,** in order to present financial statement elements in dollars that have the equivalent purchasing power.

1. **Constant dollar restatement formula.** Nominal dollars are converted to constant dollars by means of conversion (restatement) factors obtained by dividing the general price-level index at a target date (e.g., the end of current period) to be adjusted to by the one at the original transaction date to be adjusted from. The general price-level index suggested by the **FASB** is the **consumer price index for all urban consumers** (i.e., **CPI-U**). The general conversion formula is thus:

   HC/CD amount
   = HC/ND amount x Conversion factor
   = HC/ND amount x CPI-U adjusting to / CPI-U adjusting from

   For example, land acquired for $10,000 in 1985 (when the **CPI-U** was 160) could be restated to 1992 dollar (when the **CPI-U** was 200) as follows:

Land at HC/CD
= Land at HC/ND x Conversion factor
= $10,000 x 200/160
= $12,500

2. **Balance sheet items.** HC/CD accounting requires that balance sheet items be divided into two categories--monetary and nonmonetary:

   a. **Monetary items** are assets and liabilities whose amounts are fixed, by contract or otherwise, in terms of a specific number of dollars. Examples of monetary items are cash, receivables, notes payable and bonds payable. Since monetary items, by definition, represent a fixed number of dollars regardless of price-level changes, they are already stated in units of current purchasing power and do not require restatement.

   b. **Nonmonetary items** are those items not considered to be monetary. For example, land, buildings, and inventory do not represent fixed claims to cash and therefore require restatement in constant dollar accounting. Note that contributed capital accounts are dealt with as nonmonetary items, whereas retained earnings is the balancing amount on the balance sheet. In the previous example, the land purchased for $10,000 in 1985 would be restated to $12,500 on a 1992 balance sheet to reflect the fact that it would require 12,500 "1992 dollars" to buy what only 10,000 "1985 dollars" bought.

3. **Purchasing power gain or loss.** Although monetary items do not require restatement in constant dollar accounting, these items do give rise to purchasing power gains or losses. If net monetary assets are held during a period of inflation, for example, those assets will command a lesser amount of goods or services following the price rise, creating a purchasing power loss. Conversely, holding net monetary liabilities through a period of rising prices creates a purchasing power gain because those liabilities can be repaid in "cheaper" dollars.

ILLUSTRATION 1 -- Purchasing power gain or loss

Assume the books of Jakovac Company carried the following:

Net monetary items:

January 1, 1992	$10,000
December 31, 1992	14,000
Purchase of equipment for cash, January 1, 1992	5,000
Purchase of merchandise occurred evenly throughout 1992	20,000
Sales occurred evenly throughout 1992	35,000
Cash dividends paid on October 1, 1992	6,000

The **CPI-U** are as follows:

January 1, 1992	100
July 1, 1992 (average for 1992)	110
October 1, 1992	115
December 31, 1992	120

Based on the above information, a schedule can be prepared to compute purchasing power gain or loss for 1992:

Schedule to Compute Purchasing Power Gain/Loss

	HC	CF	HC/CD
Monetary items (net), January 1, 1992	$10,000	120/100	$12,000
Add: Sales (average)	35,000	120/110	38,182
Total available	$45,000		$50,182
Deduct: Purchases of merchandise (average)	$20,000	120/110	$21,818
Purchase of equipment	5,000	120/100	6,000
Paid cash dividends	6,000	120/115	6,261
Total deductions	$31,000		$34,079
Monetary items (net), December 31, 1992			
Restated			$16,103
Historical	$14,000		14,000
Purchasing power loss			$2,103

Note that, on the schedule, **CF** stands for conversion factors, and that purchasing power gain or loss is reported in the HC/CD income statement, if provided.

4. **Income statement items.** In restating HC/ND income statement items, the assumption is made that all revenues and expenses, except allocated items (e.g., cost of goods sold, depreciation expenses, amortization of intangible assets, and bond discount or premium), occur evenly throughout the year. Accordingly, the conversion factor is the year-end CPI-U divided by the average CPI-U for the year. The restatement of allocated revenues or expenses is related to the initial purchase or acquisition of the corresponding items. Thus, the pertinent conversion factor is the year-end CPI-U divided by the CPI-U at the time of the initial transaction.

C. Current Cost/Nominal Dollar Accounting (CC/ND) [or Current Cost Accounting (CC)]

The current cost system is a response to the general criticism that the historical cost fails to reflect price-level changes. Under this system, the historical cost model is abandoned. Assets are measured at the end-of-period current cost. **FAS 89** specifies current cost for certain types of assets as follows:

1. **Balance sheet items:**

   a. **Inventory** at the current cost of replacing or reproducing the inventory owned. Ending inventory is measured at current cost by multiplying the number of units on hand at the balance sheet date by the end-of-period current unit cost.

   b. **Property, plant and equipment** at the current cost of acquiring the same service potential as embodied in the assets owned. The current cost of a depreciable asset is measured at the end-of-period current cost (new) minus the recalculated accumulated depreciation based on the current cost.

   c. **Specialized assets such as natural resources** at current market buying price or current cost of finding and developing the resources.

   d. **Other assets** generally at historical cost, if not significant in amount.

   The current cost may be determined (a) by using price-level indexes for specific goods or services or (b) by direct pricing (price lists, standard costs, etc.).

2. **Income statement items.**

   a. **Revenue** -- Current cost revenue is the same as under the historical cost system.

   b. **Cost of goods sold** -- Current cost of goods sold is measured by multiplying the number of units sold during the period by the average current unit cost.

c. **Depreciation expense** -- Current cost depreciation on a straight-line basis may be measured by dividing the average-for-period current cost of the asset (beginning-of-period current cost plus end-of-period current cost divided by 2) by the estimated useful life of the asset. Note that average-for-period current cost is used to measure depreciation expenses only. End-of-period current cost should be applied to measure the accumulated depreciation of the asset.

d. **Other expenses** -- generally use historical cost, if not significant.

e. **Holding gain/loss** -- Holding gains or losses represent the increase or decrease in the current cost of assets during the period. Following **FAS 89**, the increase or decrease in the current cost amounts of inventory and property, plant, and equipment represents the difference between the measures of the assets at their **entry dates** and **exit dates** for the year. Entry dates means the beginning of the year or the dates of acquisition, whichever is appropriate; exit dates means the end of the year or the dates of use or sale, whichever is applicable.

A holding gain or loss is realized if the asset is used or sold. Otherwise, it is unrealized. Holding gains or losses currently realized and any increase or decrease in unrealized holding gains or losses should be reported in the current cost income statement.

D. Current Cost/Constant Dollar Accounting (CC/CD)

Although the **CC/ND** model is an improvement over the historical cost models, it fails to separate the effects of general and specific price-level changes. **FAS 89** encourages use of a **CC/CD** model as introduced briefly below:

1. **Balance sheet items.** As in HC/CD accounting, each of the balance sheet items is classified as either monetary or nonmonetary. However, nonmonetary items such as inventory and property, plant and equipment are reported at current cost, and other assets and liabilities are generally reported at their historical costs.

2. **Purchasing power gain or loss.** Under the CC/CD system purchasing power gain or loss should be determined and reported in the same manner as under the HC/CD accounting.

3. **Income statement items.** The CC/CD model differs from the CC/ND model mainly in the determination of income statement items. Under the CC/CD model, (1) the current costs of revenues and expenses are restated using the general price-level indexes, (2) purchasing power gain or loss is included in income statement, and (3) the inflation effect is adjusted to the holding gains or losses.

ILLUSTRATION 2 -- Accounting for inventory under the current cost systems:

Assume AAA Company's records show the following:

January 1, 1992:	Purchased merchandise for $2,000.
December 31, 1992:	The merchandise remained unsold. Current cost of the merchandise increased to $3,000.
December 31, 1993:	Sold the merchandise for $7,500, when the current cost was $5,000.

CPI-U:

January 1, 1992	100%
December 31, 1992	120%
December 31, 1993	150%

Required: (1) Prepare a comparative income statement under the CC/ND system.

(2) Prepare a comparative income statement under the CC/CD system.

Solutions:

(1) **CC/ND system:** A simplified comparative income statement under the CC/ND system is presented below:

	1992	1993
Sales	$ 0	$7,500
Cost of goods sold (current cost)	0	5,000
Gross profit	$ 0	$2,500
Realized holding gain	0	3,000 [2]
Total realized profit	$ 0	$5,500
Increase (decrease) in unrealized holding gain	1,000[1]	(1,000)[3]
Net income	$1,000	$4,500

Notes:

[1]Increase in unrealized holding gain (1992) = \$3,000 - \$2,000 = \$1,000.

[2]Holding gain realized (1993)
= Current cost when merchandise was sold - Historical cost of goods sold
= \$5,000 - \$2,000
= \$3,000.

[3]Decrease in unrealized holding gain (1993)
= Ending unrealized holding gain - Beginning unrealized holding gain
= \$0 - \$1,000
= (\$1,000).

(2) **CC/CD system:** A simplified comparative income statement under the CC/CD system is presented below:

	1992	1993
Sales	\$ 0	\$7,500[2]
Cost of goods sold (current cost)	0	5,000
Gross profit	\$ 0	\$2,500
Realized holding gain	0	2,000[3]
Total realized profit	\$ 0	\$4,500
Increase (decrease) in unrealized holding gain	600[1]	(600)[4]
Net income	\$ 600	\$3,900

Notes:

[1] Unrealized holding gain adjusted for general price-level changes
= \$3,000 - (\$2,000 x 120 / 100) = \$600.

[2] Sales and Cost of goods sold (1992) are not restated because the sales were made at the end of the year.

[3] Realized holding gain
= Current cost - Restated historical cost
= \$5,000 - \$2,000 x 150 / 100
= \$2,000.

[4] Decrease in unrealized holding gain (1993)
= Ending unrealized holding gain - Beginning unrealized holding gain
= 0 - \$600 = (\$600)

ILLUSTRATION 3 -- Accounting for depreciable assets under the current cost systems:

Assume BBB Company purchased a machine on January 1, 1992 for $20,000. The machine had a useful life of 10 years with no residual value and the straight-line method was applied. At the end of 1992, the current cost of the machine (new) was $30,000.

CPI-U are as follows:

January 1, 1992	100%
July 1, 1992	110%
December 31, 1992	120%

Required: (1) Determine holding gains or losses under the CC/ND system.

(2) Determine holding gains or losses under the CC/CD system.

Solutions:

(1) **CC/ND system:** Determine holding gains or losses:

To compute holding gain of the machine for 1992:

Depreciation expense:

CC/ND: {[($20,000 + $30,000) / 2] / 10}	$ 2,500
HC/ND: ($20,000 / 10)	(2,000)
Realized holding gain:	**$ 500**

Ending book value of machine (net):

CC/ND: ($30,000 x 90%)	$27,000
HC/ND: ($20,000 x 90%)	(18,000)
Unrealized holding gain at end of period	$ 9,000
Less: Beginning unrealized holding gain	0
Current increase in unrealized holding gain	**$ 9,000**
Total holding gain ($500 + $9,000)	**$ 9,500**

(2) **CC/CD system:** Determine holding gains or losses:

To compute holding gain of the machine for 1992:

Depreciation expense (restated)	
CC/CD: {[($20,000 + $30,000)/2]/10} x 120 /110	$2,727
HC/CD: ($20,000 / 10) x 120 / 100	(2,400)
Realized holding gain:	**$ 327**
Restated ending book value of machine (net):	
CC/CD ($30,000 x 90%) x 120 / 120	$27,000
HC/CD ($20,000 x 90%) x 120 / 100	(21,600)
Unrealized holding gain at end of period	$ 5,400
Less: Beginning unrealized holding gain	**0**
Current increase in unrealized holding gain	**$ 5,400**
Total holding gain (machine)	**$ 5,727**

KEY CONCEPTS

Current cost accounting (CC/ND) An accounting system that abandons the historical cost model, and measures each of the financial statement elements in terms of its current cost, or in price-level dollars specific to the element being measured.

Current cost/Constant dollar accounting (CC/CD) An accounting system that abandons the historical cost model in favor of current cost and, in the meantime, makes adjustments to transform nominal dollars to dollars with the equivalent purchasing power.

Efficiency (activity) ratios Financial ratios that provide information about how efficient the firm is using its assets. The most used efficiency ratios include accounts receivable turnover, inventory turnover, working capital turnover and asset turnover.

Equity position ratios Financial ratios that measure the firm's long-term solvency and stability. The most used ratios include debt to equity ratio, debt to total assets ratio, and book value per share of common stock.

Historical cost/Constant dollar accounting HC/CD) An accounting system that adjusts financial statement elements from the nominal dollar to the constant dollar basis, i.e., to dollars with the equivalent purchasing power.

Horizontal analysis Each item of a comparative financial statement is expressed as a percentage of the same item of another period. This analysis involves scrutiny of not only the resulting percentages but also the relative importance of the item being analyzed.

Liquidity ratios Financial ratios that measure the firm's ability to pay short-term obligations when mature. The generally used liquidity ratios include current ratio, acid-test ratio, working capital ratio and defensive-interval ratio.

Monetary vs. nonmonetary items Assets and liabilities whose amounts are fixed in terms of a specific number of dollars are referred to as monetary items. Assets and liabilities other than monetary are nonmonetary items. Under the constant dollar system, monetary items are not restated. Nevertheless, they do give rise to purchasing power gain or loss.

Profitability ratios Financial ratios that measure various aspects of a firm's profit-making activities, including profit margin to sales, return on investment in terms of total assets or stockholders' equity, and earnings per share of common stock.

Vertical analysis Each item of a financial statement is expressed as a percentage of the appropriate corresponding total or base amount on the same statement. This analysis reveals the changes in the composition of items on the statement over time.

REVIEW QUESTIONS AND EXERCISES

TRUE-FALSE

Indicate whether each of the following statements is true or false by circling the correct response.

T F 1. Vertical analysis refers to the analytical technique of comparing accounting numbers over a period of years.

T F 2. When using ratio analysis as a means of comparing one company with another, it is important to consider the accounting policies and methods employed by the two companies.

T F 3. The current ratio generally is more useful than the acid-test ratio in assessing short-run liquidity (solvency) due to its more narrow definition of liquid assets.

T F 4. In the calculation of the acid-test ratio, marketable securities and prepaid expenses are both excluded from current assets before dividing by current liabilities.

T F 5. The receivable turnover ratio indicates how quickly accounts receivable are collected on the average.

T F 6. If the times of inventory turnover are high relative to industry standards, the risk to "stockout" is higher than the industry average.

T F 7. If Company A has EPS of $10 and Company B has EPS of $5, Company A is twice as profitable as Company B.

T F 8. The profit margin is one indication of management's efficiency in controlling costs and expenses.

T F 9. Historical cost/Constant dollar (HC/CD) accounting abandons the traditional historical cost concept.

T F 10. Reporting on the basis of current cost/nominal dollar (CC/ND) accounting has the advantage of presenting the effect of changes in the general price level.

T F 11. Monetary items are already stated in dollars of current purchasing power, therefore, they are not required to be restated in a constant dollar balance sheet.

T F 12. The conversion factor used in constant dollar restatement of depreciation expense is based on the index at the time the related depreciable asset was purchased.

T F 13. Historical cost/Constant dollar (HC/CD) accounting ignores the effect of specific price-level changes.

T F 14. The current cost/constant dollar (CC/CD) model takes into account changes in both the specific price level and the general price level.

EXERCISE 1

Match each of the following descriptions with the appropriate concept by indicating the letter of the concept.

Concept

A. General price-level index
B. Current cost/Constant dollar
C. Historical cost/Nominal dollar
D. Monetary items
E. Specific price-level index
F. Historical cost/Constant dollar
G. Current cost/Nominal dollar
H. Purchasing power gain/loss

____ 1. Model which focuses on specific price-level changes.

____ 2. Adjusts financial statements for general price-level changes only.

____ 3. Model which ignores both the general and specific price-level changes.

____ 4. Measures changes in the purchasing power of the dollar.

____ 5. Measures changes in the price of a specific good.

____ 6. Model which adjusts for both general and specific price-level changes.

____ 7. Effect of holding monetary items during inflation.

____ 8. Cash and receivables with fixed dollar amounts.

EXERCISE 2

Given the following comparative income statement and balance sheet for Barsorti Retailers, compute the requested ratios for 1992. (Additional information: 10,000 shares of common stock have been outstanding since 1990. Income tax rate was 40%).

Income Statement

	1992	1991
Net sales	$240,500	$201,000
Cost of goods sold	(132,000)	(111,500)
Gross profit	$108,500	$ 89,500
Selling and general expenses	(50,500)	(44,000)
Interest expense	(9,500)	(8,500)
Income before tax	$ 48,500	$ 37,000
Income tax	(19,400)	(14,800)
Net income	$ 29,100	$ 22,200

Balance Sheet
December 31

	1992	1991
Cash	$ 13,000	$ 12,500
Accounts receivables (net)	35,000	34,900
Inventories	34,800	29,000
Prepaid expenses	9,500	13,000
Total current assets	$ 92,300	$ 89,400
Property, plant and equipment (net)	115,000	105,250
Other assets	700	850
Total assets	$208,000	$195,500
Current liabilities	$ 51,000	$ 45,000
Long-term debt	107,000	100,500
Total liabilities	$158,000	$145,500
Stockholders' equity	50,000	50,000
Total liab. and SE	$208,000	$195,500

Required: Compute the following financial ratios for 1992:

a. **Current ratio** __________

b. **Acid-test ratio** __________

c. **Working capital to total assets ratio** __________

d. **Accounts receivable turnover** __________

e. **Inventory turnover** __________

f. **Debt to equity ratio** __________

g. **Book value per share** __________

h. **Profit margin on sales** __________

i. **Return on total assets** __________

j. **Return on stockholders' equity** __________

EXERCISE 3

The following incomplete balance sheet is obtained from Halfy Corporation:

Assets:

Cash	$ 10,000
Accounts receivable (net)	(?)
Inventory	(?)
Property, plant and equipment	30,000
Total assets	$120,000

Liabilities and stockholders' equity:

Accounts payable	$ (?)
Accrued wages payable	8,000
Bonds payable (long-term)	15,000
Common stock, par $10	50,000
Retained earnings	(?)
Total liab. and SE	$120,000

Additional information:

Current ratio	2 to 1
Ending inventory to net sales	15%
Net income to net sales	25%
Gross margin to net sales	30%
Gross margin	$ 24,000

Required: **Determine the following:**

a. Net sales: __________

b. Inventory (ending): __________

c. Current assets: __________

d. Accounts receivable (net): __________

e. Current liabilities: __________

f. Accounts payable (net): __________

g. Retained earnings: __________

h. Cost of goods sold: __________

i. Net income: __________

j. Earnings per share: __________

MULTIPLE CHOICE

Enter the letter corresponding to the response which **best** completes each of the following statements or questions.

____ 1. The ratio that best provides an indication of the balance between resources provided by creditors and resources provided by owners is:

a. time interest earned.
b. the debt to equity ratio.
c. profit margin.
d. the inventory turnover ratio.

____ 2. If average inventories increased from $70,000 to $80,000 during the year just ended, which of the following statements best describes the effect?

a. the acid-test ratio decreased.
b. the current ratio decreased.
c. the acid-test ratio increased.
d. inventories have no effect on the acid-test ratio.

____ 3. For a firm with a current ratio of 2 to 1, which of the following transactions would most likely cause an increase in this ratio?

a. the declaration of a cash dividend.
b. the sale of capital stock.
c. the collection of accounts receivable.
d. the issuance of a 30-day note payable for cash.

____ 4. A very high receivable turnover ratio relative to the industry average indicates:

a. the declaration of a cash dividend.
b. that the firm's credit policy may be overly restrictive.
c. that the firm's management utilizes its assets efficiently.
d. a sluggish inventory.

____ 5. The ratio least likely to be of concern to those interested in projecting a firm's future profitability is:

a. the current ratio.
b. profit margin.
c. investment turnover.
d. rate of return on investment.

____ 6. How are inventories used in the calculation of each of the following?

	Current Ratio	Inventory Turnover
a.	Numerator	Numerator
b.	Numerator	Denominator
c.	Denominator	Numerator
d.	Not used	Denominator

____ 7. During an inflationary period, a firm will incur the greatest purchasing power loss by holding:

a. accounts payable.
b. inventory.
c. accounts receivable.
d. land.

____ 8. Included in the classification of monetary items for the purpose of constant dollar accounting are:

a. cash, receivables, and inventory.
b. current assets and current liabilities.
c. accounts receivable, wages payable, and bonds payable.
d. accounts payable and inventory.

____ 9. Champion Company earns a 10% return on total assets. If net income is $26,000, and Champion has no interest expense and the total assets at January 1, 1992 is $250,000, the ending balance of the total assets is likely to be:

a. $250,000.
b. $260,000.
c. $270,000.
d. $280,000.

____ 10. Moolah Company began the accounting year with $100,000 in monetary assets and $110,000 in monetary liabilities. The price-level index rose evenly during the year from 120 to 130. If no increases or decreases occur in either monetary assets or monetary liabilities, the purchasing power gain or loss will be a:

a. $833 gain.
b. $833 loss.
c. $400 gain.
d. none of the above.

_____ 11. Selected information from the accounting records of Denikay Company is as follows:

Net sales for 1992	$160,000
Cost of goods sold for 1992	80,000
Inventory at 12/31/1991	10,000
Inventory at 12/31/1992	6,000

Denikay's inventory turnover for 1992 is:

a. 8 times
b. 10 times
c. 20 times
d. 6 times

_____ 12. Curry Corporation bought equipment for $210,000 on January 1, 1992. The equipment has an estimated useful life of ten years, with no residual value. The current cost of this equipment at December 31, 1992 was $270,000. Using straight-line depreciation on average current cost the depreciation that should be charged to current cost income for 1992 is:

a. $21,000.
b. $24,000.
c. $27,000.
d. $48,000.

_____ 13. Based on the same information as in question 12 above, what is the accumulated depreciation of the equipment presented on the current cost balance sheet at the end of 1992:

a. $21,000.
b. $27,000.
c. $24,000.
d. none of the above.

_____ 14. Melding Corporation purchased a machine at January 1, 1991 for $12,000, when the general price-level index was 120%. The asset has a useful life of 4 years and no residual value. If the price-level index was 144% at the end of 1992 and the straight-line method is applied, the depreciation expense for 1992 under historical cost/constant dollar (HC/CD) accounting would be:

a. $3,000
b. $3,300.
c. $3,600.
d. $3,800.

SOLUTIONS TO REVIEW QUESTIONS AND EXERCISES

TRUE-FALSE

1.	F	5.	T	9.	F	13.	T
2.	T	6.	T	10.	F	14.	T
3.	F	7.	F	11.	T		
4.	F	8.	T	12.	T		

EXERCISE 1

1.	G	5.	E
2.	F	6.	B
3.	C	7.	H
4.	A	8.	D

EXERCISE 2

a. **Current ratio:**
($92,300 / $51,000) — **1.81**

b. **Acid-test ratio:**
($92,300 - $34,800 - $9,500) / $51,000 — **.94**

c. **Working capital to total assets ratio:**
($92,300 - $51,000) /$208,000 — **20%**

d. **Accounts receivable turnover:**
{$240,500 / [($35,000 + $34,900) / 2]} — **6.9 times**

e. **Inventory turnover:**
[$132,000 /($34,800 + $29,000) / 2] — **4.1 times**

f. **Debt to equity ratio:**
($158,000 / $50,000) — **3.16%**

g. **Book value per share:**
($50,000 / 10,000) — **$5/share**

h. **Profit margin on sales:**
($29,100 / $240,500) — **12.1%**

i. **Return on total assets:**
[$29,100 + $9,500 x (1 - 40%)]
/ [($208,000 + $195,500) / 2] **17.25%**

j. **Return on stockholders' equity:**
{$29,100 / [($50,000 + $50,000) / 2]} **58.2%**

EXERCISE 3

a. Net sales:

Net sale
= Gross margin / Gross margin ratio to net sales
= $24,000 / 30%
= $80,000

b. Inventory (ending):

Inventory (ending)
= Net sales x Ending inventory to net sales ratio
= $80,000 x 15%
= $12,000

c. Current assets:

Current assets
= Total assets - Property, plant and equipment
= $120,000 - $30,000
= $90,000

d. Accounts receivable (net):

Accounts receivable (net)
= Current assets - Cash - Inventory (ending)
= $90,000 - $10,000 - $12,000
= $68,000

e. Current liabilities:

Current liabilities
= Current assets / Current ratio
= $90,000 / 2
= $45,000

f. Accounts payable (net):

Accounts payable (net)
= Current liabilities - Accrued wages payable
= $45,000 - $8,000
= $37,000

g. Retained earnings:

Retained earnings
= Total assets - Current liabilities - Long-term liabilities - Common stock
= $120,000 - $45,000 - $15,000 - $50,000
= $10,000

h. Cost of goods sold:

Cost of goods sold
= Net sales - Gross margin
= $80,000 - $24,000
= $56,000

i. Net income:

Net income
= Net sales x Net income to net sales ratio
= $80,000 x 25%
= $20,000

j. Earnings per share:
= Net income / Common shares outstanding
= $20,000 / 5,000
= $4

MULTIPLE CHOICE

1.	b	5.	a	9.	c	13.	b
2.	d	6.	b	10.	a	14.	c
3.	b	7.	c	11.	b		
4.	b	8.	c	12.	b		

Computation:

9. (c)

Net income	$ 26,000
Divided by: Return to average total assets	10%
Average total assets	$260,000
Multiplied by:	2
Sum of beginning and ending total assets	$520,000
Less: Beginning total assets	250,000
Ending total assets	**$270,000**

10. (a)

Monetary asset (beginning)	$100,000
Less: Monetary liab. (beginning)	(110,000)
Net monetary liabilities (beginning)	$(10,000)
Conversion factor	130/120
Net monetary liabilities (restated)	$(10,833)
Less: Liabilities at historical cost	10,000
Purchasing power gain	**$(833)**

11. (b) Inventory turnover (1992)
= Cost of goods sold / (Beginning inventory + Ending inventory) / 2
= $80,000 / [($10,000 + $6,000) / 2]
= 10 times.

12. (b) Depreciation expense (1992) -- current cost
= Average current cost x Depreciation rate
= [$210,000 + $270,000) / 2] x 10%
= $24,000.

13. (b) Accumulated depreciation (12/31/1992) -- current cost
= Equipment current cost at year end x years used
= \$270,000 x 1 / 10
= \$27,000.

14. (c) Depreciation expense (1992) -- historical cost/constant dollar
= Depreciation expense (HC) x restatement factor
= \$12,000 x 1 / 4 x 144 / 120
= \$3,600.

CHAPTER 26

Special Topics: Segment Reporting, Interim Reporting, and Disclosures

CHAPTER OBJECTIVES

This chapter is designed to enable students to:

A. Understand the nature of the problem of standards overload and some actions that might be undertaken to relieve the problem.

B. Be familiar with the information overload issue that has resulted in some accounting standards not being required for some firms.

C. Understand the SEC requirements for financial disclosure as is captured by the Form 10-K report, and the rationale for and components of the Summary of Significant Accounting Policies.

D. Be familiar with the alternative concepts that might be applied in preparing interim reports, and what concept is to be followed.

E. Understand the rationale for the implementation requirements for the areas of segment reporting disclosures.

CHAPTER OVERVIEW

PART A: Full Disclosure

A. Due to the complexity of business transactions and the need for timely reports, there has been a substantial increase in financial disclosure requirements prescribed by governmental agencies, mainly the SEC, and the accounting profession, mainly the FASB.

B. **SEC Disclosure Requirements.**

The Securities and Exchange Commission (**SEC**) was created in 1934 to administer securities acts and to regulate the disclosures of significant financial information by companies issuing publicly traded securities. Although the SEC has delegated much authority for prescribing the accounting principles and reporting practices to the FASB, it continues to have legal responsibility and final say in these matters.

The office of the chief accountant of the SEC is responsible for providing advice concerning accounting and auditing. It provides assistance in establishing administrative policies regarding accounting matters, and is directly responsible for the Regulation S-X, which addresses financial statement requirements including the forms and content of financial statements filed with the SEC.

As indicated in Regulation S-X, companies are required to file with the SEC a **registration statement** (Forms S-1, S-2, S-3, and some special forms), and **periodic reports** including Forms 10-K (an annual report), 10-Q (a quarterly report), and 8-K (a special report of significant events that occur during the year). The most important financial disclosure is perhaps **the annual report (i.e, Form 10-K)** which must be reported to the SEC within ninety days of a company's fiscal year-end with certain financial and nonfinancial information. The form consists of three parts, part II of which discloses the following:

1. **Market for common stock.** Identification of market(s) where corporation common stock is traded, including number of shares, frequency of trading, and amounts of dividends.

2. **Selected financial data.** Five year summary including net sales, income from continuing operations, earnings per share, total assets, cash dividends, and long-term obligations.

3. **Management's discussion and analysis.** Discussion of liquidity, capital resources, results of operations, and impact of inflation as needed to understand the company's financial condition, change in financial condition, and operating results.

4. **Financial statements and supplementary data.** Consolidated financial statements including balance sheets for two years, income statements, cash flow statements and statements of changes in stockholders' equity for three years, and related notes. Also, selected quarterly data and the auditor's opinion.

5. **Disagreements on accounting disclosures.** If auditors are changed due to disagreements on accounting principles, a description of the disagreements and summary of the effects on the financial statements.

C. **GAAP Disclosure Requirements.** **APB** Opinion No. 22 requires the disclosure of significant accounting policies. The conceptual framework of the FASB includes a full disclosure principle, which calls for the disclosure of any financial information that is potentially significant enough to influence the judgment of an informed reader. Many of the standards issued by the FASB have required various disclosures in addition to providing guidance on methods of measurement. These required disclosures are presented in the **notes, supplementary schedules** and the **tabular portion** of financial statements.

Notes to financial statements. Financial **notes** are an integral part of the financial statements. They are audited by the independent auditors, and must be included if the statements are to be complete. Notes provide verbal, descriptive explanations of various items included in the body of the statements which are deemed to be potentially meaningful to users. Information can be provided in qualitative terms, and the reader can make his or her own assessment of the potential quantitative ramifications of the information presented. Financial disclosures contained in the notes typically include the following:

1. **Summary of significant accounting policies.** A general description of all significant accounting principles and methods that involve:

   a. A selection from existing acceptable alternatives.
   b. Principles and methods particular to the industry.
   c. Unusual or innovative applications of GAAP.

2. **Notes on specific accounts.** Following the summary, there is a number of disclosures on specific accounts or groups of accounts such as:

   a. Accounts receivable. This note often breaks down the accounts receivable balance into trade receivable, notes receivable, accrued interest and allowance for doubtful accounts.

   b. Inventories. This note states inventory valuation method and whether lower-of-cost-or-market rule is being applied. Other disclosures include LIFO liquidation, purchase agreements, inventory pledged for collateral and related party transactions.

   c. Property, plant and equipment. This note presents a breakdown of property, plant and equipment into various categories, and, for each major category, the acquisition cost, accumulated depreciation, depreciation methods and estimated useful lives of the assets, if not disclosed elsewhere.

   d. Creditor disclosure. There are usually one or more notes providing information on the nature of various creditor claims on the firm, including long term debt, employee obligations, and lease obligations.

e. Equity disclosure. This note discloses information regarding outstanding stock options, convertible debt and preferred stock, redeemable stock and specific equity transactions, as well as any restrictions that affect the amount of retained earnings available for dividends.

f. Other notes. Changes in accounting estimate and principles, correction of prior accounting errors, contingencies and commissions, and significant events that occur subsequent to the balance sheet date but before the financial statements are issued. Note that a subsequent event resulting from conditions existed at the balance sheet date should be presented in the tabular portion of the statements.

3. **Unusual or sensitive transactions and events.** Next in the notes are transactions and events which create especially difficult reporting problems for the firm such as:

a. **Related party transactions.** **FAS 57** requires the following disclosure:

(1) The nature of the relationship(s) involved, e.g., a firm and its principle owners, a parent firm and its subsidiaries, and between subsidiaries of a common parent firm.

(2) A description of the transactions, including transactions to which no amounts or nominal amounts were ascribed, the dollar amounts of transactions and amounts due from or to related parties as of the balance sheet date.

b. **Errors, irregularities and illegal acts.** Unintentional accounting errors, irregularities that distort financial information, and illegal acts such as illegal political contributions, bribes, kickbacks and other violations of statutes and regulations are all required to be disclosed when discovered.

D. Fraudulent Financial Reporting

Fraudulent financial reporting is defined as intentional or reckless conduct, whether act or omission, that results in materially misleading financial statements. Briefly, fraudulent financial reporting can generally be traced (a) to the existence of conditions in the internal environment of the firm such as poor internal control, (b) to the external environment, such as recession, or (c) to the extreme pressures on management such as unrealistic profit or other performance goals. The accounting profession is faced with the problem of first trying to prevent it, and second, determining responsibility when it occurs. The AICPA has issued new auditing standards with an attempt to strengthen communications with the audit committee of the firm on the one hand, and with the users of financial statements on the other. The SEC in the meantime adopted new disclosure requirements to assure appropriate consultations between the firm and its auditors.

E. Financial Disclosure Requirements and Standards Overload

The ever increasing requirements for financial disclosures, including notes and supplementary information, give rise to a phenomenon known as **information overload** on the users of financial reports, and to the problem of **standards overload** on the managements of firms. Standards overload is more serious to the smaller firms than their larger counterparts as many disclosure requirements, which are mainly imposed on larger corporations, are nevertheless equally applied to smaller companies.

To encourage full disclosure on the one hand, and to avoid standards overload on the other, the FASB has recommended that companies disclose voluntarily certain financial information, or limit the applicability of certain standards to publicly held larger companies as indicated in the interim and segment reporting.

PART B: Interim Reporting

A. Annual financial statements often do not satisfy users' need for timely information because investors cannot wait until after the end of each annual reporting period to make all their investment decisions. Therefore, the SEC requires certain companies to file quarterly financial reports (Form 10-Q), whereas the accounting profession provides guidelines for interim reporting.

B. **The Nature of Interim Reports.** Interim reporting is to provide financial statements for periods of less than a year. There are two opposing views of the nature of an interim period:

1. **Discrete view** -- Each interim period is viewed as a basic reporting period, which stands separate and alone. Revenue and expense recognitions for the interim period follow the same principles and procedures as for an annual period, and an expense incurred in one interim period usually would not be allocated to the other interim periods.

2. **Integral-part view** -- Each interim period is viewed as an inseparable part of the annual reporting period. Revenue and expense recognitions are affected

by judgments made at the end of each interim period about the results of operations for the remainder of the fiscal year. An expense incurred in one interim period may be allocated to other interim periods within the fiscal year.

C. **Guidelines for Interim Reporting.** Based mainly on the integral-part view, **APB Opinion No. 28** provides guidelines, instead of prescriptions, on interim reporting as summarized below.

In general, the accounting principles and practices used in preparing annual financial statements should also be used for interim reports. However, in order to better relate the reported results for the interim period to the results for the fiscal year, some modifications are considered necessary or desirable.

1. **Revenue.** Revenue from products sold or services rendered should be recognized as earned during an interim period on the same basis as followed for the full year.

2. **Costs and expenses:**

   a. Costs that are associated directly with the interim revenue should be reported in the interim period. While companies should generally use the same inventory pricing methods and make provisions for write-downs to market at interim dates on the same basis as used at annual inventory dates, the following exceptions are appropriate:

      (1) Use of the gross margin method for computing cost of goods sold. The method, however, must be disclosed.

      (2) If LIFO is used and LIFO inventory is liquidated during an interim period and it is expected to be restored by year-end, cost of goods sold for the interim period should be debited for the anticipated replacement cost of the liquidated inventory, and an estimated liability should be credited.

      (3) Inventory losses from market declines, unless temporary, should be reported in the interim period in which the decline occurs. Recovery of such losses in later interim periods should be recognized as gains, but not in excess of the previously recognized losses.

      (4) Companies that use standard cost accounting systems should defer the planned variances (e.g., purchase price, volume and capacity variances) at interim reporting dates. The unplanned variance, however, should be reported at the end of an interim

period following the same procedures used at the end of a fiscal year.

b. Costs that are not directly associated with the interim revenue should be reported as follows:

(1) Costs and expenses that can be readily identified with time expired, benefit received or activity should be allocated among interim periods. Arbitrary allocation, however, should not be made.

(2) Costs and expenses that cannot be reasonably allocated should be assigned to the interim period in which they incur.

(3) Gains and losses that arise in any interim period, similar to those that would not be deferred at year-end, should be recognized in the interim period in which they arise.

(4) Income tax expense for each interim period should be based on an estimate of the annual effective rate as made at the end of each interim period. The effective rate should be applied to interim ordinary income on a current year-to-date basis. The income tax for the interim period is the difference between the income tax year-to-date and the amount recognized in the previous interim period(s).

3. **Special items:**

a. Significant unusual or extraordinary items, and gains or losses from disposal of a segment of a business, should be reported, net of tax, separately in the interim period in which they occur.

b. Cumulative effect from accounting principle changes made in **any** of the interim periods should be determined by the effect of the change up to the beginning of the fiscal year and recognized in the first interim period. If the change was made in an interim period other than the first, previously reported interim information should be restated.

c. The effect of a change in an accounting estimate should be accounted for in the interim period in which the change is made. No restatement of previously reported interim information should be made.

d. Contingencies and other uncertainties should be disclosed in interim reports in the same manner required for annual reports.

4. **Minimum disclosure:** When a company reports summarized interim information, the following minimum data should be disclosed:

   a. Sales, income taxes, and net income.
   b. Disposal of a segment of a business and extraordinary, unusual or infrequently occurring items.
   c. Primary and fully diluted earnings per share.
   d. Seasonal revenues, costs, or expenses.
   e. Significant changes in estimates or provisions for income taxes.
   f. Changes in accounting principles or estimates.
   g. Significant changes in financial position.

PART C: Segment Reporting

A. Many large firms diversify their operations and engage in more than one line of business. Since each of these business lines may possess different growth rate, risk and profitability while firms are generally required to present aggregated financial statements, investors are faced with the difficult task of analyzing and interpreting the aggregated financial data. Many believe that information about the relative proportions of company resources committed to operations to the various business lines, and the success the company has experienced in each business line would contribute to investors' informed decisions. As a response, the **FASB** issued **FAS 14** requiring diversified firms report segregated information, known as segment reporting, in terms of reportable segments, foreign operations and major customers.

B. **Reportable Segments (or reportable industry segments) and Segment Reporting**

1. **Industry segments and reportable segments.** **FAS 14** defines an industry segment as a component of a business engaged in providing a product or service or a group of related products and services primarily to unaffiliated customers for a profit. An industry segment meets any of the following tests shall be identified as a reportable segment:

   a. Its revenue is 10% or more of the combined revenue of all of the enterprise's industry segments.

   b. The absolute amount of its operating profit or loss is 10% or more of the greater, in absolute amount, of:

      (1) The combined operating profit of all industry segments that did not incur an operating loss, or

      (2) The combined operating loss of all industry segments that did incur an

operating loss.

c. Its identifiable assets are 10% or more of the combined identifiable assets of all industry segments.

It is noted, however, segment reporting is required only if the reportable segments represent a **substantial portion** of the enterprise's total operations, i.e., the combined revenues from sales to unaffiliated customers of all reportable segments constitute at least 75% of the combined revenues from sales to unaffiliated customers of all industry segments. Note also that segment reporting is not applicable to **interim reports (FAS 18)**, and it is not required for **nonpublic companies (FAS 21)**.

2. **Segment Reports**

If required, the following information for each of the reportable segments and for the company in the aggregate should be disclosed:

a. **Segment revenue,** i.e., sales of product or service to unaffiliated customers and sales or transfers to other industry segments of the enterprise. It does not include interest revenue on loans to other segments.

b. **Segment operating profit or loss,** i.e., the difference between segment revenue less all segment operating expenses. Segment expenses include:

(1) Operating expenses that are directly related to a segment's revenue, and

(2) Operating expenses incurred by the company that can be allocated on reasonable basis to the segment.

Segment revenues and expenses do not include general company expenses, interest expenses, income taxes, equity in income of unconsolidated subsidiaries, extraordinary items and cumulative effect of a change in accounting principle.

c. **Identifiable segment assets,** i.e., the tangible and intangible identifiable assets of the segment that are used exclusively by the segment or jointly by two or more segments. Excluded are those assets used for general company purposes and loans to other segments.

d. **Other related disclosures:**

(1) The aggregate amount of depreciation, depletion and amortization expense.

(2) The amount of capital expenditures during the period.

(3) The company's equity in the net income and investment in unconsolidated subsidiaries and other equity investees whose operations are vertically integrated with the segment.

(4) The effect on the segment of changes in accounting principles.

C. Segment Reporting -- Foreign Operations

An enterprise's foreign operations include those revenue-producing operations that (1) are located outside of the enterprise's home country, and (2) are generating revenue either from sales to unaffiliated customers or from intraenterprise sales or transfers between geographic areas. If the revenue from foreign operations is 10% or more of the combined revenue of all segments of the entity, or identifiable assets of the foreign operations are 10% or more of the combined identifiable assets of the entity, the entity shall report the following on its foreign operations:

1. Revenues

2. Operating profit or loss.

3. Identifiable assets.

D. Segment Reporting -- Major Customers

If 10% or more of the combined revenue of an enterprise is derived from sales to a single customer, that fact and the amount of revenue from each such customer shall be disclosed. But the identity of the customer need not be disclosed.

E. All the required information about a segment may be reported in any of the following ways:

1. within the body of the financial statements.

2. entirely in notes to the financial statements

3. in a separate schedule.

Whichever way is used, the segment disclosures must be an integral part of the financial statements.

KEY CONCEPTS

Foreign operations disclosure An enterprise's foreign operations include those revenue-producing operations that (a) are located outside of the enterprise's home country, and (b) are generating revenue either from sales to unaffiliated customers or from intraenterprise sales or transfers between geographic areas. If revenue from foreign operations is 10% or more of the combined revenue of all segments of the entity, or identifiable assets of the foreign operations are 10% or more of the combined identifiable assets of the entity, the entity shall report the revenues, operating profit and identifiable assets of the foreign operations.

Fraudulent financial reporting Intentional or reckless conduct, whether act or omission, that results in materially misleading financial statements. Fraudulent financial reporting can generally be traced to the existence of conditions in (1) the internal environment of the firm such as poor internal control, (2) the external environment such as decrease in demands, or (3) extreme pressure on management such as unattainable sales and profit goals.

Full disclosure Financial statements, including footnotes and supplementary schedules, should contain all information which is relevant to statement users for informed decision making.

Industry segment A component of a firm that engages in providing products or services primarily to unaffiliated customers for a profit. An industry segment is reportable if its revenues, operating profit (loss), or identifiable assets represent 10% or more of the corresponding combined total of all industry segments.

Interim reports Financial statements issued for interim periods of less than a year, typically a quarter. An interim period may be viewed as a discrete reporting period, which stands separate and alone. It may also be viewed as an integral part of the annual reporting period.

Major customer disclosure If 10% or more of the revenue of an enterprise is derived from sales to any single customer, that fact and the amount of revenue from each such customers shall be disclosed.

Notes disclosure An integral part of financial statements disclosing financial information including a summary of major accounting policies, explanation on specific accounts, unusual and sensitive transactions and events.

Securities and Exchange Commission (SEC) A governmental agency created to administer securities acts and to regulate the disclosures of significant financial information by companies issuing publicly traded securities. Companies are required to file registration statement and periodic reports with the SEC.

REVIEW QUESTIONS AND EXERCISES

TRUE-FALSE

Indicate whether each of the following statements is true or false by circling the correct response.

T F 1. A summary of significant accounting policies is an integral part of the financial statements.

T F 2. In general, current interim reporting guidelines are based on the premise that each interim period is a discrete time period.

T F 3. An extraordinary gain occurring in the first interim period should be allocated equally to each interim period in the year.

T F 4. The cumulated effect of accounting principle changes should be reflected in the first interim period, even if the change occurs in a later interim period.

T F 5. In computing income taxes for interim reporting, the tax rate used should be the annual effective rate estimated at the end of each interim period.

T F 6. Segment reporting would be required for a division with identifiable assets of 20% of the company's total.

T F 7. Information required to be disclosed for a reportable segment includes revenues, operating profit and identifiable assets.

T F 8. The gross profit (margin) method is acceptable for interim reporting purposes.

T F 9. Subsequent events occurring after the balance sheet date but before the financial statements are issued, are generally disclosed in footnotes to the financial statements.

T F 10. A contingent gain or loss, if probable but not measurable, is generally disclosed in footnotes to the financial statements.

T F 11. An industry segment is reportable if it meets the 10% of revenue, operating profit or identifiable assets test.

T F 12. The effect of a change in accounting estimate should be accounted for in the period of change, and previously reported interim information should not be restated.

T F 13. The revenue of interim periods should be recognized on the same basis as followed for the annual period.

T F 14. Costs and expenses that are not directly associated with interim revenue **must** be allocated to interim periods.

EXERCISE 1

Indicate with the appropriate letter the phrase that most appropriately describes the activity:

A. Full disclosure
B. Form 10-K
C. Regulation S-X
D. Standards overload
E. Related party transactions
F. Fraudulent financial reporting
G. Interim reporting
H. Major customer disclosure
I. Footnote disclosure
J. Management discussion and analysis

____ 1. Annual report of financial and nonfinancial information that must be filed with the SEC within 90 days after the end of the firm's fiscal year.

____ 2. Transactions involving a firm and its principle owners, a parent firm and its subsidiaries, and among subsidiaries of a common parent firm.

____ 3. Disclosure of the fact that 10% or more of the combined revenue of an enterprise is derived from a single customer.

____ 4. A phenomenon resulting from the ever increasing burden of financial disclosure requirements on managements of firms, especially small companies.

____ 5. Financial reports should contain all information which is relevant to statement users for informed decision making.

____ 6. Intentional or reckless conduct, whether act or omission that results in materially misleading financial statements.

____ 7. Document prescribing the reporting requirements including the form and content of financial statements to be filed with the SEC.

____ 8. Discussion of liquidity, capital resources, and results of operations that are required to be disclosed as a part of annual reports filed with the SEC.

____ 9. An integral part of financial statements that presents a summary of significant accounting policies, explanation of specific accounts, and/or unusual or sensitive transactions and events.

____ 10. Financial statements issued for period of less than a year.

MULTIPLE CHOICE

Enter the letter corresponding to the response which **best** completes each of the following statements or questions.

____ 1. Which of the following would probably **not** be found in a **summary of significant accounting policies?**

a. that long-term equity investment is carried at cost.
b. that LIFO is used in inventory valuation.
c. that accelerated depreciation is used for financial accounting purposes.
d. that an operating asset is disposed of for a gain.

____ 2. Which of the following is a true statement concerning interim reporting requirements?

a. All companies that issue an annual report should issue interim financial statements.
b. The same accounting principles used for the annual report should generally be used for interim reports.
c. Costs and expenses that are not directly associated with interim period must be allocated to interim periods of the same fiscal year.
d. Interim reporting guidelines are based mainly on the assumption that the interim period is a discrete reporting period.

____ 3. In reporting for business segments, the operating profit or loss of a reportable segment should include a deduction for:

	Interest expense	Income tax expense
a.	Yes	Yes
b.	Yes	No
c.	No	Yes
d.	No	No

____ 4. In financial reporting for segments of a business enterprise, which of the following is not required to be disclosed for each reportable industry segment?

a. operating profit or loss.
b. sales.
c. net profit or loss.
d. identifiable assets.

____ 5. Which of the following is not a periodic report to be filed with the SEC?

a. Form S-1.
b. Form 10-K.
c. Form 10-Q.
d. Form 8-K.

____ 6. Which of the following is **required** for a segment report?

a. Industry segment.
b. Reportable industry segment.
c. Reportable industry segment which represents a **substantial portion** of the enterprise's total operations.
d. None of the above.

____ 7. Subsequent events should be:

a. Disclosed in the notes to the financial statements if they result from conditions that did not exist at the balance sheet date.
b. Presented in the tabular portion of financial statement if they result from conditions that did not exist at the balance sheet date.
c. Disclosed in the notes to the financial statements if they result from conditions that existed at the balance sheet date.
d. Presented in the tabular portion of financial statements regardless of whether conditions existed at the balance sheet date.

____ 8. Extraordinary gains and losses that arise in an interim period should be:

a. Recognized in the interim period in which they arise.
b. Allocated to interim periods of the fiscal year.
c. Excluded from interim period reports.
d. None of the above.

____ 9. For interim reporting, income tax for an interim period is determined by:

a. multiplying the estimated annual effective tax rate to ordinary income of that period.
b. multiplying the estimated annual effective tax rate by year-to-date ordinary income, less income tax recognized for the previous interim period(s) of the fiscal year.
c. multiplying the estimated annual effective tax rate by the estimated total ordinary income for the year and then allocate to the interim period.
d. none of the above.

____ 10. For quarterly reporting, the cumulative effect of a change in accounting principle should be:

a. recognized and included in the first quarter's reported income, even the change is made in a later quarter of the fiscal year.
b. recognized and included in the reported income of the quarter in which the change is made.
c. allocated to the four interim periods of the fiscal year.
d. excluded from quarterly reports.

____ 11. Under which of the following circumstances is information about foreign operations required to be reported:

a. the profit from foreign operations is 10% or more of the net combined operating profit of all segments of the entity.
b. the profit from foreign operations is 10% or more of the net combined operating profit of all segments of the entity that did not incur an operating loss.
c. the identifiable assets of the foreign operations are 10% or more of the **total assets** of the entity.
d. the revenue from foreign operations is 10% or more of the combined revenue of all segments of the enterprise.

____ 12. Which of the following is not a test used to identify a reportable segment:

a. Its revenue is 10% or more of the combined revenue of all segments.
b. Its operating profit is 10% or more of the combined operating profit of all industry segments that did not incur an operating loss.
c. Its identifiable assets are 10% or more of the combined identifiable assets of all industry segments.
d. Its expenses are 10% or more of the combined expenses of all industry segments.

____ 13. Which of the following is not required to be presented on the financial statements under segment reporting:

a. revenues.
b. operating profit or loss.
c. identifiable assets.
d. identifiable liabilities.

____ 14. Which of the following is not an allowed modification for interim reporting?

a. using the gross profit method for interim inventory pricing.
b. deferred recognition of permanent inventory market declines.
c. recognition of a gain due to the recovery of market price to the extent of a loss recognized in a previous interim period of the same annual period.
d. including the expected cost of replacing the liquidated LIFO base inventory in the interim cost of sales.

SOLUTIONS TO REVIEW QUESTIONS AND EXERCISES

TRUE-FALSE

1.	T	5.	T	9.	T	13.	T
2.	F	6.	F	10.	T	14.	F
3.	F	7.	T	11.	T		
4.	T	8.	T	12.	T		

EXERCISE 1

1.	B	4.	D	7.	C	10.	G
2.	E	5.	A	8.	J		
3.	H	6.	F	9.	I		

MULTIPLE CHOICE

1.	d	5.	a	9.	b	13.	d
2.	b	6.	c	10.	a	14.	b
3.	d	7.	a	11.	d		
4.	c	8.	a	12.	d		